D A

Not Fade Away

A memoir of my time in the Sixties, being with Brian Jones of The Rolling Stones and the heartbreak of forced adoption

Photographs by	Terry O'Neil/RexUSA
Photographs by	Bill Wyman Archives
Photographs by	Scott Nelson Photography
Photographs by	Tony Keeley/Lebrecht music & Arts
Photographs by	City of London Metropolitan Archives

© Copyright 2015 Dawn Young
Published by Keywords Publishing 2013
Coeur d'Alene ID, USA
Printed Edition ISBN 9780989660617
eBook Edition ISBN 9780989660600
ISBN: 0989660613
This book is sold subject to the condition that it shall not, by way of trade or otherwise, be lent, resold, hired out, or otherwise circulated without the publisher's prior consent in any form, binding or cover other than that in which it is published and without a similar condition including this condition being imposed on the subsequent purchaser.

For Peter my rock, you will always have my heart

My Boys, John & Arron

*From the beginning of their lives they took my breath away
they have always stolen my heart.
I am proud to say they have grown into strong,
independent, loving men.
My dream for them is to be loved, and to know my love is forever.*

My Girls, Tara, Samantha & Nadine:

From the moment they were born they have always been a source of love and wonder to me.
I have watched them grow into the most beautiful, intelligent women.
My dream for them is that they will always have love in their lives and know who loved them the most.

TABLE OF CONTENTS

(Chapter titles are the names of songs recorded by
The Rolling Stones)

Not Fade Away

Chapter 1	Nineteenth Nervous Breakdown	1
Chapter 2	Yesterday's Papers	6
Chapter 3	Salt of the Earth	23
Chapter 4	Good Times Bad Times	30
Chapter 5	Around and Around	38
Chapter 6	The Singer Not the Song	52
Chapter 7	Stupid Girl	61
Chapter 8	The Spider and the Fly	66
Chapter 9	Everybody Needs Somebody to Love	76
Chapter 10	Let's Spend the Night Together	87
Chapter 11	Beast of Burden	98
Chapter 12	I Am Waiting	113
Chapter 13	Its All Over Now	123
Chapter 14	Can You See Your Mother Standing in the Shadows?	133

Chapter 15	High and Dry	140
Chapter 16	Out of Time	147
Chapter 17	It's Not Easy	169
Chapter 18	You Can Make It If You Try	175
Chapter 19	I'm Free	187
Chapter 20	Mother's Little Helper	193
Chapter 21	Paint It Black	198
Chapter 22	You Can't Always Get What You Want	209
Chapter 23	Something Happened To Me Yesterday	215
Chapter 24	That's How Strong My Love Is	224
Chapter 25	We Love You	235
Chapter 26	Pain In My Heart	244
Chapter 27	Blue Turns to Gray	254
Chapter 28	Not Fade Away	258

Chapter One

Nineteenth Nervous Breakdown

It's bittersweet that I have the house to myself this sunny, Southern California morning. After all, who wouldn't enjoy a few quiet moments away from the clamor and exuberance that is typical in a home filled with happy memories and love? I bustle around the kitchen trying to keep my mind occupied, my hands busy. With towel and polish, my fingers dance over the appliances - buffing the spotless stove, rubbing the sparkling refrigerator, flicking the last piece of dust off of the counter and into the gleaming sink. Motion and activity is what I need to banish static thoughts and idle moments. I must keep occupied, so as not to be engulfed by the dark clouds of regrets and sadness that stalks me.

    I pause to watch through the kitchen window the sun's filtering rays threading through the palm trees, cutting over the rock waterfall spa, and splinter into a million diamond fingers that bounce into our swimming pool. But the break from my busy work lasts too long. Now, I think of him - my lost son. Twenty-nine years have passed and, despite what 'they' promised me, the wound is as raw and my heart as fragile and brittle as the day he was taken from me.

"Get on with your life."

"This is the best thing for you and your family."

"No man will want a woman tied down with a child that is not his."

"You will forget all about it, and have no regrets."

That is what 'they': the church, our sixties society, my mother, told me. The telling must have been easy, because thousands of girls heard those same words and were taken in by them - taken in to the hiding part of the predicament, the part where being sent away from prying eyes and talking lips, was designed to contain the situation, shove it under the rug and thereby make it vanish. But the truth is that the vanishing part, the aftermath, the living with it - now that is another matter.

Oh for a house full of kids now! I need the joking, laughing and larking about the pool! I need someone to sit close beside me on the couch, drink a cup of tea and share what has happened during *their* day, so I can put *my* day behind me and delight in stories that aren't my own. I need someone right now to banish these dark clouds of mine.

Peter, my supportive husband of twenty-nine years, has taken our youngest son out to look at cars. Arron, now twenty and a volunteer firefighter for the California Department of Forestry, is seldom home. My other kids, not actually children anymore, are scattered. Our oldest daughter, Tara, is married and living in her own home now. Our second daughter, Samantha, is away at Loma Linda University working on her Bachelor's Degree. Our third daughter, Nadine, is still at home, but not today. My family is all grown up and living their own lives, yet it seems like only this morning when we relocated them as teenagers away from England and out to California.

House in Riverside CA 1994

Tara, my affectionate daughter, her mother's girl, had been heartbroken by the move. Being forced away from friends and her chance to study classical music and attend the Royal School of Music in London had devastated her. I wept at her pain, but there was nothing I could do. Peter had opportunities in the United States. Despite the sadness and heartache, she soon adapted. We have all adapted in our own ways.

Samantha, a rare beauty with an independent, free and loving spirit, has taken to the American lifestyle easily.

My youngest, Nadine, was not such an easy fit. She was always somewhat insecure, seemed to be a follower, and usually only had one friend at a time. But soon, she surrounded herself with a close circle of friends. As a cheerleader hanging out with a popular crowd, she could easily have been one of the Beach Boy's, California Girls.

So, I suppose, upon reflection, that it wasn't totally surprising that Nadine, at the tender age of nineteen, presented us with our first grandchild, Ashley. The news of her pregnancy hit us really hard. I felt as a parent the need to voice my disapproval and fears, that this pregnancy would change things for her forever. I wanted to tell her just what having a baby meant in terms of responsibility. Of course, I didn't. How could I? I knew exactly what she was going through. For that reason I tried desperately to be as supportive as I could.

I can still remember the day Nadine flippantly delivered the bombshell that she was going to have a baby. My heart felt as if it had fallen hard and fast into the pit of my stomach. I shoved my feelings down into a place of safety for myself, and for my daughter. I would be a loving and supportive mother. I would not, could not, repeat the sins of the past. No daughter of mine would endure what I had. My daughter would never know what it felt like to be cut off from family and friends and be forced to give (did I say give?), I mean experience her child being pried away from her loving arms and delivered to the care and home of strangers.

Now, less than two years later, Nadine's life has, more or less, not missed a beat. Nadine has married the father, Peter has employed him, Ashley has come along, and we are one happy family.

Living with us has allowed Nadine a great deal of freedom from the responsibilities of child rearing. Nadine has taken full advantage of the freedoms afforded her from living with us. Her social calendar is barely dented, because Peter and I can't help doting on our beautiful granddaughter.

Earlier this year, she'd burst into the house, breathless with excitement." I have tickets to see the Rolling Stones! I have tickets to see the Rolling Stones!" she danced and sang "I definitely have got some satisfaction!!" I restrained myself

Nadine could never have guess why, and hopefully would never know the reason, her father's and my extensive record collection

NINETEENTH NERVOUS BREAKDOWN

didn't include one single Stone's record was not because we did not like their music. If she had known the truth, perhaps the ecstasy of her Stones ticket would have been kept to herself.

It was amazing that, after nearly thirty years, I am still trying to survive my "Nineteenth nervous breakdown."

CHAPTER TWO

Yesterday's Papers

Rigid faces peering from old photos are all that's left of the Molloy and William's story. As I stare at the faces staring back at me, I imagine the Rosary Beads clutching tightly in weathered and wrinkled hands folded stiffly on the laps of the William's grandmothers, aunts and sisters. My father's family, the Molloy's, didn't possess such religious devotion. So, I suppose it was to be the Williams family's destiny to possess the strongest legacy that would be handed down through any family tree.

That inheritance was the all knowing, all seeing, Catholic Church, which ruled their households from the moment the presiding father sprinkled the Holy Water of Baptism onto infant's forehead right up to the Last Rights were prayed over the deceased. Invisible, but ever present in the background of each photograph, the Father, Son and Holy Ghost lurked, waiting for sins not yet committed to be perpetrated.

My Grandmother, Daisy, most certainly had an intimate commitment to the lighting of candles for prayer. I have often imagined her lips reciting the Hail Mary's over and over again while kneeling before the illuminated alter.

Born in 1891 to hard work and harder times, she spent her youth 'in service' working as a seamstress for a rich society family a few miles outside the heart of London in Chelsea. Her dainty fingers must have flown over her holy beads as dexterously as they flew over the fabrics she used in creating perfect seams for those more financially fortunate than she. Catholicism coursed through her veins and was passed down to her descendants as part of their DNA. Church ritual and doctrine created the rules of her life and dominated the lives of her children. No matter how far away or how hard they bucked against the chains of the great Mother Church, somewhere in the familial bands of the twisted double helix, the nuns in their habits and the fathers in their robes held the family generationally.

In her late teens, Daisy married a strict Catholic man, and soon after had her first child, Raymond. Within three years of the consecration of her wedding vows, her husband was dead, and at the age of twenty, Grandmother and Raymond were alone.

Fortunately, Grandmother was an attractive woman, with fiery red hair and a personality to go with it. Her Catholic beliefs allowed that as a widow she could remarry, and so she did within a year, and soon after had another son, Clifford, followed by a daughter, Renee. Next was a set of premature twins, who only lived a few hours, before being blessed by the Church and buried. Survival for pre-term babies in those days was rare, but her faith brought her through and was called upon once more when her second husband died of a heart attack.

Redoubling her religious fervor, this hardworking woman gave what extra time she had to involvement in Church affairs. I can imagine her sitting by the firelight, dutifully and skillfully sewing vestments and alter clothes. Two years later, Grandmother's good looks and Church devotion secured her another husband. He was a commendable man, a good Catholic, willing to take on the care of a young widow and her three children. Another marriage sanctified, and Daisy became the wife of John William, my grandfather.

After their successful union in the eyes of the Church, daughter Mable soon arrived, followed by another set of premature twins, who were suitably blessed, when they did not survive. After the twins, my mother Joyce was born, and then followed their last child, Peggy. My grandparents' family totaled six children.

As a wife and mother, Daisy gave up working outside of the home. The mantle of raising children lay heavily upon her shoulders. Sunday Mass, prayer and communion was the thread that wove the family together. Hard work and long hours kept them fed and clothed. Grandfather, bent and crippled from scoliosis, could not hold down a job. So, all of the domestic and financial burdens were placed firmly in Grandmother's lap, which added another bead for her to pray on her rosary. Grandmother opened shop in the front parlor of their tiny home, where she worked at dressmaking. Locally, she was known for her exquisite handiwork and was thereby kept busy with alterations and garment creation.

In addition to dressmaking, Grandmother created a small housecleaning business. Once the girls were old enough, and as soon as school let out for the day, they were put to work scrubbing floors, beating carpets and hanging laundry. There was no waste in my grandparent's home: clothes were handed down, vegetables were grown in the garden, fruit was picked from the trees, and the children saw their childhood slip through their calloused fingers.

In the autumn of 1928, all of the William's family offspring contracted diphtheria. The family was quarantined, and all they could do was to kneel before the family alter, light candles and pray that they only had mild cases. Unfortunately, Mable passed away and six-year-old old Peggy's hearing was irreparably damaged

Time went on, and Grandmother's faith continued as the dominant thread that provided life with meaning. All of her children attended Catholic school, prayed at Mass, accepted communion and obeyed (at least while in sight) Church doctrine. Parental emotional distance, uncompromising religious beliefs, and grueling work conditions caused the children to chafe at the hard lives they had been born into. To move out and create their own lives was foremost on each of their minds. The Church made all of the rules and, despite rebellion by the younger generation, was never far from the family threshold and would ultimately shape my destiny.

Raymond was the first to claim his freedom. He'd never gotten over the death of his Father, and didn't like his Mother's choice in stepfathers. Possessed with an independent spirit, at the age of fourteen he joined the Merchant Navy and was soon stationed in Singapore. This exotic country suited him - he was far away from an unhappy home and managed to become successful. Other than returning to London on special occasions, Singapore is where he stayed for the rest of his life.

Renee, a flamboyant dresser with a wild personality, made her escape by becoming a Tiller Girl, Briton's equivalent to the Rockettes high kicking dance team. An actress on and off stage, she did as she pleased and stood out in the drab days of pre-war Britain. Her lime green wedding dress, made by Grandmother, was fashioned around the green pearl headdress she wore at a mermaid show she was appearing in. She loved the color and the costume and was determined to wear it for her wedding. She married a handsome officer in the Royal Air Force.

Clifford gained his familial escape through a temporary Royal Navy enlistment, when the war broke out.

Mother, a talented singer, received a scholarship in 1933, which paid for private voice lessons. Her dream had been to move away and become a professional singer. Music was Mother's primary pleasure in life. Music was in a way to her, what the Church was to Grandmother.

When she was seventeen, Mother met my father, Colin Molloy, a temporary trumpet player for a local band she was singing for at a dance hall near her parent's home. Mother was instantly attracted to the handsome, twenty-three- year old musician, who had played in the Isles of Sheppy Boy's Band as a child and had been a member of the Queen's Scots Guard Band since the age of sixteen.

The union was met with immediate disapproval. Grandmother was shocked and horrified that Mother would consider taking up with an atheist *and* a musician. Minnie, my dad's mother, was appalled that my father would consider marrying into a Catholic family.

The two would not be dissuaded they became engaged. Despite her protests of the marriage, Grandmother Williams made Mother's bridal gown, but of course not until my parents were coerced into agreeing that the children would be brought up Catholic and that the wedding receive blessings from the Church. Mother was working at a textile factory making parachute fabric. As a wedding present, she was given her choice of any cloth available, so that a suitable outfit might be created for the nuptials. In April of 1937, Joyce Williams, and Colin Molly became man and wife.

Colin and Joyce April 1937

Mother finally had what she'd been yearning for - complete and total freedom from her childhood home and all of the drudgery connected with it. Free at last, her nights were spent singing and dancing with her handsome young husband. She felt absolutely no remorse for younger sister, Peggy, left home alone to deal with the after work chores and Grandmother's hard ways. Peggy eventually managed her escape by marrying a draughtsman.

As a married couple, my parents lived life in the fast lane. Entertainment and fun were first priority, followed by smoking and drinking, with work and responsibility trailing behind. In 1939, less than two years after their marriage, World War II broke out, and a year later, and not intentionally, Mother got pregnant with my brother, Michael.

They rejoiced in the fact that he was a boy, and raised him as if he could do no wrong. Dad, being an only child, proudly passed on the Molloy family name. Michael spent most of his infant years safe with his Paternal Grandmother, Minnie, who lived in the Isle of Sheppy Kent, far way from London and the imminent threat of bombings.

Since my Father was on active duty, he lived in Wellington Barracks. Mother kept her job at the textile factory. On weekends, they visited Michael. This went on until they were able to find housing outside of London, where they could live together and Michael would be safe.

Six years later, and once again unexpectedly and this time not happily, my Mother was pregnant with me. Another child would restrict Mother's lifestyle - the last thing she wanted. I was born in March of 1946, in Epsom Surrey England.

The war with Germany was over, and Father resigned from the Scots Guards, in order to try his hand at being a hotelier at Great Yarmouth. This was my dad's first plunge into the world of commerce. Indeed, it was his first trek out of the relative comfort and security of military life, as a musician in the Royal Scots Guards, into the life of a civilian. I suspect that his decision to move to a far away seaside village and start a new vocation might possibly have been encouraged by a distant relative, whom everyone called Aunt Eva.

※

Aunt Eva lived in the English East Coast holiday resort of Great Yarmouth, where she owned and ran "The Acacia", a well-established guest house that could accommodate up to thirty visitors. Located on Princess Street, it ran adjacent to Britannia Pier, one of the town's fashionable entertainment spots and a major tourist attraction.

Aunt Eva's house was an extremely popular port of call for those lucky enough to be able to afford a seaside holiday in early post war Britain. Year after year, the same people returned to sample the delights of Auntie's home cooking. Her homemade steak and onion pies in particular were the talk of the guests who stayed there, along with her kind and heartfelt hospitality.

Great Yarmouth was a town determined to put the Second World War behind, and quickly set out its stall as a major resort for holidaymakers, in an effort to rebuild its reputation as one of Britain's major seaside attractions. It was a town full of color and bright lights with a buzz of people from all areas of the UK, hoping to enjoy their well deserved holiday.

Although it hardly seems credible, in a small town with around 34,000 people, Great Yarmouth, during the summer season, was a scene alive with activity. Marine Parade Street was bordered with stands of cotton candy, penny ball machines, fortunetellers and all manner of beautiful exotic parrots, used for holiday pictures. Kiosks of fish and chips, Ferris wheels, merry go rounds, and bumper cars competed with the fishermen's paradise of rods, dangling down into the ocean below in hopes of catching Cod for a good meal.

In preparation for the influx of travelers, theater owners sought out the newest and most interesting shows. Famous entertainers arrived in their expensive cars, creating a buzz among the locals and visitors. Great Yarmouth boasted two competing entertainment piers, along with the Baron's Amusement Park.

The Britannia Pier was located at the far end of Marina Parade, had a small indoor amusement area. A short distance behind was the box office, where the theater stood followed by its musical attractions.

The Wellington Pier was located at the far end of the Boardwalk. This stately white building was home to amusements and also boasted its own theater, where such greats as Billy Fury and comedian Tommy Cooper performed. It was also home to the famous Winter Gardens.

My Father played his trumpet every night at one, or another, of the pier theaters, or at the Hippodrome Circus.

Oh how I loved the circus! I remember the multitude of clowns and the smell of the horsehair matting that was used on the floor of the center ring, to secure good footing for the performers and animals. I never tired of the show.

First, I was dazzled by a white horse rhythmically trotting around the ring, while a pretty young woman, dressed in a sparkling pink costume, stood tall and steady on his back. She danced and turned in time to the music being played by the live band.

Once the horse and his rider pranced out and away, the Bengal tigers and lions performed center ring. I held my breath as their trainer cracked his whip, causing them to snarl and strike out with unsheathed claws and leap through hoops of fire.

As the big cats left the ring, out came the baby elephant, amble and trotting everywhere, showering the clowns with trunks full of water from buckets placed around the ring.

The last act, the one that inspired me most of all, was when the high wire appeared bathed in spotlights high above our heads. The tight rope artists! Dressed in thin white stocking suits, they dazzled us with their dangerous feats, somersaulting back and forth, and standing on chair rails on one foot with no net to catch them.

While we gawked in awe skyward, down below the clowns lifted and dragged the heavy horsehair mats out of the ring. Of course, we didn't see them do it. When the daring performers completed the last flip and spin, we looked back to the center and as if by magic, the circus stage began to slowly sink down, to be replaced by a rising lighted fountain.

Mermaids swam through the fountain, dressed in glittering turquoise swimming costumes, their hair covered with white swim caps dotted with blue silk flowers. These water nymphs danced in synch with Frankie Avalon's *Voyage to the Bottom of the Sea*. A full orchestra created the musical luster, and often Dad, my own luminary, joined in with his trumpet. All was all spectacular, and I thought it was wonderful. Great Yarmouth was a splendid place to live, a town steeped in a rich and colorful history.

As a busy port, Great Yarmouth had flourished for hundreds of years. Famous for its herring fishing and dating back to medieval times, kings and queens had visited and met ships from the Orient selling arrays of exotic delights. It was the wealthy Victorians, with their insatiable desires to discover and sample new and foreign pleasures, who originally appreciated the tiny township's potential as a holiday resort. They transformed the port of Great Yarmouth into a magical little jewel - a beloved gem.

While trying to make a success of the boarding house, for which they had neither the business acumen nor the personality, my parents practiced sloppy child – minding, in an effort to preserve their "pre-Dawn" lifestyle. Mother once admitted that having me was one of the greatest sorrows of her, life and that she had tried some "remedies" to eliminate her pregnancy.

My parents lacked the hominess and family orientation, that was the bedrock of Aunt Eva's personality, and which also was the essential ingredient of the hospitality industry. They spent more time out at places like the Winter Gardens than they did at home taking care of business.

Mum and Dad loved the Winter Gardens, a huge glass conservatory erected in 1903 and used for family, as well as adult, entertainment. The bandstand housed the resident musicians and an evening of hop was always at the ready on the dance hall floor.

The Winter Gardens: Originally built 1904 Closed 2008

The Winter Garden pavilion housed tropical banana trees and flourishing creeping plants that wound their way around the steel frames surrounding the marquee. Shifting colored lights created a romantic, glamorous atmosphere. Surrounding this enchantment were tiled tables and iron chairs, where smoking, drinking and dancing patrons congregated. My parents would ballroom at every opportunity, loving to waltz and quick step the night away.

During the summer season, the twenty-piece Neville Bishop Band became the resident orchestra. They performed to packed audiences. Neville Bishop held three daily shows. Mornings were for children, and afternoon and evening performances were for the adults. The place was bursting from the moment it opened, until the time it closed. He was fantastic. He was hilarious. It was especially full on Sunday's when one hundred foot long queues of fans waited to get in. On occasion Mother sang with them.

While my parents neglected their responsibilities, flourishing establishments strove to pry as much cash out of the holidaymakers as possible. The competition was fierce, and each venue clambered to book the biggest stars of the day. For my Dad, a talented and respected musician, rubbing shoulders with such greats as Jerry Lee Lewis, comedian and musician Norman Wisdom, Lucille Ball and husband Ricky Ricardo with his Latin Jazz, was nearly a nightly occurrence.

Great Yarmouth, the little seaside town, had been created into a Mecca for the rich and famous. My parents, with aspirations to further their musical careers, were in the hub for professional musicians. They even cut a disc called "Anything You Can Do I Can Do Better" just as their own personal keepsake.

Social fetes, music, singing and dancing had precedence over everything else. A story from my infancy goes that my parents were attending a big event one afternoon and took me along. They slipped away, while I slept in my carrycot in their old Ford car. I eventually awoke and being hot, wet and hungry, began to cry. My crying turned into wailing, and my wailing into hysteria. Alarmed, passerby looked inside the closed and locked vehicle, stunned to find an unattended and screaming infant.

Taking control of the situation, a man pried the quarter window ajar and was able to open the car door and liberate me. Drenched in sweat, soiled and seriously close to hypothermia, I was not easily calmed down. A woman bystander checked my carrycot and discovered all the necessities to clean me up. She changed my nappy and soothed my hysterics. Somehow, my parents were found and confronted. My mother's response was that she had simply forgotten that I was in the car.

If my parents found me inconvenient as an infant, imagine the problems they encountered, as I grew older. As a three-year old, I was inquisitive and into everything. This was regarded as trouble. To negate the nuisance factor, they devised an ingenious method of restraining me. Leather reins strapped around my upper chest, with over-the-shoulder restraints, were connected by a slip lock that could easily attach to any kind of rope or string. I was often tied to a clothes pole in the courtyard at the rear of the boarding house. With the Great Yarmouth attractions almost at our doorstep, the reigning was doomed before it was started. Wiggling and twisting, I found that I could simply slip off my clothes and be free. Relieved from captivity, I would scamper off to the seafront attractions to ride my favorite child sized carousel with its six tiny ponies. The Police were called and off to police the station I would go, until they contacted my parents. After the second time, my parents were warned that next time RSPCC (Royal Society for the prevention of cruelty to children) would be informed

As I grew older, I watch through a crack in the bedroom door, as Mother got ready to go out. On a dressing table were jars of Pond's cold cream and heavy pan stick make up. She took her time getting ready, working as an artist would with oils on canvas. Between steps, she took long drags from her cigarettes: mascara . . . puff . . . rouge . . . puff . . . powder. . . puff, until, after the last inhale and exhale of smoke, she finished with bright red lipstick and a liberal dousing of Channel No 5. She then set her thin reddish hair in tight, fashionable permanent waves. For her evenings at trendy parties, she wore floor length silk gowns, completed with a fox fur wrap. The finishing touch were six inch, ankle strapped heels that complemented her tiny size five feet.

Whether for daywear under bright flowered dresses or a night outing under fashionable gowns designed for women half her age, Mother wore suspenders to hold up her fine fifteen denier back pencil lined silk stocking hose. The finishing touch to any of her costumes was always a huge hat. Her favorite was black and tipped on one side with black feathers, and a fine black net that could be pulled down over her face.

I was embarrassed by her over-the-top fashion sense. As I watched her, I wished she would give me half of the attention she exerted to make herself look glamorous. Hiding behind the door and peering unseen into her room, I remained a shadow in her life.

Despite having married an atheist musician, Mother still remained a practicing Catholic, and kept her promised to the Church and her mother that I would be brought up in the faith. As early as was possible, I was enrolled in and began attending, St Mary's Catholic Convent in Great Yarmouth. The nuns in their perfectly pressed black habits with large bead belts around their waists frightened me. They glided through classes and down church hallways, with their metal cross hanging from their necks tinkling as they passed. Not a hair showed from underneath the habits that clung tightly around their faces and necks. Most were from Ireland, had heavy Irish accents and never smiled. From my point of view, their true and only vocation was to terrify young children into confession and prayer.

The school was adjacent St Mary's Catholic Church, which was as unwelcoming and frigid as the cold stone flooring. I hated going, but knew, if my absence was noted, come Monday morning the nuns would be waiting to cane my knuckles or those of any child, who didn't go to Mass on Sunday.

St Mary's Church was very old, with traditions that demanded respect. The statues of the Saints, the tombs, the stained glass windows depicting the Stations of the Cross, the echoes on the stone floors, the flowers, the candles and the smell of incense would have created a beautiful atmosphere, if it were not for the emotional iciness I constantly felt there and the threat of retribution I knew always awaited, if I did not comply with Church dictates. When the choir sang and the organ with its massive pipes was played, the fear of God was instantly instilled in me. As a result, by the age of five, I had become a good Catholic.

At eleven, it seemed that Michael, my brother, was old enough to look after himself and, as an afterthought on his part, me as well. Our parents made a point of sending us outside to our own devises as much as possible. One day, Michael was told to go out and play and to take me with him. He generally didn't mind so long as I played whatever game he chose. But, that day, I wanted to stay at home. Mother wanted us out, and not wanting a scene promised us chips. I begged to stay inside, promising to be as quiet as a mouse, but my pleas fell on deaf ears. Father escorted us off the premises, and I was left in the charge of my brother.

I may have been forced to go with him, but I planned to do as I pleased. The seeds of rebellion were taking root within me, and I would do as I wanted as often as I could. Neither of us wanted to be together, so within minutes of leaving the house I started acting up. My brother paid no attention to what I was doing. Spotting a doll in a shop on the opposite side of the road, I dashed into the street, my thoughts only on getting to the toy. The poor lorry driver didn't have a hope in hell's chance of reacting quickly enough to prevent hitting me. The lorry's wheels ran over my knees. After being rushed to the hospital, it was found that I had no broken bones.

The distraught driver was totally beside himself with worry. Michael, who had witnessed the event, was petrified. He also had the worry of facing our parents, when they found out that he had "allowed" me to run across the street. So, where were my parents while this was going on? They had been gaily socializing with friends at a cocktail party.

After the accident, at my Aunt's request, I spent more time at her house and less at my parents'.

Thank God for Aunt Eva Jones, by far and away the most important person to me during those formative years. She may well have been the single most influential woman in my life, helping me develop my fashion sense, my make-up style, and the person I grew up to become. Eva Jones was a shining light of hope to me. Her heart and mind were made up of goodness, caring and understanding. I felt safe and loved, when I was around this adorable woman. Remembering her now, I marvel at her patience and her quiet serenity. Nothing seemed to faze her, or cause her to raise her voice. Auntie was the complete opposite of my natural mother.

After four seasons of "trying," my parents admitted defeat as hoteliers. There had been plenty of arguments leading up to the decision to quit. My mother had a short fuse, a sharp tongue, and absolutely no patience with customers. They had "tried" and failed, so it was time for Father to re-enlist in the Scots Guards Regiment. Just like that, my parents moved back to Surrey, taking my brother and I along.

Given the chance, I would have stayed with Aunt Eva, but I was not given the choice. However, most conveniently for my Mother and most happily for me, Auntie wanted me with her during the summer months. I counted the days I was forced to stay with my parents during the school year. Once the last bell rang at School, Mother deposited me on the first Grey-Green bus headed east for Great Yarmouth.

Aunt Eva was much older than my parents. She was also much wiser. Actually, she was my great aunt, because she had married my paternal grandmother's brother. The reality was that she was not related to me by blood, and yet she loved me unconditionally, as if I were her own child. It was Eva who gently guided me through life's education and showed true care to my emotional needs. Where she mustered the strength and gentility to love me and care for the steady stream of happy visitors staying at the Acacia I will never know. She didn't live under the best of circumstances. I found this out on the day her husband, Uncle Percy, was buried. Aunt Eva returned from the funeral and praised the Lord that "that Bastard was six feet under" and no longer part of her life.

I knew my Uncle Percy was a foul mouthed, hard drinking fisherman, but it never occurred to me that he was coming home after fishing trips and boozy nights and taking his bad temper out on my beloved Aunt. She always dismissed the bruises and cuts as accidents. But that was always the way things were in those days: domestic violence and child endangerment were private crosses to be bore in silence, and heaven forbid that they pass the threshold to the outside world.

My holidays with my aunt were filled with happy hours helping her and the maid with the general chores involved in maintaining the guesthouse. I tidied, cleaned, dusted and made up the beds. I enjoyed these domestic chores; it felt good to be of help and appreciated, too. Auntie praised me for the good work I did and gave me warm hugs when I became frustrated and upset when things didn't go my way. In contrast, at home with my mother was like living in a house made of stacked cards, liable to topple down without warning. I was always ill at ease with Mother and not quite sure when, or why, she would slap me for some imagined misdeed.

The only task Auntie would not allow me to help out with was the ironing, but the fascination of watching her tackle this laborious job has never left me. I can still see her in my mind's eye during those days before electric irons were widely available, which certainly would have been a luxury item in post war Britain. Anyway, my Aunt had a tried and tested method that she'd have been loath to abandon to a new fangled idea that used electricity.

She used two heavy steel irons, which were heated on the coals of the range and used one after the other. Taking a sizzling iron out of the fire, she deftly pressed linens, towels and pillowcases. When the iron became too cool to finish the task, she adroitly exchanged the cool with the hot and continued on. To avoid burning her hands, Auntie had made thick, heavy hand-knitted mittens. Her movements were practiced and flawless, and the garments with their perfect creases piled high in no time. With each exchange of the flat iron, her cheeks flushed becoming rosier and rosier.

The best bit for me would come when her task was complete. She'd slip off her heavy gloves, kiss my forehead and put her warm hands on my cheeks, which would soon flush and take on a similar glow as hers had. Aunt Eva also allowed me to put the enormous gloves on while they were still toasty and warm. She did warn me not to put them on, until she said so. She said that the heat would be too much for my soft skin. Such a small piece of thoughtfulness that made me become aware of the touching love I was receiving for the first time in my life. As a result, I began to feel safer and more myself, as toasty warm as those marvelous mittens.

When not making the Acacia more inviting and homey, my Aunt was a dressmaker. In addition to making many beautiful dresses for me, she made wedding gowns. Watching her patiently sew hundreds of sequins onto the delicate white fabric stirred in me a passion for weddings. I had an eye for pretty things, and thoughts of someday having a bridal dress made especially for me became an obsession.

Every Saturday morning, during those early summer years before I learned about boys and fell in love with all things musical, I walked down the street to the corner where the Sandringham, the largest and most expensive hotel in Great Yarmouth, was located. My treks were to see if a wedding reception was being held. Stooping down and peering between the iron railings, I would scan the ballroom basement, hoping to get a glimpse of a lucky bride. Memorizing the tiniest details of each adorned gown, I ran as fast as I could back to the guest house to tell Auntie all about what I had seen. On every occasion, she smiled and chuckled at my glee and told me that I would make a bonnie bride one day and have the prettiest wedding dress in the world. These words were always music to my ears.

Sadly, summers in Great Yarmouth were always too short, and eventually the day arrived when the Grey-Green bus waited for me to board. Waving goodbye and looking out the back window through eyes clouded with tears, I sadly watched Aunt Eva fade, as I left her behind along with my peace and security. Once again, I would find myself returning to London and a troubled life.

CHAPTER THREE

Salt of the Earth

The rebuilding of London post war was slow. The national economy, still reeling from WWII, was stumbling to get back on its feet. It was eerie and odd how one house would be standing alone on a street bombed by the Blitz, with all signs of past habitants obliterated. Residents who chose to stay in their homes were allowed to, providing they had clearance from inspectors, employed by the government, and their building had not been flagged for demolition.

My brother and his mates spent hours going through the rubble and ruins that made up our neighborhood, even though he had been told repeatedly not to go near them, out of respect for the land owners. They went anyway, looking for "trophies" of tools or jewelry. Most children did it, but if caught by the police they knew it would mean big trouble with their parents. We were afraid of the police, and, in those days, parents were responsible for anything their children did. Warnings to children and parents were the first line of action, but if warned too many times, there was a good chance that The Royal Society for the Prevention of Cruelty to Children would take the young offender from the family.

One day, Mike threw a rock at a house that had not been flagged, breaking a window. The owner brought him to our door and threatened our mother to pay for a new window or be reported to the authorities. Money was taken from our piggy banks and from household funds to pay the home owner. My brother received several slaps and a loud angry lecture. This did not deter him one bit, because he still came home with his pants torn and shoes scraped from climbing and falling.

Bomb site in London 1949

1952, King George VI died. George had dramatically become England's King in 1936, after his older brother, King Edward VIII, who had been king from January twentieth through December eleventh scandalously fell in love with American Wallace Simpson.

King George was not prepared for the role that was thrust upon him. He was a good man, but lacked confidence and had no charismatic appeal. His reign was particularly difficult due to a speech impediment. His fear of stuttering in front of a crowd or over a microphone was paralysing. Neither he nor his subjects were happy with the situation. Making matters worse, Britain was soon plunged into war with Germany, which created years of bombing, ration books and the Black Market. The nation was plummeted into depression and sadness.

George's lacklustre reign might have gone largely unnoticed by the British public had it not been for his effervescent, cheery and ever smiling wife, Elizabeth, and their two charming daughters: the oldest and future queen, Elizabeth the II, and her sister Princess Margaret. How the crowds would buzz with electric fervour each time these two endearing young ladies appeared on the balcony at Buckingham Palace.

At the time of his death, George's England was a mass of broken buildings, populated by a broken hearted people trying to dig their way out of six years of war and uncertainty. The populace needed some kind of new hope to nurture and bolster them. This was the time when Princess Elizabeth acceded to the British throne and became Queen Elizabeth the II. The 1953 Coronation ceremony for the new queen was just what was needed. The nation was going to have a party the likes of which hadn't been seen since the celebration of VE-Day. A feeling of hope and optimism was in the air. It would be the last such event of the twentieth century. The new monarch would take her reign into the new millennium. Not that the future was occupying the thoughts of most of the Queen's subjects. They had Coronation Day preparations to consider.

For me, seven-year-old Dawn, this was going to be a truly memorable day. Mother had been in a really good mood. She was looking forward to Coronation Day. It was going to be extra special because Mother's half-brother Raymond and his family were coming over from Singapore. He'd done well for himself, and Mother wanted to make a good impression on him by showing off her own little family. Neither fourteen-year-old Michael nor I had met this uncle from the mystical, magical realm of the Far East. Play acting my own little Royal Princess Coronation and imagining my meeting with family from mysterious places, I was excited as any young girl would be.

Our treat for Coronation Day was to pay a visit to the Chessington Zoo, near to our home in Surrey. It was going to be lovely seeing the animals and spending a carefree day with Mother and my brother. There would be lots of stalls and treats to be had, and, thrillingly, it was where we were to meet our uncle and his family for the first time.

However, for me, the most exciting part of the whole adventure was undoubtedly going to be my outfit. My loving Aunt Eva had come up trumps as ever. Her sense of occasion was reflected in the beautiful garment she had created for me. I was going to be a "Coronation Belle of the Ball." I knew that everyone would be in awe of little Dawn and her lovely dress. I felt special.

The dress itself was really a simple enough affair. It was made from a good quality white Taffeta, with a nice sheen and body to it. My clever Aunty had added red, white and blue checked ribbon around the sleeves and waistband, to reflect the colours of the Union Flag. My little dress was an eye- catcher and perfect for the little princess I had been pretending to be. I couldn't wait for Coronation Day to arrive, so I could get into my costume. Mother fussed over me, making sure I looked perfect in my royal outfit.

Dawn's Coronation dress 1953

The celebrated day arrived, and we drove up to Chessington Zoo. It was my first time visit ever.

We met my uncle and his family, who seemed pleasant enough. Of course, they commented on my dress and how patriotic I must feel. I didn't know what they meant; I was just pleased to receive a compliment and some attention. My joy, however, was to be short-lived, and soon after was to turn into my worst and most likely my Mother's worst, nightmare. All of the children in our party had been given a bottle of a new American drink called Coca Cola. We all loved it! Things were idyllic we were a happy normal group, until I ruined it all by spilling my drink all over the red, white and blue trimmed puffed sleeves. The perfect sheen of my white Taffeta dress was spoiled by a creeping brown stain. I had spilled my Coca Cola. How I had done it only the Lord knows. Was I distracted by all that was going on around me? It was such a busy day, such a busy place. In retrospect, I know any seven-year- old might have done the same, but to my mother I'd done the inexcusable.

I was devastated. What had I done to Auntie's dress! I was also terrified at the retribution my mother was about to pour on my head. My prayer was that she might overlook the mishap, as the simple clumsiness of an excited child and that, for once, I would be forgiven my misstep, and our day would continue as if nothing had happened. No such luck. The backlash wasn't long in coming. My mother held her temper just long enough to see our relatives out of earshot. They must have been quite a ways away, because, when her explosion came, the ferocity of the screaming was considerable.

"Why did you spill that drink? Can't I trust you with anything? Why are you such a clumsy, hapless child?"

Her questions hammered into my spirit. It was her most effective form of berating me. There was no way I could answer even one of the series of questions being fired at me. I had no defence for myself. I couldn't think, and I dared not try. Of course, once I was under her angry spell, as always she would deliver the final blow. I suppose she believed this last jab, always firmly stabbed into my heart, was necessary in the total elimination of any self-esteem or confidence I might have left after her tirade. Lowering her voice, so that I would be the only one hearing her poisonous zinger, Mother, in her clearest and most precise voice, dripping with emphasis and contempt, unsheathed the final verbal dagger of the day. Without thought or remorse, plunged and twisted the dagger, as she let me know that I had let her down in front of her brother and that this had completely spoiled hers, as well as everyone else's, day.

I was truly a bad child, and was burdened by the shame of causing trouble between my uncle, who'd come all the way from Singapore, and my mother. As I shrank into myself, Coronation Day turned horrid, Chessington Zoo became my prison, and I felt the stares of people gawking at the naughty little girl, who had stained her Auntie's pretty party dress. My outfit had become the object of ridicule. All eyes were on me, and I shrank from the unwanted attention. I couldn't wait to get out of that stupid, ugly costume.

So much for the hope and optimism of a new era, and so much for my Coronation Day - memorable to me only as a harsh lesson of how a child's place in society was not an expression of their self, but a mere reflection of their parent's attitude towards them.

CHAPTER FOUR

Good Times Bad Times

There was so much tradition revolving around the Royal Family. My father was privileged to be a part of the Queen's Scots Guards Regimental Band. Father's beloved Guard was, and still is, a regiment of the Division of the British Army. Its' origins date back to 1642 when King Charles I of England and Scotland created his own personal bodyguard. In 1686, the Royal Guard was made a part of the British Army and despite being made up of some musicians was an integral part of the job description that includes the Queen's safety.

Being the daughter of a father who was part of the Queen's Military Band, which is part of the Royal Guard, doomed my childhood to compulsory attendance to most official occasions, including attending the Changing of the Guard, band concerts at Hyde Park, and annual tea parties held at Buckingham Palace for the musicians' children.

The Changing of the Guard was the most difficult function for me to attend. Taking place every fourth month at Buckingham Palace, Mother, Michael and I were *always* present as the Queen's flag, along with her safety, was assigned over to the next regiment. Tourists enjoy the pageantry, my mother enjoyed the ceremony. My father was proud to be part of the spectacle. But being a child, forced to comply with tradition, dress in clothing that was not mine (and I would not have chosen for myself), and most unpleasant of all, to be expected to act in a manner that made my mother appear to be someone better than she was, caused me to detest the very things that my father held to be most important to his life.

Hyde Park concerts held every week and the annual tea parties held for all of the musician's children were a constant part of my life. Hyde Park, a beautifully landscaped oasis, is part of the Queen's gardens, located in the heart of London. The Band Stand, built for the purpose of afternoon concerts was the only cover afforded my father, while he played in all kinds of weather. I had to behave myself and listen to the military music of pomp and pageantry. If the weather was nice, a crowd would gather and sit on the grass and listen. Mother brought books for me to read, but my preference was to watch people. I would have preferred to climb trees, but that never would have been allowed. When it rained, the audience was made up entirely of drenched family members.

The annual June tea parties, held at the Buckingham Palace gardens, were probably my Mother's favorite opportunity to show off her best outfits and largest and newest hats to other military wives. For me, it meant another "best" dress I disliked, for my brother a shirt, jacket and tie. The Royal Family was always very generous towards its' military, and that included all of us who were the musician's children. It was regarded as an honor that no one should or would miss. I believe it was an honor that would have been enjoyed more if my Mother had not been attendance. Somehow, she made a party, designed for military children, into a party meant for her.

Organized games, like the egg and spoon race or three-legged race, were standard. Tents were set up away from the main seating area and always included either a puppet show or a magician to entertain us. The main seating area was made up of round cloth-covered tables, upon which gorgeous tea sets and hot water waited for smiling parents to enjoy. Waiters circled the parent's tables with huge silver trays covered with tiny finger sandwiches of salmon and cucumber, ham and tomato, or egg and crescent. Other waiters followed with small iced cakes. Mother was dazzled. I chose to be bored.

Buckingham Palace gardens where tea parties were held.

The Queen and the Queen's Mother often attended these gatherings. Impeccably dressed, always wearing gloves, they and their Maids in Waiting walked among us, talking to us children and asking if we were enjoying ourselves. We were all quick to curtsey, bow, and not speak unless spoken to. Every child in attendance had been well schooled on how to be polite and proper. My disobedient heart rebelled, but at the periphery, the security guards always watched everything that was going on. What would happen to the child who did not curtsy properly or bow quickly enough? Luckily for me, I never had to find out

Christmas parties for us were often held at Wellington Barracks, situated across from the Palace. Wellington Barracks is the home of the Guard, recruits in training, and houses the Queen's horses. Wellington had a huge mess room, where a massive decorated Christmas tree was set up, and Father Christmas always rode in on an enormous horse. Along with Father Christmas, there was singing, games, and a small gift from the Queen for each of us. If the circus happened to be in London, the children's celebration would be held there.

I suspect that if Mother had not forced me to wear the hand-me-down dresses from people I did not know, while she enjoyed the newest and nicest clothes she had picked and purchased for herself, I might have tried to enjoy all of the festivities. However, by the time I was six, I realized that was not going to happen. It had become a battle of wills. I played my part in being the inwardly rebellious child, allowing just a hint of grumpiness, which only my mother could discern, to show. Mother loudly cooperated in her role by castigating me as being an "ungrateful child."

Not everything about my Father's military duties created sad memories for me. My favorite recollections involve those times when Father got ready to go to work, particularly if he was to be in a parade. The preparations took hours, and I was entranced watching him whiten his belt with a chalk-like substance and polish all the brass buttons on his bright red coat, under which he would slip a special flat piece of brass to protect the red fabric. He spit polished his black patent leather shoes to a mirror shine, and with a damp towel deftly pressed his thick blue worsted trousers, until the creases were crisp and straight. He brushed the Bearskin to perfection. I watched mesmerized, as he attended to each detail, and all between drags of his cigarette. These were special times for me, as I had him to myself. His life with the Scots Guards afforded him a camaraderie he did not get at home. The Guards was his second family, and he spent as much time with them as possible. Essentially, my Father's life was that of a musician and a patriot.

He never left the house without his trumpet in the boot of the car. He and Mother continued to party every night - Mother dancing, drinking and smoking, father playing his beloved trumpet. This was my parents life. My brother and I stayed home - alone. We were two young children getting up every morning, fending for ourselves, going off to school.

My school, a newly built Sutton Secondary School for Girls was a public school. Its religious studies were Church of England. But because I was a Catholic, and out of respect for my faith, I was excused from opening assembly every morning, I thought this was ridiculous and decided to attend morning assembly anyway. I enjoyed singing the hymns which weren't part of a Catholic service. My favorite was *Morning Has Broken*. Aside from this morning ritual, l didn't like school too much. I felt like an outsider and didn't make many friends. I wasn't trendy and, because I started classes mid-year, I did not have a history with the other girls.

In the early sixties, the choice in classes was limited: boys had classes suitable to the "male sex" and girls took classes revolving around domestic chores. All of the girls took classes in cooking, needlework, ironing and flower arranging, while the boys focused on such things as carpentry, engineering and home repair. I was very good at needlework, thanks to Auntie who had been so patient in teaching me how to use her sewing machine. Domestic Sciences taught girls how to be homemakers and mothers. We were also taught how to iron a man's shirt and cook meals. The age of women's liberation was not yet on the horizon and girls were brought up to find a man, get married, stay at home, look after the house, and have children. Boys were taught to be breadwinners, and expected their wives to wait on them hand and foot.

At thirteen, l had ear problems and had to have my tonsils removed. This was followed by a mastoid operation at St Anthony's Hospital in Cheam Surrey. While there, the hospital held a summer garden party with Petula Clark as a guest singer. I was thrilled to see her. She came up to the ward to say "Hello" to all of the patients. She asked if I was feeling better after my operation, and told me I was very pretty.

In accordance with medicine of the sixties, my recuperation from the mastoid and tonsil surgery was to take five weeks. Post-op I was taken by ambulance to a convalescent home in Woking, which was out in the country about fifty miles away from home. I was the youngest there, and was desperately lonely. I spent my time reading, doing needle point, and walking around the massive grounds. Mum and Dad drove out to visit on Sundays and brought me new books to read. I thought the time would never end. Despite their weekly visits, my parents failed to tell me that, during the time I was "locked away" recuperating, they had up and moved our family to another part of Surrey, to a place called Sutton.

They moved us to the nicer side of Sutton. The house and garden were much bigger than any of the places we had lived before. Our other homes had always been in less expensive areas, with the rent being supplemented by the Guards, because Father wouldn't have us living in the barracks.

Our new home turned out to be a huge Victorian house. We didn't have many furnishings, and the place seemed empty. Despite the heavily lined floor to ceiling mustard colored curtains, the massive glass windows and the tall, white, filigreed ceilings made the place impossibly cold. I was grateful for the large radiators that had to run nearly non-stop in order to keep any semblance of warmth.

One positive to the move was that my parents had purchased a television. It was quite small compared to those of today, just a twelve-inch square box- no color, just a black and white picture. To make the picture seem larger, my father attached a big magnifying bubble to the front. The downside to having a bigger picture was that anyone who wished to watch television had to sit directly in front of it in order to see the picture.

In addition to having a television, we also had a telephone. Mother was so excited. It was a third party share line, which could be annoying if someone picked up and interrupted the call or quietly listened in. I remember it being large, black, heavy and expensive. To make a call we had to put our finger into the appropriate numbered hole and dial around to zero. There were no push buttons or talking to phones to make a call out in those days. I was always startled by the high-pitched ringing bell, which that let us know when someone wanted to talk to us. Little did I realize that, in very short order, the telephone would be one of my most treasured inventions.

In addition to being moved without warning, I also discovered that I had to walk almost a mile to the bus stop to get to school. It was a nice quiet neighborhood, but I knew no one, and once again did not make any friends. I walked back and forth through soaking rain terrifying thunder and lightning storms. I just knew that at any moment I would be struck dead, because the tree lined street was a perfect target for lightning to strike. Walking alone, I kept my eyes open for strangers in case they might want to talk to me, while paddling my way in shivering misery to and from the rain soaked bus stop, feeling I had to put up with it and brave it on my own.

In Sutton, Mother found work in a newsagent's shop. Her job was to sell newspapers, magazines, books, cigarettes and sweets. Dad took the train into Wellington Barracks or drove, depending on the weather, or if he had a music gig in the evening.

Because there was nothing else to do, Mike, who had not yet left home, took up ballroom dancing. The Rendezvous on Sutton High Street was about forty-five minutes away. How he found the place I will never know, as the ballroom was wedged in between shops on High Street. Future dancers trekked through a door that led downstairs to the basement. The walls were mirrored with light strips running over the top of them. The ceiling had a huge mirrored globe in the center, which turned slowly during the dancing. The Waltz, Foxtrot, Tango and Cha Cha were taught. Many times girls met Mike at the studio. He often took me along for something to do, too. Our dancing careers were short lived, because by the next summer Mike had enlisted in the Royal Engineers and was gone. As an Engineer, Mike was trained to maintain the railways, roads, water supply, bridges and transport. Royal Engineers also operated the railways and inland waterways.

If Dad was not working, especially in the springtime, we were loaded into the car and drove an hour out to the country to my favorite picnic place, Box Hill. The countryside was beautiful. The lanes were lined with hedges, all grown to separate one homeowner's property from another. Once we got into the woods, the hedges fell away, and I remember in April the hills would be covered with Blue

Bells. Blue Bell time, I loved it! The beauty of seeing and walking through all those dainty blue flowers, growing wild in the woods as far as the eye could see, was something I would never forget.

However, as much as I enjoyed going to such wonderful places, the car travel was always a hardship on me. Invariably I would get car sick. When I think of car sickness, I think of my parents constantly lighting up and puffing away on their Woodbine's. The good side to this, I suppose, is that I have never had any desire to even try to smoke, I always hated the smell of cigarettes and the residual odor it left. I vowed I would never smell that way. It was such a fashionable thing to do back then. All the movie stars smoked their way through films, while newspapers, billboards, buses, buildings and businesses promoted one brand over another. Everywhere we went: in pubs, at restaurants, in stores, there was always a cloud of smoke and stinky ashtrays. It was the expected thing and no one back then considered their health and the harm smoking cigarettes might do.

As soon as school let out, and the summer holiday began, I was on the first bus headed for Great Yarmouth and my Aunt Eva. Because I had grown up, I no longer went downtown to see the latest in bridal design and had lost interest in watching Aunt Eva iron. Instead, I hung out with schoolmates at Leo's Coffee Bar. The name "coffee bar' is not an entirely correct description - it was more like an ice-cream soda shop. We were a fashionable crowd. The boys greased and combed back their hair, and we girls wore tight pencil skirts and twin tops, which were matching short sleeve sweaters with cardigans. We danced to the juke box, and made our way up to the market place for a plate of cockles - a very small shell fish splashed with vinegar. Our favorite choice was fresh fish, with chips red hot, wrapped in newspaper. We ate while we walked down High Street to the Marina Parade entertainment, all the while talking about the new American singing groups.

CHAPTER FIVE

Around and Around

When my brother Michael came home on leave, he frequented a smoky pub called the Red Lion, in Sutton Surrey, where we still lived. It was 1962 and I was sixteen years old. My first exposure to the Stones was with Mike at that pub. The Stones didn't mean anything to anyone then. They were just a few lads with longish hair and unkempt clothes playing together. I loved their music from the first. When my brother wasn't around, I went to hear them with my girlfriend Bronny (Blodwin Owen). She loved them from the beginning as well.

My first memories were of Mick Jagger and Brian Jones sitting at a table drinking, smoking and discussing which of the musicians, that had auditioned for bass and drums, would be the best fit for the band.

I remember Mick as being a tall lean college boy, dressed in tight trousers, a sweater, and wearing a scarf with one end thrown over his shoulder. He stood out in the crowd, with his flamboyant clothes and confidant demeanor. When he walking into a room, the atmosphere changed. It seemed as if everything was supposed to stop, so as to take notice that he had arrived. He could be funny and sometimes cutting in his speech and manner - one of those kinds of people you either loved, or hated.

The Red Lion where the Rolling Stones played in 1962

    As I got to know him, I learned that he was a student the London School of Economics. The way he talked, it seemed that he knew where he was going in life and exactly how he was going to get there. He was charismatic, confident, and never at a loss for words.

    Mick had a close friend, Keith Richards, who was part of the group and was also sitting in on the conversation that first day I saw them. He was a skinny boy, with dark messy hair. In his dark gray corduroy trousers and a crew neck t-shirt under a long black leather jacket. he had a roguish, rough appearance. Leaning into the conversation, he was agreeing with everything Mick was saying about band member selection. Keith was a chain smoker and always had a cigarette nearby. As a matter of fact, the entire group smoked constantly, and they didn't care about the brand. They smoked whatever they were able to beg or borrow.

Brian was quietly sitting, observing Mick and Keith, while listening to what they had to say. As the Stone's founder, he had the last say regarding the musicians who would be joining the group. In a way, he didn't look like he belonged with the other two boys. His style wasn't Jagger flamboyant, nor was it even close to the Keith Richards rebel look. He was impeccably dressed - his trousers didn't have a wrinkle or crease, his t-shirt looked new, and his shoes were spotlessly clean.

From the beginning, Brian had visions of a bluesy type band. All of the boys were fans of the Delta blues musician Muddy Waters, and I believe it was his influence that brought the diverse group of lads, that the Stones were to become, together.

Right from the start, I noticed the boys did more talking, smoking and drinking than playing. Just a few of us hung out to listen to them. 'Carol' were crowd favorites. People often wandered in off of the streets to get a drink, and then stayed to listen if the boys decided to perform. Eric Clapton dropped by from time to time.

While hanging out, Bronny and I also got to know the keyboard player, Ian Stewart, otherwise known as Stu. Stu was one of the kindest men I've ever known, and always made us feel welcome when we showed up and hung around talking, while he organized the group's setup, he fixed guitar strings and found parts for the drums. A truly gifted pianist, he loved playing blues, jazz and boogie-woogie for us. He was the only one of the group who owned a vehicle, a Volkswagen van he had purchased to haul the boys and their equipment to gigs in.

When Bill Wyman joined, he brought his own guitar- a fretless bass he'd made himself, which provided a distinctive sound that the boys loved. He also had his own amplifier. This contribution made him a "keeper." He was nice, seemed a bit shy, quiet, and more into his music than socializing.

The same was true of Charlie Watts, the new drummer. He loved the music more than the "scene" of what was going on around him. He had a steady girlfriend, Shirley Shepherd, and, unlike the other boys, never cheated on her. Mick, Brian and Keith were more interested in the limelight.

During those early years, my parents imposed a curfew of ten o'clock in the evening on me. Not that the curfew made a bit of difference. My rebellious streak was never far away and sneaking out of the house wasn't hard, since my parents were doing what they normally did - party all night. I played at going to bed, waited, and was out as soon as they were. More often than not, I pretended to be spending the night with Bronny, and that gave me carte blanche to do as I pleased. What I pleased to do was find the boys and listen to them play hour after hour.

In late 1962, my parents moved again, this time to Belgravia Chesham Place, near Slone Square, in borough of Westminster, right in the heart of London. I don't think I became aware of class status until then. We had always lived in middle class homes, where the neighbors were friends and no one was better than anyone else. But, at the age of fifty, my father had been honorably discharged from the Scots Guards. No longer eligible for military housing, he needed to find a job and a place for us to stay. Chesham Place was the solution to both of his problems. His job was to take care of the building and repair anything that went wrong in tenant flats. He kept the front entry spotless and locked the tenant entrance after eight in the evening. Mother served as housekeeper to Mrs. Hopton, the wife of the landlord. Mr. Hopton our employer, was the owner of Chesham Place and a wealthy Member of Parliament.

Chesham Place, Chesham Close, was situated on the Lyall Street corner. A private driveway meandered up to a charming paved courtyard. Lush shrubs scaled the surrounding walls and, alongside the black polished front doors, stood two massive potted fir trees. The doors opened onto a grand marbled foyer, adorned with a large chandelier dripping with diamond shaped crystals. Built in the Victorian era, Chesham Place was designed so that the exquisite view of the square's park could be enjoyed. Surrounded by a black wrought iron fence and gated for the use of tenants of Chesham place only, benches were situated under the shade of magnificent trees, which were surrounded by grassy areas and lined by flowerbeds, filling the seasons with different colors.

My parents, being staff, were housed in a basement flat and had their own entrance, which was entered from Chesham Place and down a wrought iron staircase to the basement yard and into our own front door. The magnificent front door and grand square were barred from our use. Despite their position as employees, our flat was actually quite large. The kitchen was the prominent feature when we entered our home. A cozy living room waited for us to the left of the hallway, and my parent's room was on the right near the bathroom. The flat had only one bedroom, so my room was located outside my parent's flat - down the hall, past an office and across from another flat. It was a cozy setup for a teenage girl. There were also stairs and a service elevator in this hall that employees were to use when doing work for the tenants.

Since I was sixteen, and done with my schooling, Mother decided that it was time I found a career for myself, so that I could move out and find my own way. That's how things were then - once a student left school they were expected to go to work. My aspirations were in the field of nursing, followed eventually by becoming a midwife. However, at sixteen, I was too young to attend nursing school, as the entrance age was eighteen. Mother wouldn't hear of me waiting almost two years to begin a vocation, since she wanted me contributing to the household finances as soon as possible. She explained that I could attend nursing school in two years, if that was what I still wanted to do.

Since I had no idea as to what kind of career I might want to undertake, Mother decided my future for me. She determined that I was to become a hairdresser, because I liked to play around with hair. Therefore, the next step in my life was to become a stylist.

Having decided my future decided for me, I was informed the next day that I would apprentice at Clariages, one of the oldest and most expensive hotels in London. In the early sixties, schools to teach hairdressing were non-existent. The place was old, and smelt stuffy, Nothing about it fit my personality. I wanted out and lasted a week.

Not to be deterred, Mother wasted no time and marched me down to Michele of Park Lane, a very posh and expensive location in a well-to-do part of town. They were old fashioned and boring, again just not me. I hated it and only lasted a month.

Vidal Sasson opened his first salon in Mayfair in 1954

My next port of call was with an up and coming stylist located in Mayfair, London - Vidal Sassoon. My starting wages would be two pounds a week and increasing every six months. Mother collected my wages for use on the household expenses leaving me enough cash for the tube train and lunch.

I was one of a group of apprentices that year for Vidal. We spent our first three months sweeping floors, gathering towels and making tea, while watching the salon. Unlike the salons I had been at before, this was big, and modern. As new apprentices, we were not allowed to interact with clients. However, once we had mastered the art of tea making and towel handling, Vidal began to allow us to shampoo clients and then trained us in the art of passing pins to him, while he combed out hair. It was only after such menial tasks had been mastered to his standards that we were allowed to learn to cut hair.

His style was very unique and was fast becoming all the rage. He cut the hair very short at the back, graduating to long in the front. Being a perfectionist, he was hard to work for None of us ever knew if he was going to throw things across the room, humiliate one of us, or be nice. He was a temperamental man, who was all smiles and conversation to clients and then, when they were gone, would turn two-faced behind their backs. We never knew what each day would bring, and the stress was enormous.

My Friend Bronny, who was still living in Sutton, often took the train out to meet me after work. Sharing my love of music, she was my accomplice of choice in going to various venues to see the newest bands play. She knew of a place called the Marquee Club, where Alex Korner had an up and coming band. The front of the club was indistinguishable from any other storefront, except for the bill posters advertising such groups as John Mayall. We went as often as we could, taking the underground to Oxford Street.

The Stones began to play there regularly, so, in addition to watching the boys, we began to make friends with other music industry hopefuls. Bronny began dating a boy, who wanted to be in a band. I was happy hanging with Stu, Mick, Brian and Keith. As the Stones sound began to improve, they played more gigs. Stu told us when and where, the group was going to be playing next, and would ask us to come and support them. Of course we were more than happy to accommodate.

*Marquee Club opened in 1958 and moved
to Wardour St London in 1964*

Bronny and I didn't just spend our time at the Marquee. The Flamingo Club was a short walk over to Wardour Street, Soho. Jammed between two shoe stores, it was better known for its jazz over pop music.

When we felt more adventurous, we caught the train out to Windsor and hung out at the Ricky Tick Club. The Ricky Tick was small and dark, and located in an upstairs room at the Star and Garter Public House on Peascod Street. The ride to Windsor was long for two teenage girls with limited funds. Traveling in London in those days was relatively easy and safe. I don't know what my parents would have thought if they knew that, while they were out night after night enjoying the music they loved, we were traveling around London in pursuit of the music and groups we admired.

Crawdaddy Pub was called The Station Hotel the present day it's The Bull & Bush, the Rolling Stone first played there July 21st 1962

Another club that was popular with us, as well as many other fans, was located in Richmond, it was opposite the train station in the Station Hotel, and this was called the Crawdaddy Club. It had a great atmosphere but was quite small. As the groups they featured became more popular and as followers increased, queues began to form outside around the street. Such popularity forced the Crawdaddy to relocate to the larger Richmond Athletic Club.

Also, Studio 51 was a place to see all the jazz and rock bands. While we followed the Stones from one club to another, but we never lost our affinity for the Flamingo, I guess that is because that is where things began for us.

Brian, Mick, Charlie & Keith (Courtesy of Bill Wyman Archives)

Many times, after the shows, we were invited by Stu and one or another of the boys to the Lyon's Tea House Marble Arch, which was open all night. We were free to joke around and talk about music, usually American blues artists. Those were good times.

It was during one of those nights that Stu was told by Andrew Loog Oldem, then Stones manager who had taken over from Giorgio Gomelsky, that he was not going to be a band member anymore because his image didn't fit. Stu was rightfully upset and hurt, but I was not surprised when he stayed on as road manager. He cared about the group, kept them organized, made sure they got to where they needed to go, and to be honest, sometimes they still needed him to play keyboard. That was Stu - all heart. He was really attentive about the boys, and I also think he knew they were going to go somewhere and be something big.

At the age of seventeen, and having worked at Vidal Sassoon's apprenticeship long enough, I was sent to a Wella permanent wave course and then off to L'Oreal coloring school, both located on Oxford Street. It was there, through one of the other students, that I met Simon Boyle, a socialite who owned a successful wig making business. He asked me if I would be interested in making hair wigs and would be happy to train me. The pay was good, ten pounds a week, so I left Vidal and went to work for Simon Boyle, and his partner Luc, in a tiny little mews house off Bond Street.

I loved the work. The clients were interesting, some of them theater people, some society, and even a few royalty. Simon's wife was a beautiful tall, and lean French model named Marie Les. Simon was a kind man and easy to work for. He dressed impeccably, had a slim frame, handsome face and wore the Edwardian look of long coat jackets. He also drove a dazzling 1950's white Mercedes sports convertible. This was during the time that the Beatles were becoming famous, and the Boyle's played their new LP all of the time. One of the most exciting parts of my job was to go to the West End Theaters and pick up wigs for actors like Anna Massey and Sir Lawrence Oliver. It was the most exciting and happiest time in my life. I had no idea at the time that I was living part of the sixties history.

I also had no clue that my home in Chesham Place was also the same building where Brian Epstein lived. The Beatles were known to walk into the foyer, go up the lift to the top floor, and I never noticed. I was also unaware that Andrew Loog Oldham had been Brian Epstein's PR man before managing the Rolling Stones.

Some weekends, Bronny and I would venture to Soho and sit in the 2i's Coffee Bar on Old Compton Street. Back then they were still playing blues, like Robert Johnson & Jimmy Reed, which I loved. Before Eric Clapton became famous, he was a frequent visitor. He didn't pay any attention to us, but we noticed him.

Bill & Charlie at Studio 51 (Courtesy of Bill Wyman Archives)

    During one of our nights at the Station Hotel, Stu noticed us arriving. He was setting up the props and made a point of talking to us, excited to tell us that the boys had recorded their first single, "Come On/I Wanna Be Loved", on Decca. They were going to be on television, on a show called *'Thank Your Lucky Stars'*. He could hardly contain himself. Pacing and acting like an overgrown kid, he was all smiles and said he knew this was the start of something huge.

These were changing times, wonderful times. Mary Quant was designing clothes with her trademark daisy on them. Jean Shrimpton, the top model, was in all the exclusive magazines. David Bailey was the top photographer, and Vidal Sassoon was making a statement with his hair styles.

One of the tenants in our house was a son of Lord Serge Beddington Behrens. His father and step mother lived upstairs, while he had a flat in the basement next to ours. He was friendly, but a little awkward - tall and lanky, not at all confident talking to girls. We became friends. One night, after he and his university friends had partied one night by drinking too much and putting bubble bath down the toilets and sinks to see them overflow, I helped him clean up his place, so he would not get into trouble from his parents. It was through him that I met Lady Roxanna Lampton, better known as Bunty.

We became good friends. She was a terrific, fun loving girl, with a tiny frame, and long straight black hair. She drove around in a purple MGB sports convertible that has a tape deck. Back then, that was so wild. She knew I was the caretaker's daughter but didn't care that I was not aristocracy or in society, and often took me to Portobello Road, or Carnaby Street, to shop. Or, we'd go for a drink in the Lowndes Arms. It wasn't until much later that I learned that The Stones had played at her debutante ball three months before I knew her, when apparently Brian was ill in the car out side so Chris Andrews played instead, and the boys hung out after.

AROUND AND AROUND

Rolling Stones at Tin Pan Alley (picture courtesy of Terry O'Neill/Rex USA)

CHAPTER SIX

The Singer Not the Song

The summer of 1963 found me as usual on holiday visiting, my aunt at Great Yarmouth. I needed the break from the long work days I had been putting in at Simons and staying on guard against my mother's antagonism. Life in general had become a mindless treadmill. Visiting Auntie, making some new but never close friends, at least provided relief.

Just days before my leaving Yarmouth and my return to the "real world" of London, I saw a flyer at Leo's Coffee Bar advertising that the Rolling Stones were scheduled to play at the Grand Hotel ballroom in Lowestoft the following night, September sixth.

I showed the flyer to a couple of the girls, who had attended school with me, and whom I loosely considered to be friends.

"I know these boys, they're friends of mine." I shared, my enthusiasm getting the better of me. "I used to hang out with them at the Marquee Club in London."

"Yeah, I bet." was their sarcastic reply. Their father owned The Baron's Amusement Park on the promenade. They'd grown up with money and I suppose the thought of an insignificant nobody, like Dawn Molloy, hanging out with the increasingly famous Rolling Stones was ludicrous.

"I think I might go and see them." I'd made the statement without thinking. It had been a spur of the moment idea not one I'd intended on sharing, at least not to the likes of the Baron's girls. These were not girls to disclose anything to. They'd always been taunting, sarcastic and stuck-up towards me.

"We have front row tickets!" they revealed in triumph "We'll give you a lift to the Lowestoft so you can see your old *friends*."

This, of course, was meant to embarrass me. Instead, it made me mad and, giving in to my impulsive nature, I took them up their offer for a drive to the hotel, hoping after the fact to purchase a ticket and see if I could get backstage once the concert was over, The thought "What if no one remembers me?" flashed through my mind, but there was no turning back.

The Grand Hotel Lowestoft.

True to their word, the Baron girls picked me up to take me to the concert. As we entered the The Grand Hotel driveway, I spotted Stu, with an armload of equipment, unloading his van. It was as good a chance as any to find out if I was remembered or not. I told the girls to drop me off, which they did, gladly. I'm sure they watched as I strolled over to Stu in the parking area. He was so surprised to see me that he nearly dropped the amp he was holding.

Putting it down, he embraced me in a hug that made it quite clear he remembered who I was. I never turned around to see what the reaction was in the car that had just dropped me off.

"You are the last person I would ever expect to see so far away from London." He laughed.

"I'm visiting my aunt. I saw your flyer at the coffee bar and thought I'd see the boys play, before I take the train back home tomorrow."

"Oh ride back with us, don't bother with the train." And just like that my plans changed, and I helped unload the van. Following Stu up the stairs to the lounge, carrying drum parts, I saw the boys. Bill was tuning his guitar. Mick and Keith were sharing some personal joke, and Charlie was concentrating on something he was writing. Stu said that Brian was sick again, with an asthma attack, and not making the gig. The boys were going to have to work harder, not having the extra guitar on stage.

"Look who I found." Stu announced, and when the boys looked up, their heartfelt greetings and surprise, followed by questions as to why I was so far from the Marquee, put us all right back as if no time between us had passed.

"You will enjoy the show, Dawn," Stu assured me with pride "We've have come a long way since you saw us last."

I did have to admit that I was surprised at how much things had changed with the group. I certainly took notice that their hair had grown considerably longer, and that they were all dressed differently - more to their own personal style, completely dissimilar to the suit thing that manger Andrew Loog Oldham had pushed on them in the beginning.

Paying customers began to fill the Ballroom, the air was filled with smoke and anticipation, fans were everywhere in the lounge. A photographer and a couple of reporters from local television stations arrived. I could feel the expectation. Stu led me back downstairs. The crowd was loud and tense, keen for the show to begin. The equipment was set, and, with no opening act to warm up the audience, the energy level from just beyond the curtain was heating up. As the boys took to the stage, the voices of screaming girls assaulted our ears. Stu put me stage left, affording me a preferential place to see the boys and the crowd in action.

My excitement spiked, as the curtain drew back and the deafening roar of screaming girls running towards the stage trying to touch the boys, erupted. I had never seen anything like it before. Bouncers pushed the excited fans back, dragged them away, and then returned to remove another mass of hysterical teenagers. Fans were throwing flowers, love letters and stuffed toys onto the stage. Looking out into the crowd, I couldn't help smirking, as I glanced down at those two snooty Baron girls sitting in the front row, mouths wide open in shock at seeing me side stage. The expression on their faces was classic.

The boys *had* changed, since I had seen and heard them last. They were more confident on stage - not trying to second - guess what each one would do individually anymore. They were a band now, taking the lead from Mick - the born showman. He had always been a bundle of energy, able to hypnotize the audience with his facial expressions and lean gyrating frame. I was captivated by his hands, shaking the maracas in time with the music willing it all: sound, music, motion, into an extension of his body. Mick, wiggling and jumping to the beat of the music in those tight trousers, oozed sex. He was everywhere at once, relentless, and never seemed to tire.

During the slow songs, he teased the girls, leaning towards them, cupping the microphone in his hands, his eyes luring them in with a 'come on' look. Responding to the bait, the girls surged forward, reaching and stretching towards their deity. Mick, on dancing feet, slipped back and away, flipping his chin and tossing his hair across his smiling face. 'Come on' his body reiterated, enticing and suggestive. Girls fainted, screamed and collapsed in tears.

Mick Jagger singing with Keith Richards on guitar.

Energetic Keith shadowed Mick titillated the crowd, playing the rhythm guitar, undulating and interacting off of Mick's dance moves, enticing the crowd into a surging frenzy.

Bill, on bass, played as he always did, his focus, demeanor, and passion were given over to the music. He seemed immune and unaffected by the histrionics engulfing the audience. Standing stage right, moving to the beat, playing his riffs, trying to hear the song over the pandemonium, he chewed his gum and smiled at the unseen faces beyond the stage.

In the back, hammering out the beats, and driving the momentum forward, was Charlie lashing out the tempos that propelled the energy in Mick's feet around the stage. The primal thrusts of the drumbeats drove the girls to greater madness, until, in a climax of energy, the Lowestoft crowd was engulfed and encapsulated.

Together before frenzied, swooning onlookers, The Rolling Stones had taken the basic blues music of such greats as Bo Diddley and Howling Wolf, infused it with some of America's deep south Louisiana classic sound, and made it their own.

When the show ended, I stayed back stage and helped Stu pick up the flowers, letters and toys thrown by love struck fans. Despite being hot and tired and I'm sure needing rest, the boys had snatched up a Teddy and were throwing it back and forth between them, laughing and jumping as their tosses went over heads, under feet or at each other.

With things cleaned up but the parking area still full of excited girls, we all retired to the lounge to enjoy the cool breeze wafting in from the open bay windows. The boys unwound by enjoying a few whiskey and cokes, while I drank Tizer. Girls began to show up, actually they seemed to be everywhere - some were friends, others complete strangers. What shocked me was that they all seemed 'available.' The boys came and went as each potential conquest flew into their radar.

Mick and Chrissy, his girlfriend at the time, had quite a row on the phone, "I don't get it," he said to me. "What is her problem? She gets jealous over everything." I really didn't know what to say. Couldn't he see how his behavior towards other girls and how his cheating would cause her not to trust him? Chrissy had every reason to be upset, angry and sad over Mick's conduct. As a matter of fact that very night he left to his hotel room with a very leggy blond.

It seemed to be the norm for the boys now, and that was another change I saw in them. Keith would sit in the lounge with two girls all over him, not having to work at trying to get them to come up to his room and to his bed.

Bill was doing pretty much the same thing. I wondered how girls could throw themselves at someone they didn't know and why they would do that? I guess I was always the dreamer, looking for a relationship, seeing my man and I being only with one another. This Rock and Roll lifestyle where girls offering themselves as a one night stand was as alien to me as the idea of men walking on the moon.

Charlie was not like the rest of the boys. He didn't say much, always reserved and pleasant, and didn't make jokes about people the way Mick and Keith did. I remember him talking to the reporter from the local paper with Mick after the show, and going to his room alone.

Stu left the lounge and took all of the boy's equipment to the van. By then it was the early morning hours. The hotel grounds were finally free of girls and everyone had gone to bed. I was parked in an overstuffed chair, tired but happy. Stu sat down on the couch opposite me.

"We've been back at the recording studios to cut another disk. It's called *You Better Move On*, and is going to be released later this year." he told me I could hear the excitement in his voice, he was so proud of everything that was going on. "We are booked in so many places, I'm not sure how we are going to fit it all in Andrew had not considered travel time between the shows," at this he sounded worried. We stayed up talking most of the night about Stu's worry about not getting all of the gigs in that they were booked for, they were also wondering why there was no money for all the work they were doing, about the places they had played, the girls, the fame and how they still liked playing the small Clubs the most.

I don't know when I fell asleep, Stu was gone, probably off to his room I had supposed alone, and I was still in the overstuffed chair. I awoke to the sound of a vacuum and the clattering of china plates by the maids laying out tables in the dining room downstairs, getting things ready for breakfast. The evening seemed almost dreamlike, but there I was alone in a chair wondering what to do next. I decided I might as well get up and stretch my legs.

The dining room, with floor to ceiling windows, overlooked the beach. It was quite warm and sunny for early September, and looking out at the breakers after a night of such frenzy was surreal. It wasn't long before everyone began to trail in. I didn't have much money with me and, since we were all paying for our own meals, I just had and toast and tea. Mick was awake and full of his usual self, taking the piss out of the waiter, who was acting flamboyant and flirtatious. The boys were in hysterics, and of course Keith jumped right in, helping to wind Mick up tighter, taking the jokes a bit further. I loved their sense of humor - witty and very dry. It was fun to watch and be part of their larking about. They didn't care who their target was when it came to a joke. Birds with big breasts were a favorite.

Seeing riders pass by on horses gave Keith the idea that they should get some horses and ride along the beach at the water's edge. The idea didn't go far because, just as quickly another leaped into Keith's mind and out his mouth. It was all too funny and over much too quickly, we all had to get back to London. Vidal Sassoon and Mother had been lurking at the edges of my mind - time to return home.

Mick now drove a dark green Ford Zephyr he borrowed from his Dad. He'd parked it out in the back lot, and brought it around for the drive back to London. Mick and I were in front, with Keith, and Charlie in the back. Stu followed with Bill in his rickety van with all the equipment. Before we left, we threw in money for petrol, and hoped that Stu's van wouldn't break down. It was amazing, with how many gigs they were playing, that none of them had any money. Money was an issue that the boys had decided would be discussed with Andrew, as soon as they returned to London.

It was a memorable trip. With each crossing, or stop light, we were vulnerable to dive bomb attack from frenzied girls. Spotting Mick's car full of Rolling Stones created a magnate for screaming females trying to claw their way inside, clinging to the windows crying and screaming. At first the boys thought it was hilarious. They had no idea they'd become so recognizable. They laughed as Mick took extra precautions not to drive off with a girl still attached to the car.

Despite the hilarity of making fun of dive-bombing girls, Mick and Keith found time to play practical jokes on each other. At one point, when everyone was sleeping, Mick flicked his cigarette butt out the window. Whether it was on purpose or not, the cigarette reentered the car through the open back window and landed on Keith's lap. Keith nearly knocked himself out jumping to the roof, trying to get the burning butt out of his crotch. Not too funny in Keith's mind, but side splitting in ours. The more Keith swore at Mick, the funnier it became.

Listening to the radio and hearing, *Come On* their first hit to reach the charts, we all felt a surge of pride and gyrated, laughed, yelled and sang with the song. It was their lucky break. They were going to be famous and I knew them - all of the hours of practice and playing were paying off.

Eventually, we arrived back in London. Stu's van had managed to stay in one piece, but Mick's car was badly scratched by the out of control fans. Mick and the boys drove me back to the house at Chesham Place, and Mick made a remark about me being a rich kid, as they dropped me off. I never let him know that I was only the caretaker's daughter. Maybe it was because we were all too busy saying our "goodbye's", or maybe it was because of my hurried retreat into the downstairs flat, so that my father wouldn't see who had brought me home. I didn't want to explain what I was doing in a car full of longhaired boys. As they drove away from the front entrance, I ran around to the servant's entrance and went inside.

CHAPTER SEVEN

Stupid Girl

Life was changing in England. As a generation, British youth were pursuing their own dreams and seeking independence from the beliefs of their elders. Most boys were letting their hair grow, a visible rebelliousness that our parents hated. This was the time when the Mods and the Rockers were coming into their own. Whether Mod or Rocker, teen groups set themselves apart by the dress and hairstyles they chose.

Mod girls wore their hair board straight, with a thick fringe hanging down their foreheads. I learned to iron my hair by spreading it out on the ironing board, placing brown paper on top, and applying a hot iron. Dark eye makeup, false eyelashes, pale lipstick, miniskirts, boots and empire dresses created our wardrobe. Mod boys, not afraid of color, dressed in trousers of bright purples and pinks, and wore sports jackets or parkas.

Mod interests revolved around the music of the day, mainly rhythm and blues, soul and beat. Scooters were a favorite mode of transportation, which was completely opposite from the Rocker boys whose preferred mode of transport were Triumph's and BSA's.

Rockers greased their hair into pompadours, dressed in black leather jackets and motorcycle boots. The Rocker girls wore next to nothing under their leather jackets, and set themselves apart by wearing loads of make-up and big hair. Fifties songs and rock and roll were their music of choice.

Working in London, I was exposed to many different fashion statements. My friend Bronny had always been very modern, and as often as possible I emulated her style. Working at the salon, I met women from all walks of life, who had an elegance and flair adapted to reflect the current trends while retaining their own personal tastes. I learned, from observing how these women dressed, to adapt my own clothes to reflect *my* individual take on contemporary trends.

November of 1963, the Stones were playing at the Leyton Baths. Bronny told me that her friend, Alan, wanted to know if we would like to come. I remember how we giggled and laughed over that question. Who wouldn't want to go and see the Stones play?

Alan and his girlfriend, Andrea, often went with Bronny to Soho to listen to the blues. Alan was everything proper English parents feared. He loved the Mod style and dressed the part to perfection, from his fourteen-inch bell bottom trousers, tab-collared shirts (that made his neck sore), to the penny round collars held together with a pin. He also had a Beatle Jacket that sported a low round collar and four buttons going down the front. But Alan's clothes were not the ultimate high point of his wardrobe. What put his attire over the top were the prized Anello boots, which he had purchased with his mates at Drury Lane from a shoemaker called Anello & Davides.

Those boots were the ultimate in trendy with their gusset sides at the ankle, their Cuban-heeled high arches and a seam running from the top of the boot along the foot to the toe. The popular label for them was" Beatle Boots", because the Beatles had worn them on stage, thereby making them an instant must have. The boots came in black, brown or blue, and due to their popularity were limited in the number available. The fact that Alan had a pair was big news to all of us.

Leyton Baths Closed in 1991

November twenty-third, the day of the Stones concert arrived. We all met at the bus going to the east end of London. Getting off at the Leyton Baths, we felt the excitement of the crowd. It was electric, and rushed out and engulfed us. The air smelled of petrol, two stroke diesel oil, fish'n chips, and beer fumes from the surrounding pubs. It was five-thirty and we wasted no time in getting in the queue. By six-thirty, the queue had grown to almost a hundred teenagers, milling around and waiting for the doors to open.

From our vantage in queue and from what seemed to be coming out of nowhere, a gang of "Scooter Boys" riding chromed Vespers and Lambrettas, all sporting tall aerials decorated with flowing foxtails, sped past. As we watched them disappear into the darkness, a gang of Rockers, or Greasers, as we often called them this because of all the hair crème they wore, thundered by. The vibration from their BSA's, and British Norton's shook through our bodies, and we worried that they might stop and accost us "Mods" as we waited in queue. Our concerns were not without merit as the Mod's and Rockers had clashed up and down the coast nearly every weekend, causing many adults in Britain to worry that these two groups would "bring about the disintegration of the nation's character," as news reports stated.

As soon as the doors opened we surged forward, the growing queue disappearing as we moved. The venue, called the Leyton Baths, had been a swimming pool. The pool was covered with wooden planks that served as a concert and dance hall. The old style 1930's building stank of bleach, and our ears were assaulted by the now familiar sound of screaming girls. As we moved ahead, the smell of cigars, cigarettes, beer, highly lacquered hair and cheap perfume nearly gagged us. Burly rough looking bouncers were stationed around the auditorium and in front of the, for the moment, empty stage.

We paid our five shillings and squeezed onto the dance floor. Down front was a cluster of Rockers. My fear was that they would start taunting the Mods, calling them "queers" or "fruity" and cause a riot. Packed elbow-to-elbow, if a disturbance broke out we would be trampled before we could make a move to get out. Directly in front of me swaying back and forth was a large Rocker girl with heavily lacquered back-combed hair. Alan lit up a cigarette, dodging as she moved so as not to set her hair on fire.

Spying footwear shuffling beneath the stage curtains ignited a louder swell of screams from the audience. The band was tuning up, and how they heard the "one, two, three," as they did their sound check, I will never know.

As the curtains drew open, the crowd of girls unleashed an even more thunderous salvo of earth shaking screams. Emotions ran out of control. The Rocker in front of us toppled backwards and crashed to the floor. Other girls also dropped in unconsciousness, smashing onto the wooden boards. The fainting escalated as the concert progressed. Young males willingly lifted the limp young women up and happily took them out, while their mates were delighted by the show of bras and knickers that were paraded out the exit, stage left, to the waiting St. John Ambulance services outside the exit doors.

The ear splitting squeals the general tumult of fallen bodies being dragged out guaranteed we wouldn't be able to hear a thing. Mick's lips soundlessly moved, but his gyrating hips covered in tight trousers said everything the girls wanted to hear.

I was barely able to make out the sound of Bill's bass that, as was his style, was being held vertical as he played. In a gray jacket, blue leather waistcoat and tight leather, trousers, he stood nearly motionless. Only his eyes moved as observed the throng of teens below, all the while chewing gum.

Brian was playing next to him. Alan, a guitar enthusiast, yelled into my ear "Do you see what he is playing? It's his Gretsch!" The name meant nothing to me, but the spearmint green guitar with the white scratch protector had obviously made an impression on our fashion minded friend. "Do you see, he's wearing Anello boots!" What I had noticed was an immaculately dressed blond haired angel, wearing very fine striped trousers with matching waistcoat, white shirt and string tie.

Unable to hear above the din, and concerned that the vibrating floor might give way causing us all to end up in the pool, Bronny and I decided to leave early and beat the crowds. As we left we guessed they were playing' *Route 66'*.

Outside, chaos still reigned, as girls cried in St John's Ambulances and others begged to be let back into the show again. A group of Mods and Rockers were milling around glaring at one another, and we had the feeling that we should take the next bus back home as soon as possible.

Chapter Eight

The Spider and the Fly

On a Saturday night in late March 1964, I was home alone listening to the Stone's latest release *Not Fade Away*, having no idea what that title would mean to me in the future, when Bunty came bounding through my bedroom door, having deserted a party at Serge's.

"There was no one interesting tonight, come on Dawn let's go out and have some fun." As always she was immaculately dressed, and as usual I felt like a Quasimodo to her graceful beauty. "Come on Dawn, don't waste the night, and put on that Mary Quant outfit you bought when we went shopping. You look so good in it and I want to go to a *real* party."

I guessed that Serge's did not meet her standards, meaning that the Who's Who of London were not in attendance. "Come on Dawn, let's go." That was it, I never said no to Bunty, or did anyone else. She was The Lady, the rest of us serving as her court. As I dressed, Bunty let my father know that we would be out late.

AD-LIB Club in 1963 and now The Prince Charles Cinema.

We were off, and Bunty knew exactly where she wanted us to go - the exclusive club called the Ad Lib. How she got us in (or maybe I should say how she got me in) I will never know. As I've said, no one ever said no to Bunty. The lift taking us up to the club was ultra modern, dimly lit, and everywhere I looked I saw my reflection mirrored in the highly polished chrome. I felt like we had entered a space capsule. Music serenaded us, as we were transported to the penthouse.

The doors opened, and the usual smell of cigarettes, booze and perfume greeted us, as we stepped onto the crowded dance floor. The low ceiling echoed the music being played by the DJ, and as I looked around I saw Paul McCartney with Jane Asher and George Harrison with Patti Boyd. My boss, Simon, was there along with his gorgeous wife Marie Les, her friend, model Jean Shrimpton, and Jean's sister, Chrissy, Mick Jaggar's girlfriend at the time.

Bunty pushed through the throng heading straight for the bar. I followed behind, an attendant to her procession. The lights of Leicester Square glittered like tiny fairy lanterns below us. The view out the giant picture window on the other side of the bar was spectacular. Ready with drinks in hand, I followed Bunty as we made the rounds saying hello to everyone, with me feeling coffee at high tea. What made me think that my scalloped skirted black crepe Mary Quant suit, and trendy Mary Jane shoes, would hide the fact that I was just a commoner and did not belong in such a notorious gathering? I was no Bunty, who looked fantastic in anything she wore on her tiny frame and walked like royalty in black boots and mini dress. I visualized being tossed out like rubbish,, if anyone were to find out I was just a caretaker's daughter.

Bunty was talking to a casually dressed male friend, I scanning the room, watching the partiers dance, laugh, and chat, I felt as if a red arrow was pointing in my direction: "Don't talk to Dawn here," it said "she does not belong." As I scrutinized the room, I noticed Brian sitting at a corner table, disinterestedly talking to a girl who was obviously trying to get his full attention by leaning forward towards him. Wearing a black turtleneck sweater and light colored, trousers, he was smoking as usual. Of course, I had seen him many times before, in concert and with the boys when the band was just starting up. But this was really the first time I had ever really taken any notice of him. How had I missed his thick golden blond hair that fell around his face in such a sensuous way before? How could I have missed how his eyes smiled, as he smiled at me - at me! His attention had left the lusty young lady and his eyes, his smile and his full attention were focused on *me*. How could I have missed his sexy impish grin? All sounds faded, all smells drifted away. My entire body was alert and aware of just one thing - Brian Jones had gotten out of his chair and was heading straight towards ME.

As he said, "Hello," I noticed he was shorter than I had remembered, despite wearing his high heeled Anello boots. His voice was soft, with well spoken Queen's English. "What's your name? Do you want a drink?" He turned and ordered Babycham from a waiter.

I barely tasted the drink, because my body was quivering while he spoke, looked directly into my eyes. He had a slight lisp, which I found endearing. He seemed to read my thoughts, which I was working hard to rein in. I know it is overstated in books and movies, but we had a chemistry that radiated between us. Pure animal heat flushed my face, and I was grateful that the lighting in the club was so dim.

"I'm Dawn," were the two words I spoke, as he led me back to his table. The girl that was sitting there had disappeared. His unfinished drink waited for mine to join it. Sitting opposite him, embarrassment clutched my throat as he stared at me, into my eyes, at my lips, along the base of my chin. His lips curved up into a wicked grin. He must have known the affect he was having on me and was in no hurry to ease my tension. He lit another cigarette and offered it to me. "I don't smoke." was all my voice box could squeeze out. Giving me a crooked grin, he took a drag and then exhaled out of the side of his mouth so that the smoke did not come into my direction.

His staring, my silence, was interrupted by a reporter, who wanted to talk about the group's newest release coming out the next week, that was simply titled *"The Rolling Stones"*.

"There's no way to talk in here. Let's finish our drinks, I'll give you a lift home if you like." Would I like? "Yes," I said to myself, "I would like that very much." I waved to Bunty who was engaged in conversation with who knows whom. She smiled and waved back, as Brian and I entered the lift exiting the Ad Lib.

Brian had an older, but still impressive, dark gray Humber Hawk. The leather upholstery was luxurious and soft, and felt like an expensive comfortable chair, as Brian helped me in. His manners were impeccable. He asked if I wanted to go home right away, or drive around for a while. Of course, we drove around and, when he finally asked me where I lived, he was surprised when I told him Chesham House. It was close to where he lived just a few blocks away in a flat in Chester Street, When we arrived in the courtyard, I was grateful to see that my father had checked on things already and would not be coming out to check on me as we parked out front. We talked for three hours, sharing our personal thoughts and feelings. We both agreed that it felt as if we'd known each other all of our lives.

I learned that growing up in the Jones household had been difficult. A year after he was born his parents had had another child, a sister, Pamela, who had died of leukemia two years later. His Mother, who was a piano teacher, never really got over the loss of their daughter, and it seemed that Brian had suffered from her death as well. But later they did have another daughter, Barbara. Family life had not been easy. His mum and dad were very strict, didn't like the kind of music he loved, and most definitely disagreed with his desire to pursue a musical career. Tempers had flared, and Brian was thrown out. With nowhere else to turn, the parents of his friend (he said she was more like sister), Linda Lawrence, agreed to take him in, until he found a place of his own. He was so grateful to Linda's parents for helping and shared with me that he would do anything for them in return. It was much later that I found out that Linda was actually one of his ex-girlfriends, but in my naivety at the time, I believed the "like a sister" story.

I disclosed how my family had ended up at Chesham House, and that my Father was also a musician, that my Mother and I didn't get on well, and that every summer I stayed with my Aunt Eva in Great Yarmouth. It seemed that neither one of us could shut up. At times, I found it hard to concentrate. What had he said? What was I saying? I was totally distracted by the gorgeous man sitting across from me. He made me feel so completely understood and heard, attentively leaned forward as I vented my frustrations with working for Vidal Sassoon, and why I chose to work for Simon.

How I wanted us to just stop talking! The words coming out of my mouth did not match the thoughts dashing through my mind and overheating my body. The thought of reaching out and just caress his golden hair, tingled on my fingertips. I wanted nothing more than to stop our chatter, and just kiss the lips that had told me so much about his sad life. He revealed to me later that he had felt the same way. But at the time, he had felt compelled to just ramble on. He remarked that he remembered me coming to the Marquee and hanging out with the boys. Then he animatedly jumped the conversation to the upcoming country wide tour the band would be on for the rest of the month. At this bit of news my heart sank.

His excitement dashed my hopes that he might be attracted to and interested in someone like me.

I fell silent. Brian felt my mood drop and stopped talking as well. The night sounds replaced our amiable conversation and, as the awkwardness grew between us, I wanted nothing more than to jump out of the car, run to the flat, and close the door behind me. Then he moved toward me, cupped my face between his soft and gentle hands, leaned forward, and kissed me on the lips with such tenderness and longing, that I thought I could die at that moment and my life would have been complete.

"Give me your phone number Dawn. I want to call you." He spoke so softly, I was afraid I'd misunderstood him. "I'll call you as soon as I can." I gave him my number, but even as I did so my inner doubts slashed at my happiness, telling me he was only being polite, not to get my hopes up and just enjoy this dream while it was happening. The doubting girl inside assured me that once this night was over I would have to go back to my normal life as the caretaker's daughter who worked for Simon. This had only been a fun night out, with a fantastic man who had made me laugh, smile, and cry all in one evening.

He walked me to our door, and left me with another sweet incredible kiss. Cautiously, so as not to wake my parents, I crept down the hall and into my room. I was too excited to sleep. I lay on my bed reliving the past hours of my make believe evening. I don't know how long I lay there. I do know that my eyes hadn't yet closed when I heard my dad knocking on my door.

"What's the matter?" I asked. From the sound of the knocks, I could tell my Dad was annoyed.

"Some person named Brian is on the phone for you. He says it is important." In those days, before cell phones and multiple house lines, there was one telephone in the house. Our phone was set up directly outside my parent's bedroom door in the hallway. As Dad muttered about being awakened at such an unearthly hour, I dashed to the phone. I waited until Dad had closed the bedroom door before I answered. I'm sure that my smile flew through the phone line to Brian's ear.

"Hello," I whispered.

"Hello Dawn, it's about time you answered."

"I'm sorry. My room isn't near the phone." I was happy and disconcerted at the same time by what he said.

"Alright, listen Dawn. I can't stop thinking about you. I have a night off. Would you like to come for a drink tomorrow? Do you know of a quiet place?" It was all happening so fast. Of course I wanted to have drink with him, of course I knew of a quiet place.

"Yes. The Lowndes Arms Pub is across the street from my flat and only locals go there."

"Good," he replied softly, obviously happy with my reply. "I will meet you there at eight-thirty tomorrow evening. Good night." And he was gone, leaving me excited, and my stomach doing back flips.

All day Sunday my thoughts were on Brian. What would I wear? What would we talk about? Would he want to see me again? How could this Sunday seem so ordinary? Mum made the usual roast lamb dinner and suggested a drive in the country. Important things were going on in my life. I picked at my food, refused the Sunday drive, and was generally restless. The hours could not tick by quickly enough.

I put on, and then took off, each one of my outfits. I finally narrowed them down to three, a gray mini skirt with a white sweater and boots, a long tartan plaid skirt with white blouse, a cardigan and boots, and lastly, a maroon crepe empire dress with tiny buttons going down the front, finished off with maroon Mary Jane style high heeled shoes. Laying my choices on the bed, imagining how I would look in each, how Brian would look at me in each, my face flushed with excitement. How could I push these feelings down? At seven, I decided on the empire dress as I felt too busty in the sweater and too frumpy in the long skirt. Nothing seemed just right for such an important occasion. My make-up was not right. I straightened my hair, which didn't seem right. Nothing seemed good enough, including me.

The Lownes Arms now demolished replaced by Flats *
(Photo courtesy of The City of London Metropolitan Archives)

At exactly eight-thirty, I walked over the Lowndes Arms, not really sure he'd be there I prepared myself for disappointment. Opening the door, I scanned the room for someone I was almost sure I would't see. But there he was, leaning against the bar as if he owned it, talking to Ken the proprietor, a glass of beer in his hand, dressed in a perfectly pressed white shirt, jeans and tailored jacket. It was obvious that no one knew who he was and that seemed to suit him. He did get some odd looks - his long blond hair did not fit the atmosphere. Seeing me, he ordered a Shandy.

Used as the pub blown up in the movie *Crying Game*, the Lowndes Arms was small and tucked away in a corner of the mews. It was the perfect location for our private rendezvous. Sitting down behind the red velvet half curtains hanging from their brass rods along the front windows, we could observe the people walk by but remain unnoticed at the same time. Brian, as relaxed as I was anxious, smiled and laughed as he told me he just loved being alone there with me. He held my cold hands tightly in his warm firm grip. I looked everywhere but at his face. I could feel the blood throbbing in my throat, as my mouth went dry.

"Look at me Dawn." he said, releasing one hand to turn my face toward his. "Isn't life mad? Life has gotten so crazy. I hardly have any time to myself anymore and now look at us. Here you are with me alone, and it's so perfect." I looked at his face, at his expression, as he said those words, as his words caressed my heart into an urgency I had never felt with a man before.

I loved looking into his face and studying his expressions. I couldn't help smiling at the devilish look he made when reminiscing about a life event wherein he was the naughty boy. My heart silently cried when his mouth and eyes dropped in sadness at recalling the frustration and gloom he felt when speaking of his childhood. But then he would brighten when the subject of music came up, and he told me about Elmore James, the American Blues Man, who first ignited his dream of being a musician. The night was gone before it had begun.

The pub closed at ten-thirty. We were not ready for the night to end. He held my hand and walked me home. At the door to my flat he pulled me close, and I could feel his heart beat next to mine. His kiss, soft and slow, unnerved me, as did the smell of Imperial Leather soap, the feel of his hands holding my chin keeping my lips pressed to his just a little longer. Breaking away, he pushed a stray piece of hair from my face.

"I know this will sound crazy, but I love you Dawn."

"How can you love me? You have only just met me." I was floating on air.

"Dawn, I think about you all the time. I see your face in my mind, in my dreams. It feels so right. It is right. I love you Dawn." I felt the same way. I put my hands into his thick blonde hair, felt the soft golden locks that framed his handsome face, and he drew me closer once more, abdomen to abdomen, heart to heart, our passion wild and free, the beginning of a great and new love. He moaned at that moment and my knees nearly buckled under me.

Brian Jones

CHAPTER NINE

Everybody Needs Somebody to Love

"It just can't be true," I kept telling myself. "He's so handsome. He is a musician he is going somewhere. He couldn't possibly care about a nobody like me." I could still feel his lips kissing mine, his hand clutching my chin pulling me closer, his embrace more intimate than any I'd ever had experienced. My entire being was suffused with feelings and thoughts of him. At work, I dared not share my unbelievable weekend. A part of me was still waiting to be let down, to be brushed off and put back into my place. Yet, unbelievably, Brian called as promised.

"We're pre-recording Friday at the television studio for Ready Set Go. Stu will pick you up." Wow! *Ready Set Go* was my favorite show and probably the favorite show of every teenager in Britain. "I'll meet you when you arrive." Just like that he took control - no asking, just instructing me, knowing I would obey his command. I loved it! I adored his confidence that I would be ready to meet him. That Stu would pick me up made me feel taken care of. I enjoyed the feeling of being possessed.

Taping for the show began early, so I arranged to get Friday afternoon off. In the meantime, the week literally crawled by. Wednesday never seemed to end, and Thursday couldn't be over soon enough. Finally, it was Friday. Exactly on time, as promised, Stu arrived with his van.

As I got in he winked at me. "Brian eeeehhhh?" I blushed and then laughed, "Ah well, good for him." Traffic was bad at that time of day, and I was afraid that we wouldn't make it before taping began. Stu assured me that there was nothing to worry about. He was right. We didn't miss a thing. As Stu began to help the boys set up, my old insecurities resurfaced. How would I stay out of the way? Where was I supposed to be, what should I do? The boys hadn't arrived, and I wondered if I was supposed to be at the taping at all. What a mistake I had made. I should have stayed at work. Everyone would be too busy to care if I were there or not.

"Hello, Dawn! Brian said, as came up behind me. As I turned around, I was met by the sight of his perfect wide smile - his smile just for me. I was ecstatic and all my insecurities disappeared in an instant. How could I have doubted?

Stu came over and introduced me to Helen Berry, a lovely girl from Nottingham that Bill was dating. I loved her accent. Her thick dark brown shoulder length hair framed her dark brown eyes exotically. Her kind personality exceeded her beauty. We stayed together while the boys were being interviewed, made-up, and generally fawned over. Cathy McGowan, the host, fell over all the boys and absolutely gushed after they were done playing *"Off the Hook"* for the show.

Ready steady go taping

Soon after the taping ended, I saw Linda Lawrence for the first time. She was animatedly talking to Cathy and Mick, when Brian came up from behind and firmly took her by the arm leading her away. He did not bring her over to introduce to me. With so much going, on I didn't give her much thought, other than the passing observation that she was very pretty. But pretty girls were all over the boys all the time. Why would that be anything new? It wasn't long after that Brian and Linda disappeared and Stu came over.

"Brian is really worried about Linda." he said. "She isn't well, and he feels that he should take care of her. Her family has done a lot for him."

"I understand." I replied. "He is so kind to help his friends out." Apparently, Brian had taken Linda to get a taxi home. Helen and I made a quick getaway with the boys to go to the Palais Wimbledon, where they had another show. Hanging out, getting to know one another, kept our minds off of the constant pulse of screaming girls. After the show, Brian drove me home. I could tell that he was exhausted after the excitement of the taping and putting on a show right after. He needed some peace and quiet.

"Was that girl at the taping the Linda you told me about?" I asked.

"Yes, I just wanted to make sure she got a taxi home. You know her family is so good to me, and all. It's as if she's my little sister and I need to be there for her." His comment was sincere. What wonderful man.

"That's the right thing for you to do," I whispered, taking his hand and squeezing it.

"You know," he went on, "I think she's friends with Donavan now. I just wanted to make sure she got home safe."

Pressing his hand again, all thoughts of Linda melted away. Leaning over, he kissed me and kissed me again. We were both tired. Sliding over, I slipped into his arms. Alone in his car, I was overwhelmed by emotions for my newfound love. I relished every moment of that night, because I knew that the next day they would be off to Folkstone for a concert and then the following day,

Wednesday, they would be at the Mad Mod Ball at Empire Pool, Wembley. The Mad Mod Ball would be our last opportunity to be together for a month. The rest of April and into May, they would be on tour. I savored every second we were together.

"Tell me you will come to the Wembley and see me Dawn. I can't pick you up and Stu has to help us set up, but come anyway." How could I turn him down? Of course I would come. "I will arrange for Stu to let you in the stage door."

Taking the bus to Wembley was the easy part. The moment I arrived at Empire Pool, I could feel danger. Rockers and Mods were everywhere, and trouble was being stirred up. Scuffles were breaking out, and the police were in full force. A mass of fans heaved around the building. Pushing through the crowd I realized the stage door was heavily guarded, so there was no way I would be allowed inside. The swirl of bodies, the shoving, screaming and fighting was more than I could handle. It didn't feel safe and I caught the next bus home.

"Dawn, wake up! *He's* on the phone again. I don't like being awakened like this." My Father was irate. It was late, almost morning as a matter of fact. I sprinted down the hall and picked up the phone.

"What happened to you?" Brian asked, nearly screamed into the phone hysterically, "Are you alright? My God I've been worried! There was a lot of trouble between the Mods and Rockers! A lot of fans got hurt. I was so afraid you were out there."

"I'm all right," I whispered in a soothing voice. "When I got down there it didn't feel safe with so much chaos and police. I knew I wouldn't be able to see you, so I came straight home." I could hear an audible sigh of relief at the other end of the line. I was smiling broadly into the darkness of our flat.

"Oh, thank God you're safe. It was bloody crazy tonight! I'm sorry I didn't get to see you. We have only just now been allowed to leave. Can you believe it? This is all a bunch of bullshit! I feel better now knowing that you are safe. Dawn, I love you and I miss you. Look, I'm knackered. I'm going to bed now. We're leaving for

Swindon later today. I'll see you again as soon as we get back to London, I promise."

It was so hard to put the receiver down, even though he'd already hung up. I knew how tired he was, but I wanted just a little bit more, a few more sentences of him telling me how he loved me and was worried about my safety. Just a little bit more.

The rest of the month, during their entire tour, I slept in the hall next to the phone in a chair. I didn't want my dad awakened, and every chance I had to talk to him I wanted - no needed.

✥

April twent-second was my parent's twenty-fifth wedding anniversary. They were having a party at Chelsea Barracks to celebrate. My brother had leave from the Royal Engineers and had invited a newly formed band from his unit to entertain.

I remember thinking that it was nice of him to invite friends out to make my parents' celebration better. However, a part of me was upset that I wasn't able to invite someone to the party as well. But I did not dare as I had not told anyone about Brian. His appearance would have been out of place at my parent's ultra conservative gathering. I knew they wouldn't approve of him, and I dared not take a chance that they would forbid my seeing him ever again.

He was my entire world. I lived by the phone waiting for him to call. I listened for the sound of pebbles hitting my bedroom window at night, to let me know he was outside waiting for me to go out to his car. I'd never been in love before. The emotions, the new feelings besieged me and I had no one to talk to, and no one to share how my life had changed now that I was Brian's. Instead, I went about my life smoldering with passion on the inside, while trying to look cool and calm on the outside.

Mike's colleague's showed up ready to play. The bass player, Peter Young, was ready to play, too. Only, in addition to the guitar, he wanted to play with me, as well. I believe he was the most forward young man I'd ever met in my life. He watched my every move

Everybody Needs Somebody to Love

and when the band had its break, he bought me a drink. He talked about the band he was in before joining the Royal Engineers.

"Our group was called the Nashville Teens. My friends Ray Phillips, and John Allen, and I practiced in the garage at Woking where we went to school. We were offered a record contract playing a song called *Tobacco Road*. My dad didn't want me to waste my life on music and told me to get a proper job. I showed him, I joined the Royal Engineers." He told me how much he loved music, how much he liked me – really – liked me? He had only just met me! But his smile was nice. He had perfect white teeth, blond hair, and was a good bass player. But my mind was on Brian.

25th Anniversary party 1964. Brother Mike Molloy Peter Young & Archie Dunlop.

As the night wore on, Peter and his mates began to get drunk. The more he drank the more he followed me around, telling me how pretty I was, how much he liked me and finally became very amorous. I mean he was all over me, and I kept looking to my brother to make a rescue, to no avail. He was in his own world, and oblivious to the trouble his Mr. Young was causing.

When the party ended, Dad and Mike wouldn't allow Peter to drive home, so Mum set him up a bed on the couch and I went off to my own room, locking the door behind me. When I woke up the next morning, Mike and Peter had both left to go back to the barracks, their troop was getting ready to leave for Aden for a year's tour.

By the end of April the Stones had returned to London. I waited for Brian to call, but it didn't come. Four days passed and my mind, always on alert to remind me of how useless and unlovable I was, snatched all of the joy I had been feeling over the previous thirty days. I became depressed, imagining that he'd forgotten me. I just knew a prettier woman had replaced me, one he loved more than me. My mind was filled with visions of how he was touching her, how he was sharing his kisses with her, how he was telling her he loved her. I stayed in my bedroom playing the LP *Rolling Stones* on my Decca record player. I sulked as I listened to *Tell Me*, and I pined as I looked at the Stones prints I had cut out of teen magazines and hung on my walls. Everywhere I went I heard their latest hit *Not Fade Away*, and knew the suffering of it exactly.

"You bring one of those long-haired gits home and you're gone!" My dad had snapped after looking at the posters. They had no idea I was dating Brian, and I hoped to keep it that way. My Father was familiar with all of the new groups. He had to hear them on television every Friday night, because I rushed home to watch *Ready Steady Go*, and *Top Pops*. He said he preferred the Beatles music to that of the Stones. He never made a comment about girl singers like Cilla Black or Sandi Shaw and Lulu, who were also hitting the charts.

✥

The days crawled by. Sunday afternoon I was having a pity party in my room, when I heard the lobby doorbell ring. It was Dad's day off and he grumbled all the way out to answer the door. Cindy, our excitable black poodle, twirled and spun in a flurry of excitement. Her berserk yipping echoed off of the walls, as she bounced around him towards the door. Weekdays the doors were open, weekends they were locked, and each tenant had their own key to get in.

"Dawn, it's for you," my Father announced over the din of Cindy's yelping. "There's someone here to see you." Who would be coming to see me? From behind my Father, with Cindy bouncing around his legs, yap, yap, yapping as he walked, entered Brian. I had given up and was shocked he'd come. What were my parents going to think when they saw all that hair? Coming out of the kitchen my Mother stopped in her tracks, mouth wide open. Dad stood beside him not saying a word. In a way it was a comedy- my Father meets a long haired git, right in his own house no less.

"Uh, Dad, Mum, this is Brian, Brian Jones." I squeaked, not quite sure how this meeting was going to turn out.

"Nice to meet you, Mr. Molloy." Brian said, turning on his high powered charm, as he reached out and shook my father's hand. "Mrs. Molloy" he said, kissing my Mother's hand. She still had'nt uttered a word, just openly stared at the blond locks cascading around his neck and onto his shoulders. Meanwhile, Cindy's ruckus did not go unnoticed, as she jumped onto Brian's legs, over and over, wagging her tail in exultant joy. Introductions complete, he stooped down and began to pet the thrilled Cindy. Appeased, she quieted down.

Dad had been playing his blues LP of Muddy Waters when Brian arrived. Brian commented on how much he loved the blues and just that easily my Father was won over. Of course, I'd told Brian about my Father being a musician, and Brian being a musician himself made their conversation that much easier. Dad began to talk and talk about his life - how he'd gone to New Orleans when on tour with the Scots Guards band in the late fifties, he rented a car and drove down town to a smoky dive where Louie Armstrong was playing. He happily he told the story about that evening. He'd gone back out to the rental car, removed his trumpet from its case and brought it back into the dive. Mr. Armstrong had welcomed him on stage and he'd been able to jam with the great man. Dad said, because of that experience, he could die a happy man.

Brian seemed to understand, and when Dad brought his trumpet out for him to see, Brian reached in with the care of someone picking up a valuable jewel, put the instrument to his lips and began to play. Dad was hooked. It didn't matter how long the hair, he had found a kindred spirit in Brian Jones, and I figured I wouldn't be thrown out of the house after all.

Having closed her mouth, and I assume accepted the long haired young man animatedly talking to Dad, Mom suggested I make some tea.

What was it about Brian? He had managed to charm both my Father and Mother. I think they fell in love with him as quickly as I did.

"Would you let your daughter come on tour with me to the Northern counties?" My God, had I heard right? Had he just come out with it? I could feel my palms begin to sweat. I knew my Father would be indignant and angry at how could this young man he just met be so forward. "We are booked to leave June first for our first trip to the States, and I won't be able to see Dawn before I leave." He looked over to me smiling.

"Well, for how long?" My Dad asked, as if this kind of request were quite ordinary. My mouth went dry from shock. Mother didn't say a word or show any sign that his request might be outrageous.

"We are away all month," Brian responded, as if he were just asking to take me to a movie. He looked Dad right in the eye, his face earnest with respect.

"Well, she can't take a month off work," Dad responded, as if Brian were planning on taking me out on a school night and he didn't want me tired in the morning. "I will allow her to go for a week, if she asks her boss first." I could not believe what I was hearing. He was actually going to let me go!

"Dawn, why don't you take Brian down to your bedroom?" My Mother's suggestion was her first words since the beginning of this uncomfortable conversation. Then I remembered - Holy Shit!!! I had all those pictures on my wall - wait! There was no way I wanted Brian to see them. I excused myself, saying I needed to go to the Loo, turned and nearly sprinted down the hall. I wondered what they made of my hasty departure. Did I need to "go" that badly? Belting down to my bedroom, I tore the photos off of the wall and stuffed them under my bed. Thanks, Mother! What kind of fool do you want me to look like? Just as the last piece of evidence had been hastily shoved out of sight, in walked my Mother with Brian right behind her. She turned and left, as if she had just escorted Bunty down. Brian entered, taking immediate ownership of my room and all that was in it.

"I love the purple walls Dawn, so soft and beautiful, just like you. The color suits you." Nonchalantly he studied my things, picking them up, putting them down. Making his way around the room, he went over to a chair where my Winnie the Pooh bear sat. I'd, had him since childhood he was a favorite of mine. Seizing the bear, Brian's his face lit up. "I love Pooh!" He exclaimed enthusiastically. "I love how innocent the animals are." Wow! Is all I could think, Brian Jones, the man that I love, likes Winnie the Pooh.

His eyes missed nothing. How unnerving, how intimate his inspection of my things felt. Walking to my dressing table, he opened my jewelry box and watched the little ballerina twirl around, listened to the music of Swan Lake for a few moments, and then closed the lid gently. He owned all that he laid eyes upon, even my record player. Oh, my Decca record player! I had a Stones LP right next to it. Picking the record up, he looked at the front, then turned it over checking the back. His fingers caressed the cover. Turning around he looked at me and burst into a wide smile that seemed to say, "I know what you think about when you listen to this." Of course, he was right and I gulped a bit, trying to catch my breath

"Its number one on the charts now, you know." Of course I knew. Putting the record down, he crossed the room in two steps, took me in his arms and kissed me firmly on my lips, his hands caressing my back and sides. Pulling me down onto the floor where my white sheep skin scatter rug lay, he leaned back, putting his hands behind his head, giving me that 'I'm up to something grin'.

Before I could register what he was up to he reached out and began to tickle me. Laughing, I watched his face as his look of impish joy turned into a look of wanting more and more of me. Tickling fingers firmly grasped my hands and pinned them tightly at my sides. I stilled as he moved closer, kissing my forehead, my ears, my eyes and my mouth. Oh, I was falling for this man! At that moment, the moment of my surreal ecstasy, Mother walked in.

Jumping away from each other in surprise and embarrassment, we laughed uncomfortably. How quickly our emotions could change. We both got up and sheepishly walked to the front door trying to ignore the awkward moment. Mother made no remark, she did not even make a facial expression to let me know her thoughts.

I walked Brian up stairs to his car and said 'goodbye' with a passionate kiss and a promise that I would see him in Manchester.

Brian starting his car in our courtyard.

CHAPTER TEN

Let's Spend the Night Together

There was so much to do. The first piece of this romantic, frenzied puzzle was to get permission to take time off of work. I had a month to prepare myself, to muster up the nerve to ask for Simon's consent. As always, my imagination plunged into a riot of negative thoughts. What would happen if I couldn't get the time off? How would I tell Brian? What would he say? What would he do? Would he find someone to replace me? Swirling thoughts produced jittery nerves. I could not eat and hardly slept. Finally, I managed to marshal some courage and approached my employer.

"Simon, I would like to take some time off." I was tentative, more so than normal. I didn't want to be a burden, nor did I want to let him down.

"Time off, for what? When?" My insides were churning, what would be his response?

"I want to take a week off to go on tour with my boyfriend. He's in a band called the Rolling Stones. He's asked me to go with him for a week." I was on a roll. The words spilled out almost faster than I could think of them. "After this tour, he and the boys are going to the United States, and they will be gone all of June, and I don't know when I will get to see him next. This is our last chance to be together, and my father has given me permission to go, if I can get the time off with you." There, it was said, out in the open and announced to the world. Simon stared at me in what appeared to be astonishment. I don't think he even knew that I had a boyfriend, let alone one whose group was becoming nearly a household word.

"A week you say? I can't have you gone longer than that. When do you want to go?" When did I want to go? I could hardly believe my ears. I suppose I had expected him to say "no." When did I want to go? Well, I wanted to go immediately, but of course that was out of the question.

"I'd like to leave on May twenty-third" I held my breath. He appeared to be contemplating the work that was to be done, the clients we were supposed to serve, what it might take to cover my absence.

"Well, right then, that will be fine. But just for one week, Dawn, we have a lot going on." I emitted an audible sigh. I was going. We were going to be together for one glorious week!

The plan was for me to meet Brian in Leicester. Helen was going to drive. She was meeting up with Bill, and I was going to be the happy passenger tagging along.

Never would we have guessed what was in store for us. How were we to know that a new kind of "fan" was morphing onto the music scene? The late fifties and early sixties was an era in which teens were finding their own identity and creating a new way of doing things. The Mods and Rockers were not the only changes our generation was initiating onto English society, rules were being changed. The days, when audiences sedately sat in their seats enjoying the music the sound the ambiance of a concert were over. We didn't know that yet, but twenty days before I was to leave on the biggest adventure of my life, I was about to get my first taste of what the new "fan" was like.

Sunday, May third the boys were playing at the Palace Theatre in Manchester. I was riding down with Helen. I looked forward to the quiet moments Brian and I would be sharing. Being able to kiss and hold one another, while we shared our long talks, was what I lived for, since the beginning of our relationship that past March. It seemed that we never had enough time to say all that needed to be said. The boys being on the road made our together moments fewer and farther between.

The drive down was uneventful. Helen and I talked about work and what it would be like on tour. We'd never been to Manchester and finding the hotel where they were staying was a bit confusing. It took us a few detours and wrong turns to finally make our way to the entrance. Maybe it was good we had lost our way. At least it gave us a hint of what was to come.

The venue was the Palace Theater, situated about a mile away. Between the theater and the hotel, things had gone mad. The streets were crowded with teens. Groups huddled in front of stores, smoking, and joking about. Rockers gunned the engines of their motorcycles, while leering at Mods on the sidewalks. It was utter chaos.

The Palace Theater Manchester.

Finding the entrance to the hotel was a short-lived relief. People crowded in the front of the hotel and around the grounds. Hundreds of girls were milling about looking for something or someone. Helen and I soon realized they were not just looking for *someone*, but for some "someone's," and those *someone's* were the Stones. The lobby was spacious, but upon entering I felt claustrophobic. Photographers loitered in the foyer and teens hid behind pillar. Groups mingled in front of the lobby des. A crush of women lurked by the elevator doors, while others circulated around the front entrance. It was complete pandemonium and it was about to get worse. Helen and I got our room keys and fled.

"I've contacted the police," Stu told us. "They've agreed to create a human chain from the car to the stage door." The boys started to laugh, was this some kind of joke? "No," Stu was adamant. "I've arranged for a bread van to pick you up at the back entrance of the hotel. Once the driver loses the fans, you will transfer to an ambulance where you will be driven as close to the theater entrance as possible. When the driver stops jump out, run like hell through the police barricade, and get in that stage door fast!"

We were incredulous, how could something like this be happening? None of us thought of the boys as anything other than a local band of lads come to town to give a show. When had fame found them?

"This has to be some kind of joke." one of the boys said, "We all have to pile into a bread van, drive around town, change into an ambulance - just to get someplace that is less than five minutes away?" Stu shook his head, in conformation. He was serious, as he escorted the boys and all of us girlfriends down the back stairs and out the rear exit. How could we take something this ludicrous seriously?

Stu had been wise to arrange for transportation. The rear entrance was not as crowded as the front, but, at seeing the boys, a united screech erupted from the teen females prowling near the back. As if controlled by one mind, they surged towards the van and us, Mick slammed the door shut, as they clawed and clung to the sides and back of the vehicle. The driver hit the pedal.

"This is insanity! What the hell are those birds doing?" Brian held me close, protecting me from the dangers of the stampeding rabble, as down the driveway and out and away from the theater we were spirited. The van turned left and right, ducking down side streets, speeding past corners so that onlookers couldn't identify the true contents of the bread van. Finally, arriving at the pickup point, we anxiously exited and leaped into the ambulance. Once again, we were propelled into the darkness, down one street and up another.

Twenty minutes later. we arrived at the venue. It was Bedlam, and the inmates had been let loose! Screaming women rushed the police chain, flinging themselves onto the officers. With the Palace stage entrance in view, we girls jumped out first. My feet had not hit the pavement when I was grabbed by a police officer and tossed like a rag doll into the convulsing crowd. I hit the ground hard and, as I fell. the police grabbed Helen and Chrissy, pitching them into the fray as well. The boys went crazy.

"They're with us!! Get them out of there! They're our girlfriends! What the hell!" The boys broke the police barricade, fighting the crush of screaming females in an effort to get to us. The women surged forward like a pack of wolves howling over a piece of meat. The boys were savaged. Hunks of hair were yanked out by the roots pieces of clothing were ripped from their bodies. as the frenzied girls scratched and grabbed at the boys, screeching in hysteria for souvenirs.

As I lay prone on the rigid blacktop in absolute terror for my life, I witnessed people being tripped and stomped on. Over my head the madness was deafening. Stampeding boots and heels obscured my view. I knew I was going to die. I'd literally fallen into a nightmare

As the boys shouted at the police and at the insane women, the uproar turned on us as girls realized we were a part of the group. Grasping, pulling hands reached for us, lusting after whatever they could rip off of our fallen bodies. Brian shoved and pushed a path towards me, grabbed me by the hand and yanked me up just as a fan ripped the sleeve off of my dress. Bill managed to rescue a scratched Helen, and Mick, shirt torn, had saved Chrissy. I was grateful to be alive. The boys literally fought their way through the crazed crowd to the stage access.

"Son of a bitch!" A bleeding Stu screamed, slamming the door behind us. "Are you boys okay? No one hurt? Thank God, no one was seriously hurt!" The panic and horror etched on his face told the story. We were lucky to have survived. Shocked and petrified, we stood in the total silence of the theater. I had never been so scared in my entire life. Outside, the rioting fans pounded on the door and the walls. The screams were muffled, and the background quiet of the theater was a welcome reprieve. Thank God, Stu had had the forethought to make sure there were plenty of stiff drinks available in the dressing room, along with a change of clothes. The boys were pissed and shook up.

That night was the first time I saw any spark of jealousy within the group. Once past the stage door, and once we checked and made sure that no lasting injuries had been inflicted, and once we made sure everyone was safe and accounted for, we had to climb a flight of grid iron stairs to get to the dressing rooms. I'd lost one of my shoes in the tumult. Brian and Stu had gone up the stairs in front of us. I was shakily making my way upward, when the heel of the shoe I had managed to keep slipped through a hole in the grid. I tripped and staggered backwards sliding down six steps, on my way towards crashing to the ground. Mick swiftly jumped forward and caught me under the arms, breaking my fall.

"Are you alright, Dawnee?" he asked. At that moment Brian appeared around the corner.

"Get your fucking hands off my girl!" he bellowed.

"Its okay, Brian. Mick just caught me. I fell." I tried in vain to explain. Glowering at the two of us and not saying a word, Brian stamped out of sight. "What was that?" I asked, looking at the boys. Mick just shrugged and walked away.

"Don't worry, Dawn, he'll get over it." Bill stated matter-of-factly. "He has his moods. Just ignore him." Moods, I wondered? I'd never seen Brian display any kind of anger before, and I was completely surprised by his outburst. But considering the tension of being on the road all of the time, and the harrowing experience we had just survived, it was easy to assume he was just out of sorts and letting off steam. No one mentioned Brian's outburst, and I imagined that the other boys felt the same way at one time or another. It was time to have a few drinks, for the boys to change clothes and get ready for the show. Out in the auditorium the sound of rabid fans being ushered in began.

Helen, Chrissy and I were placed stage right. The air was electric, and it seemed that the walls would burst from the foot stomping arising from the audience. It was so hot and clammy. The crowd began chanting, "We want the Stones! We want the Stones!" The place was vibrating with anticipation. It was time for the show.

The curtains were drawn and the boys opened with *Carol*. The fans went wild. The decibel level went from 75 to an ear shattering 130, in a nanosecond. The amplifiers seemed muted and the microphones useless, competing against the escalating din. Screaming themselves hoarse, the frenzied teens cried, wailed and fainted. Mick worked the crowd, clapping his hands over his head like he was playing a tambourine, moving his legs and arms in rhythm to the music, pouting at the girls as he sang. Brian looked over, smiled at me and mouthed, "I love you." We were alone, despite the raging sea of hormonal passion emanating from the audience.

"I think it will be safer for you boys if we don't arrive until after the fans are seated." Stu said, when the show was over and everyone was in the dressing room, smoking, drinking and trying to come down from the high that always occurred after a performance. "In the future we will leave before they are allowed out of the venue. I won't let what happened tonight happen again." That was Stu, always fussing over the boys, making sure the equipment was set up just so, protecting the boys from people who had no business behind the stage or in the dressing rooms. Stu was the mother hen, the Stone's biggest fan, and best friend.

However, not even Stu could staunch the inevitable affects of fame. Within months, even the most common of activities became a challenge. Enjoying a meal, without a photographer's flashbulbs bursting in their faces or fans swarming the table, had become impossible. Meals were ordered through Room Service well after three in the morning, when the boys were finally able to return to their hotel after a performance. Stu's plan to leave before the fans were released didn't work out. The boys and their group had become prisoners of their fame. They could go nowhere and do nothing, without creating a public furor. Even returning to their hotel rooms after a concert and the hours long wait for girls to leave the theaters didn't guarantee peace and quiet. Someone, somtimes everyone, always seemed to figure out where the boys were or where they were going to be. Security was lax in those days, so no one bothered to tell fawning girls to leave. Girls stalked the boys, waited for them in the lounges, in the stairs, in the hallways. There were girls everywhere, and all of them were ready to be shagged by whichever of the boys was willing to choose them.

I remember seeing Keith that night drinking with two girls, while more girls appeared from what seemed to be nowhere. Mick and Chrissy, Helen and Bill and Brian and I had slipped away (if that could be possible) to our rooms for what we had hoped would be some peace and quiet. Brian opened our room, and it became immediately apparent that, to some kinds of girls, a locked door and a girlfriend at your side means nothing.

To my horror, Brian spotted a pair of feet sticking out from under the bed.

"Come out from under there." He said kindly, and without the least bit of hesitation out rolled a naked girl who jumped to her feet, pushed up close to him and placed her arms around his neck. "All right now, time to get out of here." And opening the door he gently pushed her out. A giggle came from the bathroom. With a sigh, Brian opened the door and there stood another unclad young woman waiting to pounce upon my man. "You too," he said politely, "time to leave." And taking her by the arm he handed her the pile of clothing that had been tossed on the toilet and let her out.

"My God," I thought, "what kind of girl would sneak into the room of a stranger to have sex?" Then my mind, my old nemesis, spit the venomous thought through my heart: "Why wouldn't he want these girls? They have beautiful faces, perfect bodies and are gorgeous."

Up until that very night, that very moment, I hadn't given sexual matters much thought. Brian and I had spent our time together cuddling, talking, and had done a small amount of petting. But always the "good girl," I had honestly not held the thought of "going all the way" and having sex with Brian as the goal of our relationship. I was naive to say the least. Seeing two girls ready to, I have to say that I became scared about when and how would "it" happen. Before Brian, I had never had a boyfriend and had never kissed anyone other than my father and brother. Brian was my first in every sense of the word.

During our months together, I'd learned that, when Brian kissed me, he aroused feelings that had lain dormant under my Catholic Catechism teachings. He'd opened up a Pandora's Box of primal urges that I didn't know what to do with. I knew I wanted to share every part of me. I wanted sexual freedom. But it had never occurred to me to share such a personal and intimate part of myself with a stranger, as the girl under the bed and the girl in the bathroom had been willing to do. But Brian was no stranger. We'd already shared everything- our personal secrets, our regrets, our future dreams. I'd never felt closer to anyone in my life.

"Dawn, are you alright? Don't think about those slags. I'm here with you. You are the only one I want, will ever want." And he took me into his arms and kissed me gently and lovingly, on the lips. "Come, Dawn, lay down here with me. It's been a long day. I love you."

In his arms, safe and secure, we lay upon the bed and he covered my face, my neck, and my hands with kisses. Reaching up to pull his face closer to me, he took my hands and gently pinned them over my head. "God you are beautiful, I will never get tired of looking at you, holding you, touching you. I love you Dawn. You are mine, and I am yours."

Letting my hands go, he began to make an intimate acquaintance with my body. His fingers traced the buttons on my blouse. First the top button, a flick of the wrist and it opened. Then grazing the material downward to the next, his fingers paused considering whether to move forward or move back. A quick flick of the wrist and another button was released from captivity.

"You are mine Dawn," he smiled, setting the other buttons free. "I am yours." His hands, his mouth, his words released all of the primitive instincts that had been tamped down by my 'good girl' Catholic upbringing. "We are one." He had whispered as our love climaxed and boiled over.

"I *am* yours Brian," I whispered at last, "all yours, all of me, forever."

The following day, cuddled in one another's arms, Brian, still pleased to have been my "first and my last," kissed my cheek and told me to get dressed.

"We're going to High Street. I'm getting you a new dress. You need another one to replace the one whose sleeve was taken away. I wish I could have protected you better. You could have been trampled, killed. The least I can do is buy you a new one."

We walked into Dorothy Perkins Dress Shop. On each side of the store were racks and racks of clothes, organized according to color and style, each more lovely than the last. I was in heaven, if only Bunty could see me!

At the back of the store near the dressing room sat the salesgirl writing in a book, her dark hair falling over the counter. She didn't look up when we entered.

"Here Dawn, try this one, I know it will look fantastic on you." Brian said holding up one of the fashionable dresses. The girl looked up from her writing, and we could tell instantly that she recognized Brian. Beginning to shake, not sure what to do, she started to speak. Brian took control.

"Shush," he said. Putting his finger to his lips, he winked at her, a secretive smirk on his face. "Just help my girl find a dress, and I will give you an autograph when we pay. Please don't call your friends. Can you do that?" She covered her mouth with her hand, eyes wide, and nodded "yes". Brian and I continued our shopping, as the crying, shaking sales girl watched Brian's every move.

"Here, Dawn," he said holding up a black chiffon empire dress with delicate black sequins. "This one is perfect for you."

Brian paid for the dress and autographed the quivering sales girl's white blouse. As Brian closed the shop door behind us, we heard one huge scream and the sound of banging feet.

What else could we do but laugh and imagine her calling all of her friends, as we walked back to the hotel.

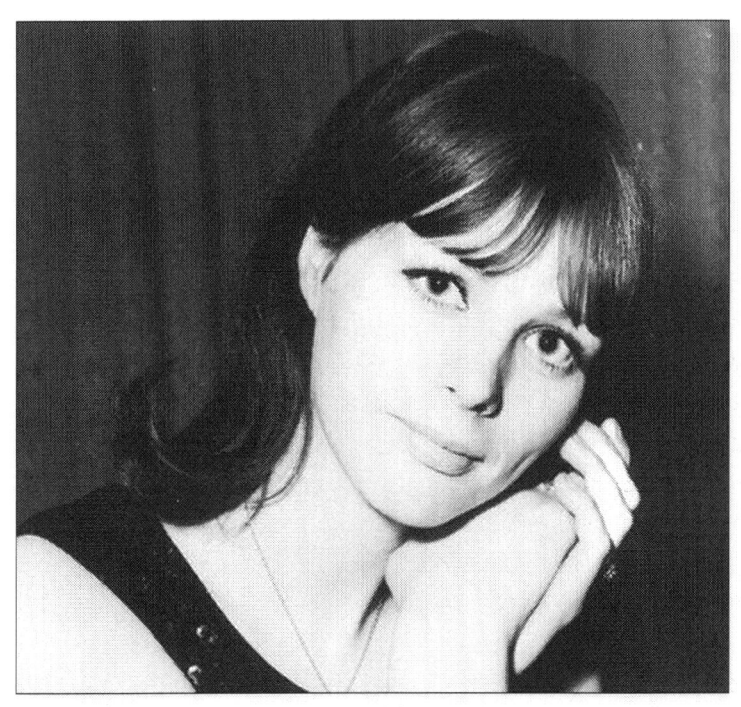

24 Dawn in black dress.

CHAPTER ELEVEN

Beast of Burden

The boys were staying in Manchester, doing a television show called *The Scene*, at the Granada Studio. Helen and I weren't allowed to watch the filming. Only the 'artists' were allowed, much to Brian's annoyance. It really didn't matter. I had to get to work and begin the long lonely countdown to May twenty-third, when we would be reunited and I would have the opportunity to finish off the tour with him.

"I'll call you every day Dawn. I can't wait until I see you again. Being away from you is complete and total hell." We kissed, but not long enough. Helen drove me home in her Mini.

Brian kept his promise, calling me most nights after the shows and again in the early morning hours, much to my father's annoyance. The boys were traveling all over England. My father kept newspaper clippings of their progress, while I heard all of the details first hand from Brian. He told me how the girls had become bolder and more unruly and the crowds louder and more aggressive. As always, he reminded me, of how much he loved me and how much he missed me, and that he was counting down the days until he would hold me in his arms and make love to me again.

In the early evening of May sixteenth, Brian was back in London and came down to the flat to see me for a few hours.

"Let's go to the Lowndes Arms and have a drink. It's nice to go someplace where we can be left alone." Hand in hand we walked to our little hide away and snuggled into what I now thought of as 'our booth.' Sitting close, he complained about how hard his life had become, how he had no time to relax and how dominating Andrew was when it came to his life and everyone else's in the band.

"He's making us get away from what we started out to be. He wants it to be all rock and roll and forget the blues. Andrew Loog Oldham just wants to sell records and make money, and it's off of my back that he's doing it. I tell him how I feel, and he just tells me to 'to get over it', or gets mad and carries on like a lunatic. He won't listen and it's taking hell out of me. He's pissing me off." There wasn't much I could do, just hold his hand, stroke his hair and let him know that I would always be there for him no matter what. He was still agitated when we left the pub.

Back in my room, he began pacing. He always did that when something was on his mind. I sat on the bed, while he walked back and forth in front of me. Then he stopped in mid-stride, turned walked up to me, closed his eyes and tipped his chin up and away. He said nothing, just moved back to his previous path. Turning again, he stopped and looked me in the eyes. What on earth was he thinking? What did he want to tell me? I knew better than to press the subject. It was for me to sit and wait, and for him to think and tell. I wanted to touch his arm, reassure him that whatever he had to say I could be trusted. Back and forth he went.

"I have to spend some time with the Lawrence's, Dawn. I hope you understand. I want to let them know what is going on with me and all." Is that what was on his mind? Of course, I understood, I was not one of those possessive girls, who would keep their guy away from all of his other friends or family.

"Oh, that's fine, Brian. You're such a good person to keep in touch with them. It's one of the many things I love about you." And with that he kissed me, and we made love not once, but two more times.

"Before I go Dawn, would you get your Dad for me? I need to ask him if I can leave my car here in the courtyard while I'm on tour in the US. Since the girls have discovered I live at Chester Street they've been stealing bits and pieces off of my car and from around the flat, and I don't want to keep replacing radio antennas and rubber washers from the tops of window screens."

As luck would have it, the owner of Chesham House, Mr. Hopton, was on a month's holiday. Dad was able to park Brian's Humber Hawk in the privacy of the enclosed courtyard. It amazed me how famous the boys had become in such a short time. It also amazed me how tiresome fame seemed to be. With his car secured, Brian left to check in with the Lawrence's.

May twenty-third, Brian picked me up at my parents' flat. Impeccably dressed charming as always to my mother and father, he looked tired. The last time we had seen one another in person was ten days before, and the change in him was palpable. His carefree 'I want you, I will have you' glint was there, but dimmed. I could tell he still loved me, and I wasn't about to let my wayward mind lead me down that usual path of insecurity. But the spark he always had, his flint to my steel, just didn't seem set to burn.

"How are you feeling Brian? Are you okay?" I asked as he opened the door to let me into his car.

"I'm fine, just tired of everything. Tired of not being able to eat or sleep without being hassled. Tired of being on the road, I hate missing you all the time. The schedule is killing me and no one seems to notice or care. I'm about done in Dawn and don't know what to do about it." Driving down to Leicester, we talked about the long hours of trying to write music, practicing, and waiting for the fans to leave just so he could get back to another nameless hotel full of clutching fans wanting a piece of him. Driving together on the M-1 motorway he was at least free of female harassment and the obligations of the band.

"I'm so glad it's just you and me today, Dawn. When we're together I can feel like I can just be myself. I know you don't judge me or expect anything. You understand me like no one else does. God it's hard being on the road without you. If you were on tour with me all the time, I know things would be better, easier.

"What could I say? Reaching across the console, I took his hand and wondered what I could do to make it easier for him-so many people always wanting a piece of him. I did my best to stay in the background, so he would never have to worry about me trying to get something from him, too.

"Hey, The Leicester Forest Service's! Let's get something to eat."

I laughed. How like Brian to be down and overwhelmed and then make a complete turn in his mood and be ready to eat. We nearly had the place to ourselves. At least there were no fans around. Finding a booth in the middle of the restaurant, Brian ordered a huge breakfast, which he ate like a starving man. I enjoyed the sudden lift in his spirits. He needed to eat one meal without being harassed, this was perfect. The side of his mouth curved up just enough to let me know that some of his old sparkle was back and that he was thinking what I was always thinking- 'I want you.'

"We need more times like these Dawn. That's why I love going to your parents' flat and hanging out. Your Mum and Dad are so good to me. They don't talk about the gigs don't expect me to be anything other than who I am. They let us be together so I can unwind. I just don't get enough quiet and independence now that we are becoming famous.

"It isn't as good as you might think you know. I just wanted to be a blues player, a musician, try and write music. I never thought it would be like this - all the birds stalking me, never having a moment's peace. It's bloody awful most of the time."

I listened; nodded in understanding, letting him say what he needed to. When he'd finished eating, the boys in the band found their way into the restaurant and his energy dropped.

It was time to go back to the very world he'd just been complaining about, time to leave and return to the clamor and chaos of what was now his 'real' life. It made me sick inside to think of how much he was suffering. If I could have taken some of the stress off of him I would have. Getting into the car, I turned and kissed him, making an unspoken promise that after the show he would have the solace he yearned for - in my arms.

Not Fade Away

The concert was at the Leicester University. Fans were everywhere. Somehow we managed to get to the hotel without being accosted. Helen was with Bill and the boys, who were doing a photo shoot. Photos, interviews, and screaming fans everywhere - nothing had changed. Helen and I hung back, waiting until it was time to go into the show.

Getting in was Manchester all over again, Manchester and every other town we'd been to before – always having to push and shove our way into the theater, then Stu putting us stage right so we could stand and watch the boys perform.

They all seemed fatigued, worn out from the tour. But, once the curtain went up, it was as if everything else in the world was erased. The boys became their alter ego, 'The Rolling Stones'. Mick owned the stage - strutting, clapping and gazing into the audience with his bedroom eyes. Bill, Keith and Brian backed him up on guitars, while Charlie kept the beat moving on the drums.

It was hypnotic this 'bad boy band' pushing the limits of what had been done, what could be done on stage, the crowds under their control while out of control. The music became the soul of the noisy, disorderly crowd running wild, throwing clothing and gifts, while offering their bodies and undying love to the boys.

Show after show, playing twice a day, the boys wooed the audiences and the girls swooned and cried. Both Helen and I were amazed at how well the boys, how everyone, was getting along on the tour. It wasn't just the boys any longer just the boys driving from one small town to another doing shows in different parts of England anymore.

Other groups had been signed on to play to the sold out, over-the-top crowds. The Baron Knights and Duke D' Mond with Peter Langford were part of the starting lineup. Peter Langford, with his novel and funny *Call up the Groups,* performed an amusing parody of the latest popular bands. They were as funny off stage as they were on. It was a good thing too, because the overly crowded airless dressing rooms, the constant inhaling of cigarette smoke and heavy drinking wasn't exactly conducive to harmony.

Peter and Gordon met us on part of the tour singing their hit song *World Without Love*. I loved listening to them sing. Peter was reserved and quiet, and Gordon was a gentleman who had no problem letting people know his opinion on things. One of those things was cussing around a female presence.

"Hold that thought." He'd say to the cusser and generally all profanity stopped. If he personally swore, he always apologized for his transgression. I liked that respectfulness about him. In such close quarters, it was nearly impossible not to hear someone swearing, so it was nice to know that Gordon was trying to make things more civilized. Tempers got short in the hot stuffy little rooms we were all crowded into. Preshow nerves sometimes brought out the worst in performers, and a little bit of chivalry went a long way. Peter and Gordon, like so many other musicians were nervous before shows. But once on stage all anxiety seemed to melt away.

The Overlanders, a five band group, with a folk sound, led by Paul Arnold with his lead guitar, played their hit song *Don't It Make You Feel Good*. Also on the bill were David John and the Mood. They seemed so young but had been signed by the Stones old manager. They played a song called *PrettyThing*, which had also been sung by Bo Diddley. The Carvavells, two girls singing there hit song *You Don't Have to be a Baby to Cry*, also performed, as did Julie Grant, only girl was only a year older than me, a small dark haired girl and quite shy. She had a minor hit called *Count On Me*.

Tony Marsh, a loud comedian, who hated the Stones was also on the tour. He said they were vulgar and dirty, and insulted them whenever he could. One night Keith had had enough and the two got into a fist fight. Keith got the better of Tony, and I assume Stu was the one who broke things up.

To say that the groups were on top of one another was an understatement. There weren't private dressing rooms or seating areas in those days. How one group kept another group's things separate was something I couldn't imagine. Stu handled the boy's, and their equipment, while making sure strangers were not harassing them.

Generally, prank playing was the favored method of breaking the tension, and everyone was on alert, never knowing who would do to what, to whom, next. Laughter was probably what kept most of the groups sane.

I don't know how they managed to tune their guitars with all the noise and commotion that went on in those cinema dressing rooms. With no windows, the rooms were stuffy and hot. They laughed while they prepared because no one would be able to hear them anyway.

Before shows the boys would peek through cracks in the heavy velvet curtains and pick out the girls they wanted to shag afterwards. Mostly the boys were on form playing jokes on one another and anyone in the vicinity.

This is how things went from one venue to the next, one town after another: two shows every day, stay at a hotel, fight through the crowds, put everything into the performance and music, then jump into the van try and evade the girls who invariably chased and jumped onto the cars. Try to get them at least out of the way, so an escape could be made, and do it all over again.

Fans literally overran the small towns where these groups were being booked. Where local police previously only had to worry about a few local drunks and unruly Rockers, the crowds being drawn by these new popular bands were unlike anything ever experienced before. Overwhelmed by the sheer numbers of people, police were kept busy trying to keep the peace as best they could.

After Coventry, where more screaming girls eluded overwhelmed law enforcement, Brian and I managed to escape the crowd early.

"Let's go home Dawn." He looked exhausted, "Let's go back to your place, where we can get away from all of this."

After driving to his flat at Chester Street, he gathered some clean clothes, returned and tossed a bag into the back seat, revved up the engine and sped over to my parents' place. Mum and Dad heard us come through the door and got up.

"Oh you're awake, thank goodness. Mrs. Molloy, would you mind if I take a bath here? My place is always swarming with people and I just want some quiet." Brian looked like a man beseeching a passing ship to rescue him from a deserted island - or in his case maybe put him on one.

"Of course," Mother answered. "I'll get clean towels." She gave him shampoo and soap. When he came into my room his hair smelt of Sun Silk shampoo and Mum had given him Dad's robe. Taking my hand he pulled me onto the bed with him. I could tell he was beat. I hadn't noticed before, but he had bags under his eyes. Kissing me, pulling me close, I felt the hair on his body and soon realized that, despite his fatigue, he was willing to share his love with me. Soon afterwards, as I lay in his arms, I heard the soft purr of his snoring. Too wired to sleep, I slipped away to Mother's room.

"He's completely exhausted Mum. You can't believe how hard they work on stage. He's asleep on my bed."

"Leave him alone, let's have a cup of tea." I told her about the concert, the girls, and the constant travel, and was soon falling asleep myself.

"Mum, can you wake me at eleven? Brian has a concert in East Ham tomorrow." And that was it for me. Being shaken awake by my Mother was the next thing I remembered

"It's eleven, Dawn time to get up" Running down to my room, it seemed a shame to wake him. He looked so peaceful, innocent and carefree, it was a pity to have to rouse him, but if he didn't get up he wouldn't make it to the East Ham on time. Kissing him gently he pulled me close making love to me once more.

Brian dressed in a nice shirt, jacket and pants he pulled out of his travel bag. He splashed on some Cedar Wood Cologne. It must have been a good night's rest because Brian was his happy talkative self again.

Setting off out the front door, he said 'good bye' to Mum and Dad. I kissed him, wished him luck, and he was off to another show.

The plans were for him to return the next day and pick me up for another leg of the tour.

"Put on one of your miniskirts, I want to look at you while we drive." He told me before he left.

I packed my bag and waited for him in the courtyard. When he drove up, I felt his eyes looking me over as he got that devilish look on his face. Getting in the car, I leaned over and gave him a kiss, and we were off to another venue.

"You know, Dawn, things aren't always going to be this crazy. One of these days, I want to travel around the United States. We can get a car and drive down the Pacific Coast Highway in one of the American open top cars, and go to New Orleans and see some real jazz musicians. I know you'll love it. Its something I've wanted to do it all my life."

"I want to be with you all of my life." I answered, smiling, feeling content.

The concert was being held in the Birmingham Town Hall. Fans swarmed everywhere. It was another lucky day because we managed to enter the hotel undetected. Stu and the boys were already checked in. Our timing was perfect the boys were scheduled to do a recording for *Thank Your Lucky Stars*, so I went to our room.

When the boys returned from the studio, Helen and I met them at the tradesman's entrance, so we could all go to the show together. As usual, security at the hotel and at the venue was hopeless. Stu did his best to find ways to trick the fans into thinking the boys would be going one place, and then leaving for another. But, once the fans caught the scent, the stampede was on and the boys had to fight their way through the crowds.

The next day, after a night of partying, I was awakened by Brian kissing my face, my eyes, and my lips. He held me close. "Let's get married, Dawn. I want you all the time." I started to laugh, "No, I mean it. Get dressed, I'm serious, let's go find the courthouse and do it." Looking into his eyes, I realized he wasn't kidding.

"You're serious, okay then let's go." And while we both dressed we talked about our future, our traveling plans, what our parents would say. As we went downstairs Brian took my hand and grabbed the flowers out of the vase at the reception desk. Laughing, we made it out the door. We were heading for the parking area as Andrew Loog Oldham drove up.

"Where the Hell are you going?" he snarled, getting out of his car.

"I'm going to get married" Brian said, showing him the flowers and kissing my hand.

"Oh no, you're fucking not." he shouted, glaring at me like I had instigated the idea 'We have a photo shoot to do! Get your shit into the van."

Within minutes, all of us were in the van on our way to the outskirts of Birmingham and the countryside. We didn't speak. Brian held my hand the entire ride.

From left Helen, Keith, Bill, Charlie, Dawn & Brian.

The location was in a gorgeous wooded field, and the shoot was to be in a vintage car. The boys were enchanted, and examined every detail, from headlights to back bumper. They took turns sitting in the driver's seat pretending to drive and honking the old fashioned horn.

Michael Ward the photographer. When he was finished, Helen asked a bystander to take some pictures with her camera. Helen stood on the board in the front and I stood behind Brian, wishing I were somewhere else rather than in front of the camera. Brian grabbed my legs and pulled me close to him.

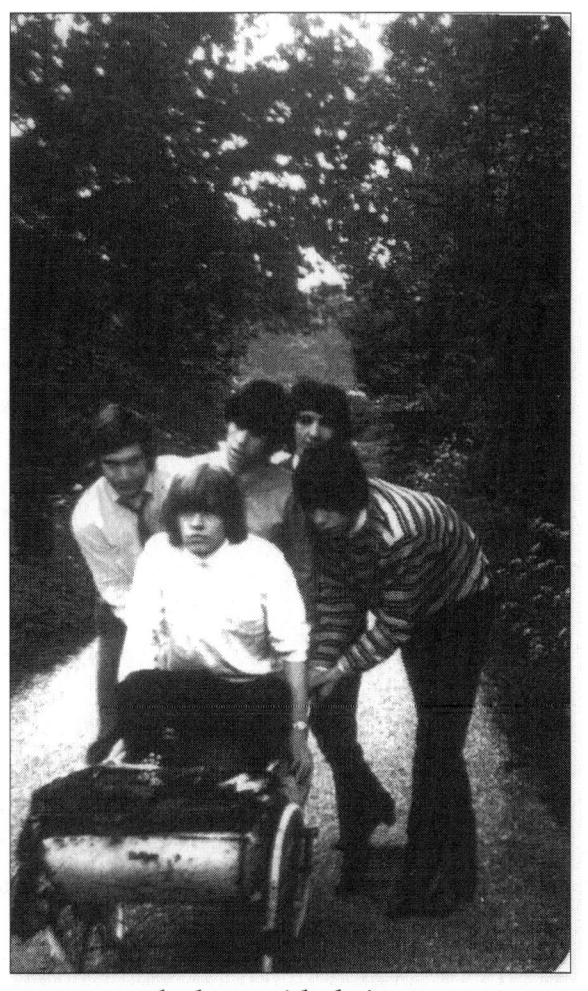

The boys with their toys

Mick and Keith had been wondering around and found an old pram in a ditch. Brian jumped in and Keith, Mick and Bill pushed him around, trying to tip him out of it. It was hilarious, and Michael Ward the photographer got more photos than he had first imagined. So did Helen.

Keith & Bill tipping Brian out of the pram while Dawn looks

Once the photo shoot was completed, Stu drove us back to pick up Brian's car, so we could make the drive to their next stop- Cannok.

After a while all of the hotels seemed to be the same and all of the names of the towns blended together. But I remember Cannok at The Danilo Theater Staffordshire. The back stage was smaller and hotter than most. We were packed together like sardines in a tin. Stu dreaded these kinds of places. Tempers would flare and there was no place to set up the equipment.

*The Danilo Theater Cannok 1964 demolished
in 1970 now retail development.*

As always, there were lots of cigarettes and the alcohol flowed freely. But even that was not enough to keep tempers cool. Again as always, girls were everywhere, like bees to a honey pot, and the noise was deafening. The back door couldn't be opened for fear of fans getting in. Stu managed to climb on a chair and open a tiny little window in hopes of getting some air. We were all floating in pools of perspiration, breathing smoke and tipsy on booze. Peter and Gordon went on stage, followed by the Baron Knights. I was standing at the side of the stage watching, when my head began to spin and I blacked out.

"Are you alright?" Suddenly I was looking up at Gordon Waller, who was holding me. Apparently, he caught me as I was toppling to the floor. Brian had been getting a drink when he heard I'd fainted. He was frantic and didn't want to go on stage for fear I'd faint again. Gordon said he would take care of me until they were done. It was so hot that I wonder how no one else passed out from the heat. The worst part of all was that, once again, we couldn't leave because the fans were milling around, trying to get a glimpse of the boys.

Privacy was probably the most sacred commodity during those times. Brian and I craved it, and with every stolen opportunity we managed to make love.

Leaving Cannok, we headed for Stockport, another movie theater but a little bigger this time. The crowds were large, but not as out of control as some of the smaller towns we had been to. There was more security, and we were able to get into the venue without a fight. As I watched the show, not being able to hear a word they sang, I marveled at how good they'd become and how well Mick worked the crowd. They were playing *I'm Alright* and the girls were frantic, as he moved back and forth in rhythm to the maracas. It was such a good song, and I felt sad that no one could hear it. They all worked hard to be heard, and the effort wore them out. But after a show they were so wired that they could not relax. As always, they had to wait for the crowd to clear out, so they told jokes, talked to the girls they had picked up, and drank whisky or rum and coke.

The Essoldo Theater Stockport demolished in 1994 now office block.

Stockport was my last concert on the tour. That night Helen was driving back to London, and I had to go back to work. We were excited and talked about the week with the boys, how Helen really liked Bill, but it was sad that she was due to leave for Australia.

The boys were traveling on to Sheffield, but they would be back in town for a show at Wembely in two days, so I didn't feel too bad. But, two days when you're in love might as well be two years, I missed Brian probably as soon as Helen drove us out of the Stockport parking lot.

He called as promised. Dad was annoyed as usual. I was in the clouds of love and nothing mattered in the world. I slept with the white shirt he'd left with me, the one he had worn on the cover of their first LP *The Rolling Stones*. His harmonica sat on my dresser and his LPs lay by my record player.

Chapter Twelve

I Am Waiting

I didn't see Brian before he set off for America. He would call to check in, always over the top with excitement, sharing the latest news in his life. "Dawn, we are going to the States! I'm going to see and hear the best blues players in the world! I wish you were coming along. It would be so much better with you at my side." I had no idea how he handled the whirlwind of trying to get ready and organized.

"I just don't have time to come by." He said sadly. As always, he never questioned if it were alright with me or not, assuming that whatever made him happy was just fine with me

I would have loved to see him, but that seemed to be out of the question. He told me how Linda was still not feeling well and how he and her family were worried about her. It was going to be hard for him to say goodbye to the Lawrence's, given her health issues. In my mind, this reaffirmed that he was a sweet and considerate man, even when his life was being turned upside down from getting ready to fly off to a foreign country. I admired and loved him all the more, because he loved and cared so deeply for everyone around him.

I watched them leave for America on the television news on June first. The police were having a job holding the crowds back. I could feel the excitement of the boys leaving London and expected their tour of the States to be a success. Two days later, I received a call in the middle of the night, he was in Hollywood.

"Dawn, you can't believe this place! Everyone has a swimming pool, the sun shines all the time, and everywhere you look there are palm trees. It's just like in the movies. We played with Dean Martin. What an ass! All he did was try and take the piss out of us. We don't need that kind of shit. He's not the one being chased by girls everywhere he goes. God, I think about you all the time. You'd love it out here. I miss you." And then as always he was gone, telling me he would call when he could, leaving me to try and get back to my normal everyday life.

"Dawn, you can't believe this place! We're in Texas! It's huge! We're riding in the bus and this place goes on forever. There are real cowboys here, and they had real guns too. God I'm tired. I miss you every second. I'm looking forward to seeing Chicago."

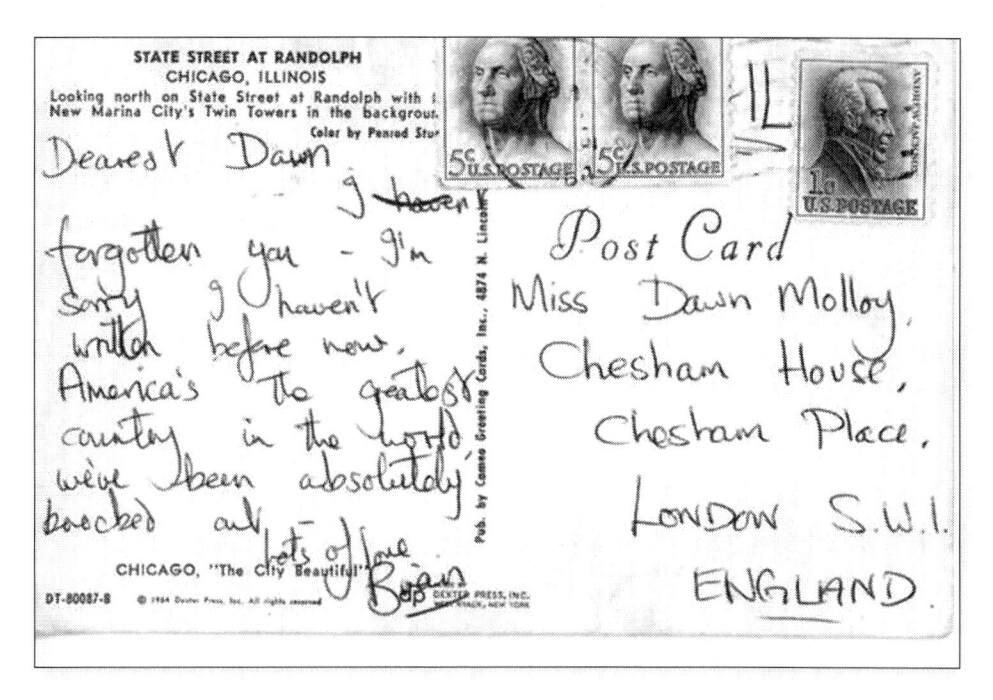

> Dearest Dawn
> I haven't forgotten you - I'm sorry I haven't written before now. America's the greatest country in the world, we've been absolutely booked out, lots of love
> Brian
>
> Post Card
> Miss Dawn Molloy,
> Chesham House,
> Chesham Place,
> London S.W.1.
> ENGLAND

Chicago post card to Dawn 1964

The next time he called was to tell me that he'd met Muddy Waters, his blues hero. He came into the Chess Studio where they were recording. I thought he was going to come through the phone he was so high and excited. A few days later, I received a post card that he had written to me from there.

Dearest Dawn

I haven't forgotten you - I'm sorry I haven't written before now, America's the greatest country in the world, we've been absolutely knocked out-

Lots of love Brian

A few days later he called from Nebraska. "Dawn, we saw a real Indian tribe - fantastic. I can't believe it. The hotels here are huge, not like the little shit holes we have been staying in at home. Believe it or not, they have security out here and they are carrying guns! Who's going to argue with someone carrying a gun! We still don't have any time to ourselves - it's always a photo shoot, television show, interview, or we're off to another concert. I'm worn out - don't get enough sleep. God I miss you every second baby. I can't wait to see you again. You would love this place. Someday we'll come back and see everything together." It all sounded so exciting, but so exhausting.

The excitement of being in a foreign country and having to do so much traveling, had changed how Brian sounded on the phone. He'd become super hyper and fast talking, jumping from subject to subject without taking a breath. I assumed he would calm, down once he returned home and had time to rest. In the meantime, it sounded like the boys lived on the go, from one show to the next, one hotel to another. To make matters worse, they had to fly back to England for two days to do a show at Magdelen College Oxford. Brian said it had something to do with a contract that they couldn't get out of. As soon as the concert was done, that very same night they had to get back on a plane and return to the United States

"Dawn, the thought of you waiting for me at home is what keeps me going. I can hardly wait to see you again."

From Nebraska he'd sent me a second post card.

Dear Dawn

Again I've just phoned you & now I'm being plagued by girls ringing me up all the time if only you were here, you'd love America,

All my Love Brian,

I Am Waiting

Nebraska post card sent to Dawn 1964

Their arrival back in England was accompanied by near riots at the crowded airport. It was all over the news. Dad and I sat in front of the television watching. "I expect you will be seeing him soon." Dad said, and he was right.

Brian showed up full of agitated energy and story after story about his adventures in America. He spent hours talking to my dad about the music greats he met, and how exhausting the entire trip was. I felt left out to say the least. I had other plans for my man, and Dad was getting in the way. Finally, Brian and Dad called the "musician's conference" to an end, and we were able to retreat to the quiet and privacy of my room.

While in Chicago, he had found the time to get me negligees. Needless to say, it did not stay on long. We made love, and made love again. It was impossible to have enough of one another.

"Dawn, have you heard our new record *It's All Over Now*? Listen carefully as the ending fades away, I did that, I love it!"

June twenty-sixth Stu picked me up and drove me to Alexander Place, where the boys had a gig. When I got back stage, I found Brian with a cute white toy poodle puppy. It wasn't more than eight weeks old and was terrified from the noise and commotion going on.

I Am Waiting

Bill talking to Dawn at Alexander Palace also included in his book Stone Alone

"Brian, the puppy is adorable. Where did you get it?"

"I got it for Linda. I wanted her to have a poodle just like yours. Do you think it's a good present to thank her and her family, for all they've done for me?"

"Why yes, that's perfect. They'll love it. Here, let me take him while you get ready for the show. The poor thing is scared to death." Handing the squirming pup over he left, only return ten minutes later in a horrible mood. He'd changed from being happy and carefree, to grumpy angry and distant.

"What's the matter?"

"Look at my damn hair. It's messed up from being so damn hot back there. Why does it always have to be so bloody hot? Look at me." I was looking at him. I was always looking at him.

Dawn drying Brian's hair with Pip the poodle

"Sit down, I'll fix it. Here, hold the puppy." I damped his hair and blew it dry, while he played with the little white fluff ball. I often worked on Brian's hair. He was so fussy, and I loved that his moods always lifted when I took care of it. This instance was no different. His black mood soon changed back to the teasing, laughing Brian I adored. Of course, the ever-present photographers used this sweet interlude to take a lot of impromptu photos.

Brian getting ready with Dawn in the back.

Time over for fussing with hair and taking photos, Brian and the boys followed Alex Korner as he exited off stage. As always the crowd erupted. The puppy wiggled and squealed in fear. I took him from Brian and went back to the dressing rooms where it was quieter. Helen hung around for a while playing with the pup, and then went and watched Bill perform. After the show, Brian was still happy and high from his performance.

"Thanks for taking care of the puppy. You are so good with him. I'm glad you were here. I don't know what I would have done. What would you name him if he was yours?"

"I'd name him Pip."

"Okay, then Pip it is." I laughed. How like him to give Linda a gift that has already been named, and I was sure she wouldn't dare change it. We hung out for a while after the show, drinking and joking with some of the other performers.

"Come on Dawn, let's go home. It's been a long day." So, Pip, Brian and I were off.

"I have to take this little pup to Linda. I'll miss you." We were at my door and he kissed me passionately, and then was gone.

CHAPTER THIRTEEN

It's All Over Now

July was a month of heavy commitments and long road trips. When Brian called, he was often distant and moody. He described the arguments he'd had with Mick and Keith over the music and the pop sound the Stones were playing. The boys were getting on one another's nerves and quite frankly it was often more than he could bear. The road trips had become grueling, and he was tired of not being able to walk the street without being spotted and asked for an autograph. Yes, things were going well for the group, but it wasn't what he wanted. I'm not sure he knew what he wanted. I know he hated not having control and despised it when things were not orderly and lined up as he felt they should be.

A quote by Keith in a newspaper report about Brian said:

Brian's trouble wasn't musical. There was something in him that meant that if things were going well, he'd make sure it screwed up. I know the feeling: there's a demon in me, but I only own up to having ONE of them; Brian probably had 45 more. With Brian it was all self-consuming pride.

He couldn't sleep without taking some kind of pill. He couldn't stay awake without taking Purple Hearts. The more drugs he took the more agitated, angry and withdrawn he became. He drank and partied and seemed to be losing touch with reality. I know he was losing touch with me. His calls had become fewer and farther between. Yes, he did have a heavy tour schedule, yes he was worn out and everyone wanted a piece of him and yes I felt guilty for wanting a share as well. I tried to understand, tried to be loving and supportive when he called, but now I never knew how to act or what to say from one conversation to the next.

It wasn't just Brian who worked hard and partied harder. The entire band was always up to something, and the news reported their escapades in great detail. They trashed places, were disrespectful, generally living up to the 'bad boy band' model that had been created around them - drugs, booze, girls and rock and roll. Brian assured me there were no other women in his life and these assurances kept me at home waiting for his calls.

On one of the days he had off, we were able to slip away and go to the Beat City Club. Security kept the fans and photographers out and only allowed ticketed people in. We found a table out of the way of prying eyes. It was good to be able to hold hands, have a drink and talk. That particular night he was once again the man I'd fallen in love with. On July twenty-forth he took me to the taping of the Ready Steady Go show again. As always, women fawned all over the boys, photographers with their flash cameras posed them in what I assume were strategic places for the best photo op, and of course there were interviews upon interviews. It was hectic and fun and Brian was still in a good mood. I had to work the next day, so Brian took me home

That night, the boys played at the world famous Blackpool Empress Ballroom to a crowd of 7,000 people. To say things did not go well would be an understatement.

"Dawn, I was scared shitless!" he yelled over the phone, after leaving the concert. "These bastards rushed the stage and this jerk started telling everyone to spit on me. Why the fuck, I don't know. Keith told them to knock it off, but they kept on. So, Keith stood on the man's hands and kicked him in the face. That's when all hell broke loose, and the fans went nuts and starting tearing the place up. We had to get the hell out of there." I could hear the fear in his voice and was so happy that he was safe in the hotel.

July twenty-fifth, the morning newspapers were filled with headlines about the riot at Blackpool and how the Stones started it and the fans tore up the seats, destroyed a Steinway grand piano and pulled crystal chandeliers apart. Fifty people were sent to the hospital and the madness only ended when police and dogs were brought in to restore the peace.

Returning home the next day, he called me so we could meet at the Lowndes Arms. As always no one took notice of either of us and we were free to just be together.

"God, the people are getting crazy. I swear to God, I thought we were going to die. We had to fight our way out of that place. I just don't believe it!" As he told the story he was unsteady and sometimes a bit incoherent. He smoked cigarette after cigarette and drank continuously in the hope of calming his nerves. I took him home. He needed peace and quiet, and I needed him.

The next couple of days he had off, and the hours I had to be at work could not tick by quickly enough. Brian rested, and visited his friends the Lawrence's. Too soon he was leaving his car in the courtyard and was back on the road again. It was a hamster wheel for him - travel, come home, stay with me, be off on the road again.

His drug abuse had escalated at this point and his dark moods were becoming more and more difficult to decipher and deal with. Sometimes he was calm, other times agitated, angry and distant. He pulled away from me at those times, but would not allow me to pull away from him. When we would lie in bed, he was silent and brooding, refusing to share his thoughts and feelings. Other times he was relaxed and silly, my old Brian - the man who was full of childishness, who instigated pillow fights, teased and tickled me until I ran around the room with him in hot pursuit.

Then he would be back to complaining - the pills weren't working as well as they had been, the touring had completely worn him out, he despised the photographers who were blatantly aggressive and rude if he refused to have his picture taken and shoved their cameras in his face anyway. The band wasn't going the way he wanted. He wanted a blues band, loved the bluesy sound. But Andrew Olden had other plans, he wanted the group to be more pop because that is what sold records. It had become about the money and Brian was over it.

"Bring the car to Longleat House. We're doing a show and Lulu will be singing. You will like it." It was August second and I'd gotten a late start. There was no way I would be able to see the show, but I'd make it in time to get Brian soon after. The parking area was jammed and getting to the gate where I was supposed to pick him up was proving to be impossible. Impossible that is until a fan recognized Brian's car and helped move people out of the way so I could get through. No sooner had I driven up than a drunk, high Brian ran out, told me to move over, and jumped in the driver's side. He was laughing uncontrollably

Longleat concert 1964 (Courtesy of Tony Keeley/Lebrecht Music & Art)

"We pissed all over the walls at that place." He was absolutely maniacal.We broke all kinds of shit, ran all over the house and no one even tried to stop us."

I read about it the next day in the paper, which described how over two hundred female fans were injured when the crowd set up such a violent clamor for the band. "We could easily have some dead on our hands, if things go on as they are." Brian had said.

All the while, the worse the boys acted the more popular they became. Honestly, after hearing the entire story I was grateful I'd arrived late.

Brian Epstein had a party at Chesham Place later the same month. Dad wasn't happy because it caused him extra work, checking invitations at the lift to make sure no uninvited "guests" made it to the penthouse. The Beatles and the Stones were invited, and after the party Brian came down to my room. I'd been waiting for him in the negligee he brought me from Chicago.

After that night, he had a few days free again. Later in the week, he went to visit the Lawrence's, and on his return would left his car in the courtyard and come down to the flat to see me. And that's how it went. Anytime he was in London, I would see him and maybe we would go over to the Lowndes Arms. But this was only if he had a night off, which was few and far between. I thought his dark moods came about because he was tired and perhaps because the pills he was taking to stay awake were not working. He was very agitated at times, and others quite calm. I believe his head was spinning with the tours and commitments they had ahead of them. Also other things like the photographers, or as they are called now Paparazzi were becoming more aggressive and the fans behavior was changing.

The roller coaster that had become my life hadn't slowed down. I worked for Simon and waited for Brian to call or drop by the flat. It made sense that I would feel "off." After all, nothing about my life with him was settled. Trying to gage his moods was a constant up or down for me. I'd notice this more since he had returned from the States. My stomach knotted when he was down, settled when he was up. My head could not handle the highs and lows, how would I expect my body to? It would be normal for a person to feel nauseated under the circumstances. I slept a lot, but who wouldn't? Brian's erratic phone calls and drop in hours had me on hyper alert. When I had the chance to rest, I did so completely. However, when my breasts became tender and my period did not make its' appearance. I began to suspect that I had gotten myself into trouble.

Why it came as such a surprise I don't know. Brian and I had never used any kind of precautions. I'd assumed Brian, being my man of the world, would know how to keep me from getting pregnant. I had no idea what the reality of things were and that 'it' had happened to me was terrifying. How could a good Catholic girl find herself in such a situation? The night I finally figured out why I had been unwell, Brian was visiting me at the flat.

"Brian…" How to begin, what would he say, "I think that I'm pregnant," Brian didn't show the least bit of concern.

"Oh, Dawn, don't worry, everything will be okay. I'll take care of you both. I love you - things will be just fine. Wait and see." Then he covered my face with kisses, my tender breasts with kisses, and made love to me as only as man who loves the woman who is carrying his child could. My fears dissipated and all my worries faded into the background noise of my ever taunting mind.

"What should we name the baby?" I was cocooned in his strong arms, safe from what the world might hold in the very near future.

"I want to name him Julian."

"Julian, what a perfect name for our boy." And it was settled. No thoughts that we might have a baby girl, Brian announced our boy to be Julian and so it was to be.

Later that evening, after we had rested, made love, rested again, my mind started her squeaky talk, her practical talk. She wanted questions answered.

"When will you tell Andrew?" I asked. Why Andrew should have any say in what was going on between us in our private moments I will never know, but Andrew had his fingers in every part of the boys' lives. We all seemed to innately know it, so why wouldn't he need to be told about this?

"Oh, my sweet Dawn, don't worry about a thing. You love me don't you?" Of course I loved him.I will take care of it all. Trust me, Andrew will be fine with it. I'm fine with it, everyone will be happy for us." I knew I was happy for us. "I need you baby, nothing and no one can come between us, especially not Andrew." He left a while after that. Alone in bed I smelled the comfort of him still on the sheets. We would be together always, why did my worry wart mind always have to try and insinuate herself into my life when things were going well?

Torquay Town Hall

Their new song *It's All Over Now* was number one on the charts. It was August twenty-eighth, and I hadn't heard from him in a month. Then, with no explanation as to where he'd been, he called." Dawn, come to Torquay tomorrow. Helen will pick you up." How so like him, giving orders as always, and as always I did as he told me to do. I was happy that he was waiting to see me the next afternoon.

Helen drove me to the town hall where the show was being held. The usual slew of ravenous fans was trolling the area, trying to get a Stones sighting. Not having the boys with us, we were of no interest and able to get to the stage door without problems. Equipment was being brought in, so we asked someone to get Stu for us.

Stu came to the door and let Helen in. As I moved forward to follow her, he turned and stepped in front of me blocking my way.

"What's wrong?" I asked surprised.

"Dawn, I'm sorry, but I can't let you through."

"But why?" I asked

"Linda's in there."

"So." Linda had been at other shows when I was there, what did Brian's friend have to do with me not being allowed inside?

"Dawn, I'm really sorry, I can't let you in because she's is in there with Brian and their baby." My entire body took a chill at those words. *Their* baby? How could that be? "Linda gave birth on July twenty-third." Stu seemed a bit annoyed as me, or maybe it was Brian he was annoyed with, or maybe because he had to be the one to deliver the bad news. "Yeah, and he told Andrew about you being pregnant now. Andrew flipped and told Brian that if he ever saw you again he was out of the band. The band already has a bad name, and Linda having a baby, and now you pregnant will make things worse. Brian has agreed, and you won't be seeing him again."

"I would never do anything to hurt Brian or the group. Doesn't Andrew know that? Why am I being sent away? I haven't done anything. Brian loves me." Then, suddenly, it made sense and I realized that no matter what I said, nothing made a difference. Brian had told me whatever it took to make me believe what he wanted me to believe. The stories about needing to take care of Linda's illness because he felt like he should do to the kindnesses of her family, the puppy, and all of Brian's things being at her parents' house was all a ruse to keep me in the dark. How could I have not seen it before? How stupid could I have been?

Helen came outside just as Stu finished giving me the bad news. I was shaking, not sure if I should cry or scream. I stumbled down into a sitting position next to the door. The tears had not yet begun to flow, but I knew that a total meltdown was soon to overcome me. I had been betrayed. I'd been played.

"What a cold and cruel person Brian is!" Helen said. He yelled at me for bringing you down here after he told me to! And Linda shows up unexpectedly and I'm blamed for all this mess?"

Bill opened the door and sat down the other side of me.

"What a bastard!" Bill said as he put his arm around me, and the sobs I'd been holding back burst through. "I'm so sorry Dawn, I had no idea he was still with her. I'm sorry how he's treating you. What a cowardly bastard!" Years later, when talking about Brian, Bill had shared his opinion that Brian was a hypochondriac, a bit of a worrier, highly intelligent and very articulate. He could be the sweetest, softest, most considerate man in the world, or the nastiest piece of work anyone had ever met. Bill stated that the boys saw that in him a lot, as he flitted from one extreme to the other. He would not give a shit about anything and then worry about the slightest detail.

Stu said, "I never really trusted Brian – mainly because he was always telling you to trust him."

Stu, Helen and Bill stayed with me until I was able to get hold of my emotions and stand up. Brian never came out to see how I was doing, or even say a last goodbye. He left this dirty piece of work to the boys.

There was nothing left for me to do but find my way home. It was a desperate, frightening, and lonely walk to the bus station. I couldn't understand what had happened. Didn't he ask me to go see him? I knew he would be in touch, I had a feeling he would call and he did.

'Jesus, Dawn. I had no idea Linda was coming and bringing the baby. I'm so sorry you had to find out about her the way you did. Please forgive me I love you." His voice made me melt.

How could I be mad a him? He continued to call, as he was touring again till the end of the month Sometimes I would go to his flat, where he would have his friends, Gordon Waller and James Phelge, stop by and they'd play tricks and lark around. At the end of September, Brian came down to the flat and suggested going the to Lowndes arms for a drink. Much to my surprise, he had James with him, who eventually went off to talk to the landlord Ken and left us alone.

"What am I going to do Brian? I'm so afraid to tell my parents."

"Don't worry Dawn, it will be alright. We will talk about it another time, when James isn't with us... I will come down and talk to your Dad. I will take care of you trust me. Your even more beautiful pregnant "and he put his hand on my stomach, smiling that wicked smile

James came back with more drinks. When the pub closed, they bought a bottle of Scotch and we went back to Brian's. As usual, there were lots of people milling around, and the record player was loudly playing the Blues. Girls were all over Brian, who was drunk, and he loved it, thinking it was funny.

I'm not a drinker and even one drink can affect me, so my first drink of straight whisky on top of what I already had, made me violently sick and I threw up all over the floor. Neither Brian nor James had any idea what to do with me. I was very emotional and realized they were getting me drunk on purpose. I sat on the steps outside feeling the world spinning and then decided to walk home, knowing from that night I was on my own.

CHAPTER FOURTEEN

Can You See Your Mother Standing in the Shadows?

Mother knew there was something wrong. She probably had for some time. Mother's Intuition, as I happily call it now, my early warning sign alerting me to some problem or other that my kids are holding back from me - something I know would be better for them to talk through with me. But my mother was rarely, if ever, in the mood for discussion. Mother was not the talking-through type. But, to be fair, not many parents took a lot of notice of their kids back then. "Children are to be seen and not heard" was the common rebuff a child would receive for interrupting an adult conversation or acting in such a way to bring attention to themselves.

There would be little chance of interrupting my Mother this particular evening. All hell was breaking loose, as she had gone absolutely ballistic on hearing of my plight. I'd endured my fair share of ranting and raging over the years, but this was something quite apart.

"Tramp!" she screamed. "I always knew you would amount to no good, you were never any good!" My mother's voice bounced off the walls in fury. "How could you bring such disgrace onto this family? We trusted you and this is how you, and this is how you repay us?" I spaced out. What was going on? What was she saying?

"What are people going to say when they find you that you've been sleeping around? What will happen if the Church finds out? Where will we be then? No! This is never going to go beyond these four walls. I'm going to make sure of that." She voiced these last two sentences in slow and deliberate tones. To this day her hateful and spiteful words live inside of me. It has always been incomprehensible to think that my mother could say those things to her daughter.

As for my father, well, at one point I thought it was inevitable that he'd hit me.

I waited for him to say or do something, to jump up, grab me by the arm, and beat me - anything. But he sat mute, staring through me, as she continued on, "You've ruined us all, just because you couldn't keep your legs closed! No man will ever want you - you are damaged goods. No one wants to marry someone who's used! You are nothing but a piece of rubbish!" She made it clear that I had repaid the debt of my upbringing by causing shame to fall on them all and everything they stood for as solid citizens, good Catholics, the perfect family.

I truly felt as if I'd betrayed them beyond repair. Tragically, Dad seemed to think the same and, to press the matter home that I was not worth the effort to him, he stood up, walked out, slamming the front door behind him and seeking the sanctity of the pub. I would have much preferred the pain of his physical anger. But to have my father wash his hands of me and abandon me to the worst my mother had to offer was the hardest blow he could have dispensed.

As day followed day, I was grateful for the opportunity to drag myself out of bed, escape to work, and hide from the boiling cauldron that constantly plagued our home. When I did have to return, it was as if I were invisible - they wouldn't even glance my way. Both were seething with anger.

Behind the scenes, mother was hell bent on finding a solution to the problem, a way to get rid of '*It*'. She'd been making inquiries. I was willing to go along with whatever she came up with, in the hope of pushing through the estrangement I'd created and getting back to a 'normal' life.

To this end, she turned to neat Gin as her first remedy for my situation. How prophetic that her cure should start with 'Mother's Ruin.' I had to drink it down, and do so rapidly. I had no idea why this was supposed to work and wondered if it was to be used as a form of anaesthesia for what would come next, which was to immerse myself into the hottest tub of water that could be run. The searing pain was intolerable, but I dared not retreat. I sat, my skin burning red, sweat breaking out on my forehead. What followed was vigorous and violent vomiting, along with painful stomach cramps.

Satisfied that she had done what she could for the moment and hoping that this violent purge would rid my body of the unwanted intruder, I was allowed to drag myself off to bed. I was in a state of physical and mental turmoil. I just wanted to wake up, go off to work the next day, and look forward to having a blast on that weekend. At least there was some sympathy to be had at work. Simon and Luc offered to keep my job open, if I had to go away. Even that small crumb of comfort that someone still needed me was a small boost to my shattered self-esteem.

Of course, eight hours at work each day, away from the looks of disgust and anger at home, brought some respite, but I still had to face my parents each night. Over the next few days, they hardly managed a passing glance, and it was plain to see they were still absolutely furious. At least after the initial volley of attrition, they were displaying some control.

Since the Mother's Ruin hadn't taken care of the problem, behind the scenes once more, Mother was able to find someone who knew a person who was willing to 'help.' After giving me the address and some money, Mother instructed to take the bus and have things taken care of. I really had no idea what she meant by this, and as yet no maternal instincts had begun to prick at my subconscious, alerting me to any possible dangers to my unborn child and making the baby my prime concern.

Mother didn't accompany me. I was to travel to the east side of town on my own. I suppose if she had come along, my story might have ended in a back street alley among the files of horrifying statistics. At the time, I had no idea that she'd sent me across town to have an abortion. I didn't even have the word in my vocabulary.

I remember looking out the bus window into the drizzling rain, such a depressing ride. All I saw were the rivulets of water running down the glass. At my stop, the rain had gone from a drizzle to an outright downpour. I didn't want to get any wetter than I already was, and quickly put up my umbrella, as I wandered down the street looking for the address on the paper.

The last thing my mother had said before I left was to make sure I didn't lose that address, I had memorized it just in case. I reached the street, and soon found the house number. It was on the opposite side of the road in the middle of a row of terraced houses. I stopped, and still can clearly remember every detail of those few minutes I stood there. My senses had become heightened, and a burning in the pit of my stomach told me something wasn't right. In fact, something was *very* wrong. The little hairs on my arms prickled up, chills ran down my spine and I had a strong feeling that, if I crossed the street and entered that house, I would be in some kind of danui. Something was wrong, but what was it?

The patter of the rain on my brolly was now quite clear and constant, picking out a crazy beat as it hit the material. I gazed, entranced by the strange, ugly, despicable looking little house. Through the descending gloom, my eyes picked out the filthy upstairs window with the equally dirty half torn lace curtains hanging limply. The front door paint was peeling away, with greasy, dirty marks around the doorknob. I stood motionless, mesmerised by the beating rain and those dank, probably once pretty lace curtains at the window. I'd become aware by now of the odour in this little street. It made me shiver and still does. Each time I think back to that evening, my nostrils fill with its aroma. I don't know what the smell was or even if there was a smell. It may just have been my body finally awakening me into maternity, but sure as hell it was stopping me crossing that road.

At that instant, a girl, younger than I, staggered out. Her face was contorted, and she was clutching her abdomen. Doubling over, she was trembling and sobbing heavily. She began to fall, but an older woman took her arm and helped her move out of the doorway and along down the road. I felt sad but I didn't know why. I've thought about her over the years and wondered how things turned out for her. I decided her plight was not going to be mine. Steeling myself, I decided that I was not going into that house, and I was not returning to mine, either. I was leaving London and heading out on the first Grey-Green bus I could find going to Great Yarmouth and my Aunt Eva. If anyone could help me make sense of what was going on with my life, of what was to happen, she would be the one with the loving, and wise answers I so badly needed.

It was October, a staid time of year in my beloved seaside town. The hour was late when I finally arrived. I had told no one I was leaving, and no one I was coming. As I made my way up the road to Auntie's, I wondered if I'd made a mistake. Aunt Eva was getting on in years. She'd given up running the Acacia. Memories of younger days and happier times filled my thoughts. She had always loved me no matter what, but, as I knocked at her entrance, I wondered how she would greet me if she knew of the news I was about to spring on her. It took her a while to get to the door. She was pleased to see me, and it didn't matter that it was late or that I'd arrived unannounced.

Being with her again was balm to my wounded spirit. Sitting me down before the fire, she boiled water and made some tea. As we shared our cups, I broke into tears and told her my story. I knelt down in front of her and put my head in her lap, and she stroked my face and hair as she had always done since I was a child, when things had been bad for me. No words were necessary. I felt warm, loved and accepted.

She called my parents and let them know that I would be staying for a little while. I didn't know what to do, but I knew I didn't want to return home. For the time being I was in her sanctuary, little Dawn again, cared for and understood. I may have done wrong, but I was still loved and accepted just the same. She was as always the sweetest, kindest, gentlest person in my life.

The following evening. I wandered down to Leo's Coffee Bar, my favourite old haunt, looking for an old friend or someone I knew. I have no idea what I would have said to them, given I was so far removed from the girl I'd been previously when out on holiday. I had run to Great Yarmouth and the tender arms of my beloved aunt, but my troubles stayed right inside of me, waiting to jump out and hit me over the head at any moment. The jukebox began playing *World Without Love* by Peter and Gordon, and just like that I was back in my hellish reality. Leo's was no refuge; I headed out to the promenade.

Being late October, the summer tourists had left, there wasn't much doing, just a few die hard dog walkers – all locals, taking no notice of the freezing wind coming in from the North Sea. It was so desperately cold, but I decided I needed to take off my shoes and walk along the shore and feel the sand between my toes anyway.

Barefoot at the water's edge, I watched as the wind whipped the swirling sea into foaming waves that lashed and tossed seaweed and shells onto the shore. This was the same beach that I had looked out upon so long ago, when I'd met the boys before their concert, talked all night with Stu, and woke up the next morning in an overstuffed chair. The sun had been shining and the water was calm. It was a happy day surrounded by friends. But that day was gone and I was now alone, my future was grim Remembering my mother's words, I knew I had nothing to look forward to and nothing to live for. My life was ruined. I had thrown it away. I had an overwhelming desire to walk into the sea and not look back. It was touch and go, as the urge to free myself from my mess was considerable. It would have been so easy to take that first step and make an end of it, stop the suffering, the turmoil and all of the unhappiness that I'd created.

Thankfully, something inside told me not to. Slipping my shoes back into my cold, sandy feet, I knew it would be a long time before my nightmare would end and there was plenty of pain still to come.

Ironically there was a Stones song that filled my mind - *Time Is On My Side* - and yes, it was.

CHAPTER FIFTEEN

High and Dry

It was inevitable that I'd have to return to my parent's home in London. I didn't have the wherewithal or resources to take control of the situation on my own. As I waited at the station for the bus to take me back, I suspected the prospects facing me when my parents picked me up were minimal. I knew my mother would be hell bent on sorting it all out in whatever manner best suited her. I was nothing more than a pawn in her personal life game.

I boarded the Grey Green, took a window seat, and watched as England's lush and pleasant pastures rolled by, unable to take the least bit of interest in any of it. Eventually, the splendid architecture of London replaced the countryside, and with each turn of the bus's wheels I drew closer to the doom my mother had most certainly sorted out for me.

The journey back provided me with plenty of time to ponder the fact that Brian had not contacted me, despite the promises he'd made while holding me in his arms in what seemed like a million years past. Taking full advantage of this, my always-tumultuous mind tortured me with recriminations. "Good girls just don't do those kinds of things," I thought to myself, "at least they didn't get caught. But then I guess they probably really weren't good girls to begin with." What would happen to me? Who would ever want me in the future? How would I take care of a baby all alone with no father for him and no husband for me?"

In her desperation to find a solution, Mother had, in my absence, sought out the sage advice of the all-knowing Catholic Church. It must have been a grueling experience for my, oh so self righteous mother. The pious Father had lent a sympathetic ear to her plight, and I'm sure had sagely nodded his head and 'tut tutted' the situation. Of course, he'd assured her, when her tale of woe was completed, that he did have the best solution for all involved.

To begin with, my sin must be kept secret from the other parishioners and, as soon as possible, Mrs. Stubbs, the social worker, should be called in so as to be of assistance. Apparently, she was a fine woman who would make a discreet visit to our home and help take care of the problem. Unbeknownst to me she worked for the National Adoption Association. Of course the virtuous cleric would pray for the family and the sins of the errant child.

Mother was grateful the church hadn't turned their back on her and had listened to her dilemma. She was more than happy to comply with the conditions set forth by the good Father - those being that I disappear until everything was corrected and returned to as it 'should be' once more.

As the family waited for the day when Mrs. Stubbs was to make her appearance, I stayed in my room laying in my bed, whimpering like Pip, Linda Lawrence's frightened puppy at the concert. She had had his baby June twenty-third and had named him Julian. Wasn't that the name Brian had chosen for our child? "Our child," what a joke that turned out to be. There was no 'our' anymore and I'd heard he was with Linda. Maybe he'd always been with her. I'd been used and hadn't even suspected. I'd believed everything he'd said and told me. What was worse, I was clueless as to how to move forward with my life.

Obviously, my mother didn't care about me. She only needed the problem removed as quickly and secretively as possible. The gin and hot bath treatment, or should I say torture, was too recent a nightmare to shove to the back of my despondent mind. She gave no kind words, provided no soft or forgiving gesture to quell my misery. I might as well have been dead to her - maybe it would have been better for all involved.

Before I knew it, the priest's answer had arrived at our front door. I don't remember if I was introduced to Mrs. Stubbs or not. Mother brought her into the flat and there she was, well dressed in an unglamorous way, with short, neat, mousy brown hair that framed a kindly face. She sat down on the chair my mother waved her to, and she opened a file.

"So, Dawn, can I call you Dawn?"

"Yes." Was all I was able to squeak.

"Dawn, I have a few questions to ask you. Who is the father?"

"Brian Jones." I replied in a quiet mousy voice.

Brows pinched together, she wrote down the answer. "How old are you? Does the father intend on being part of this?" I answered her questions dutifully, under the glare of my outraged mother.

"What are you going to do?"

'Going to do' was not a question my mother was prepared for me to answer, and she jumped into the conversation ready for battle.

"We are not keeping it!" she bellowed, using the word 'we' as if she and I were in one accord and unified in the decision. *I* had made no decision. If there was one to be made, I had hoped Mrs. Stubbs, with her experience in these matters, would have enlightened me as to my alternatives. Obviously, in my mother's mind, it had all been worked out and all that was left was for me to go wherever it was that girls in my condition went, and be done with it

I exhaled. How long I had been holding my breath? I'd hoped that Mrs. Stubbs would have provided me with something positive, something that could be done *by* me and not done *to* me. But she'd already bowed to my mother's will. As my breath left my lungs, all strength seeped out of my body, my head drooped and my shoulders slumped into submission.

Mother had Mrs. Stubbs full attention. They discussed my situation, my future, and the future of my unborn child. I might as well have been in another room - or on another planet. The sounds of outside traffic pulled me away and out of the moment. I didn't need to hear any more plans between my mother and her newest partner in crime. Tears spilled from my eyes.

Looking over and seeing me weeping infuriated Mother, who yelled into my face," Buck up! Pull yourself together! Mrs. Stubbs is trying to help you out of this mess! A mess that is all your own doing! You pull a stunt like this and we have to bail you out!"

"I think it's time to call a close to this meeting, Mrs. Molloy." Mrs. Stubbs interjected, halting Mother's tirade. "Dawn, I have some options that I think will be good for you. I'd like to come over tomorrow and discuss them with you. Maybe you will be more willing to talk to me then." And with that, she closed her file folder, stood up, calling a halt to the meeting. Maybe she sensed my despair, or maybe she and Mother had completed their plans for what to do with me.

Seeing Mrs. Stubbs out, the door was barely closed when Mother returned, raging with obvious indignation, like a bull ready to gore a red cape. "How dare you cause me to have to have a visit from a social worker!" she yelled, charging, slapping me across the face. "I don't need anyone telling me what to do with my tramp daughter!" Leaning forward, she slapped me again. "You have always been a disappointment to me. I should have known you'd end up in this condition!" slapping me once more she screamed, "You Slut! You let the first young man who looks at you do whatever he wants, and who has to take care of the problem? Me!" Slap, slap, slap, first one side of my face and then the other again.

I could take no more and ran to my room, her voice still ringing in my ears and the heat of her handprints stinging my face. Throwing myself onto my bed, I sobbed into my pillow. This time I *knew* I wanted to die. My desolation was worse than when I considered walking into the North Sea a few days before. I was at the lowest nadir in my life, truly in the depths of despair.

As promised, Mrs. Stubbs returned. She was a more efficient this time than she had been the day before, armed with all of her professional know how. This was to be the meeting wherein the final solution to the Dawn Molloy problem would be determined.

"Dawn," she began, presenting a well-rehearsed speech just how events would unfold." first you will see a doctor for an examination that will confirm that you are pregnant" The exam would confirmed that I was indeed pregnant, and that I was due on March twenty-first, 1965.

"Next, she explained I would be sent to an unmarried Mothers home that existed just for girls like me, where I would have my baby. It sounded awful, but given the fact that Mother could not bear to have me in her home a moment longer than necessary, the alternative didn't bear thinking about. There really was no point in putting up any resistance.

Mrs. Stubbs, then unbeknownst to me at the time, reeled off a montage of bare faced lies - or institutionalized, indoctrinated propaganda, that she was doing her best for me and my unborn child. Either way, she was putting together a plan of action that would affect the rest of my life, her thoughts, like those of my mother, didn't stretch that far off course

'Dawn," unless you have the full financial support of your parents or support from the child's father, nothing can be done to allow you to keep the baby. Social Services will be called in and forced to take it. The Government doesn't have the inclination, or the funds, to support unmarried mothers. If you try to take the baby and run away, you will be caught and arrested, and the child will spend the rest of its life in foster care. This is not a good solution for your child.

Turning the screws, she continued, "If you care about your baby, you will give it up for adoption, as soon after the birth as possible. That way it will have real parents, who can't have a child of their own and are happy and able to commit to the raising of a child. Your child needs to be brought up in a stable home, and you are unable to do that."The most loving and realistic answer for an unwed mother is to surrender her infant as soon as possible to a married couple who are able to care for it properly."

How gleeful Mother must have felt as Mrs. Stubbs orated. My head was swimming. I could not take it all in. It was obvious that my situation was hopeless, and I had no one to turn to.

"Dawn," she went on, "you are a smart girl, so I'm sure you understand and agree that adoption is the best plan of action for everyone involved. Once you have your baby and it is placed in a loving caring home, you will move on with your life and forget about this mistake. I've helped many girls in your position and this is for the best.

"You are young and have your entire life to look forward to. One of these days, you will meet a young man, get married and start a *proper* family of your own. You are healthy, you will have many more children in the *right* way, and you will forget all about this baby.

"I remember her emphasis on the word proper, and the use of the word mistake. She'd pulled it off. Part of me could feel my mother silently cheering in the background. My head was spinning like a top. I was a wreck I could not think for myself. I felt so bad. What had I done to everyone around me? I realized I had no choices, not with my parents against me, and Brian's back turned away. Mrs. Stubbs then opened her folder with papers for me to sign. What choice did I have?

The reality was that I was a young girl in trouble, Brian and his world of the Rolling Stones might as well have been a million miles away. I was deserted from all directions, and it made me numb.

I was assured that Mrs. Stubbs was at our house in order to help me out of my trouble. She was arranging the only "decent" solution available to someone like me. I remember her saying that word. It would be *decent* for some couple, who couldn't have children of their own to have my baby, whom they could care for properly. It would be *decent* for my family whom I'd disgraced. I wanted to be a decent person. Mother along with Mrs. Stubbs and the wheels were set in motion.

After that, as arrangements were made for me to take my confinement at an unwed mother's home called Beechwood, Mother became noticeably more relaxed. We managed at least to talk, and tension around the house subsided. I was frightened at the thought of my pregnancy, and of the idea of giving birth to a baby. Mother's only help was to tell me, "You'll see, being pregnant and giving birth is no big deal. It isn't hard at all. Women have children every day." I wasn't reassured, but since there were no books on the subject readily available and Mother had nothing else to reassure me with, I found myself on my own.

I'd never been one of those girls who were interested in children or babies. I never looked at a pregnant woman and dreamed how someday I would have a child, too, and how wonderful it would be. I didn't have a maternal bone in my body, and, with no maternal instincts, fear set in. I hoped that I'd get the reassurance and knowledge I needed from the professionals at Beechwood.

Chapter Sixteen

Out of Time

November 1964 started out colorless and drab, and then went downhill from there. Not a sliver of brightness peeked through a cloud the entire month. There was no respite, as the conditions turned grayer each day. The dull, murky weather matched the drabness of the Londoners going about their daily business - an army of trench coats in a constant march of bowed heads battling the elements, each going off to their respective places of employment, keeping the wheels of England's capital city oiled and gearing up for the long winter months ahead. The weather chilled everyone to the bones to the marrow.

I watched this London scene unfold from the relative comfort of the rear seat of my father's motorcar. Halfway through my pregnancy, my fate had been conclusively resolved by my mother. My mind had grown weary of listening to her accolades of Mrs. Stubbs and the Church, and how very grateful she was for all of their help in such a calamitous situation.

My father was ominously quiet, his tense military head and shoulders barely moving as he drove the car. He never glanced at my mother. Occasionally, I saw his doleful eyes reflected in the rear view mirror. They were the eyes of a worried man, who could not find the courage to make up his own mind and trapped between his head and heart with no right answer.

Crossing the River Thames into Wandsworth, then turning onto Putney Heath Lane, we passed through an open gate and followed the road leading up to an old Victorian home, the car's tires crunching over the small stones that made up the circular driveway. Naked, leafless trees surrounded the grounds. The place appeared lonely, cold and isolated - in tune with my aching soul. We had arrived at Beechwood, the location chosen for my confinement.

Getting out of the car, I retrieved my small brown suitcase from the boot. Inside I'd packed a few clothes for myself, four baby vests, four fleece infant nightgowns, one packet of terry towel nappies, four tiny plastic pants, nappy pins, a matinee coat, booties, shawl, baby soap, shampoo, powder and cream - all items purchased by Mother from a list sent to our flat by the Beechwood staff. Labels were sewn onto each item with my surname.

I surveyed the scene. My father did not come into the house. I'm sure he would have felt awkward. Mother ushered me up the stone steps and through the large black doors. This was an establishment of oppression, the kind of place that the hip friends I'd been hanging out with only a few weeks before raged against.

It was the biggest house I had ever been in. The mahogany doors opened onto a large hallway that led to a long and wide staircase. The dark wood floors were highly polished and had no rugs or carpets. Nothing about the place bespoke comfort. The words 'cold' and 'sterile' struck my mind. The main floor smelled of a mixture of cabbage and rice pudding.

A smiling nurse assistant, Mrs. Kent, welcomed us. As always, Mother seized the conversation, spilling her tale of woe regarding her wayward and ungrateful daughter. I stayed in the background, wishing she would get done with it and leave. A nodding, smiling, understanding, Mrs. Kent led Mother to the door. Mum said her goodbyes and assured me that she would visit on Sunday. Dumbly I stared at her. Why would I want to see her on Sunday, or any other day for that matter? I could hear my mother droning on and on, as Mrs. Kent ushered her back down the stone steps to my father waiting in the auto.

"Don't worry about your daughter, Mrs. Molloy. She's is in good hands here, and will be just fine. You've made the right decision." She opened the car door with the reassurance," I will settle her in and she will be comfortable. You and your husband have done enough, now go home and get some rest.

" Mother dropped onto the front seat next to Father. Mrs. Kent closed the door and watched as the red of the taillights faded into the distance.

"All right, Dawn," she said her voice was kind and reassuring "Come up the stairs here and I'll show you around." I followed Silent and obedient.

"Over there are the two bathrooms" She pointed them out jovially, I suppose to ease distress. "And here is the room where you expectant mothers sleep." I kept quiet. I'm sure that Mrs. Kent was properly vested in the shock of silence that must have followed her little tour each time she opened the maternity door for the unprepared pregnant girl.

Beyond the heavy wooden door was another expanse of highly polished, bare, dark floors. Not a picture hung on the cream colored walls. Two large radiators stood below windows, covered by heavily lined and worn curtains. The smell of Detol Disinfectant permeated the air. Ten identical iron beds, with ten identical bedside cabinets, lined both sides of the stark unadorned room. This home for unwed mothers would better be described as a hostel for the offending mother-to-be. "Over there, that's your bed," Mrs. Kent said, pointing to my assigned sleeping space. "You better unpack now and get settled. You need to be downstairs in twenty minutes for a meeting with the Matron to discuss house rules and regulations."

Putting my case upon the bed, I unpacked my meager belongings, placing the baby clothing in one drawer and the rest in the others. Walking over to the window, I scanned the skeletal scene of barren trees. A large garden, blanketed with orange and red, leaves, led to an out building that I correctly identified as the laundry facilities. Not another girl was in sight. I later learned they were all busy attending to their assigned jobs. I felt like the last breathing person alive in a world completely surrounded by mourning.

Twenty minutes had passed, it was time to retrace my steps down the stairs and find the Matron's office. To my left was an empty, sparely furnished lounge with two sofas, a few chairs, a couple of desks and a television. A large window afforded me another view of the back property, with its bare trees and dead garden beds. Adjoining the living room was the simply furnished dining room leading into the kitchen. Tattered and unadorned, it was a house from a Dickens's Tale.

The Matron's office, located in the front of the building, also lacked adornment, except for a set of heavily lined curtains covering the bay window that matched those in the dorm room upstairs. The bay window overlooked the driveway and framed Matron's large well-ordered desk. Along the opposite wall stood another desk which appeared to be a messy overflow station for the books and folders that occupied the many shelves around the room. The room smelt of paper and ink.

The matron didn't look up as I entered.

"Sit down there," Mrs. Kent said, pointed to a hard straight backed chair. "Matron, this is Miss Molloy, one of Rita Stubbs young ladies." Introductions complete, she turned and left. Finally looking up, Matron smiled in my direction, but not at me. Her smile never reached her eyes. She seemed detached, unemotional and rather cold, this scared me. Crisp, neat and tidy like her desk, Matron was a stocky woman in her mid-fifties. Her graying hair was neatly pulled into a bun. A stiff white nurse's hat was kept in place with four hair grips. A starched dark blue tunic dress that flared below her knees revealed perfectly polished white shoes.

I sat straight and unmoving in my good Catholic schoolgirl posture. "Miss Molloy," she began "Since you are the newest in our establishment, you will be the first to use the bathroom in the morning. This allows the young women, who came here before you, to sleep in a bit longer." Her voice held the undeniable air of unchallenged authority I had become so used to in my growing up years beneath the tutelage of nuns. "Under no circumstances will you use the telephone, neither for incoming nor outgoing calls. You are not allowed out of the house, nor will you walk about the grounds without permission. The doctor visits us every Thursday and will examine you and your progress. On Saturdays, a delivery van will arrive and you may purchase personal items. You will not be allowed to leave without permission. You are not allowed into the Nursery Area, until after your baby is born. Lights are out at ten in in the evening. No cameras are allowed.

At this point, her eyebrows narrowed. Giving me a hard look, she added, "This is what you deserve for being so foolish for getting yourself into this state." And in assurance of crushing any rebellion that might be welling up in me, she added "All girls are treated the same here, no exceptions. It does not matter who the baby's father is – no one gets special treatment. That will be all."

Her attention was back at the file and my existence was erased. Mrs. Kent returned and ushered me out. Matron failed to mention in her Beechwood House rules that all of us girls had to work "for the pleasure of our confinement." Depending upon health and stage of pregnancy, we were assigned our chores.

The newest girls polished the wooden floors on hands and knees, until they shone brightly. I quickly learned to buff lavender polish into the fine wood and then rag-polish it to gleaming.

Cook assigned us the chores of peeling masses of potatoes shelling peas by the sack load, and taught us how to prepare whole chickens. It took a lot of blister rising work to keep a house full of pregnant girls well nourished. Meals rarely varied, always comprising chicken, potatoes and a vegetable. Some evenings, we were treated to milk-based dessert. No wonder one of my favorite treats was eating fresh sweet peas from the pod, during my kitchen work duties. Meals were generally a somber affair - no larking about like a "normal" group of girls might have done at a dorm. When everyone was done eating, we picked up our dishes, took them to the kitchen and placed them by the sink for the girls on cleanup duty. Then the rest of us set the table in preparation for the next meal.

Mrs. Kent oversaw the "sweat room" - the laundry house. The washing was sorted and placed into huge boiling tubs of water. Nappy boiling dominated most of our cleaning duties. Huge wooden tongs were used to manually remove the wet items from the wash vats. Excess water was pinched out of the fabric through the rollers of a mangle, which was turned by a handle at the side. In dry weather, the laundry was hung out in the garden, on wet days we placed each cleaned item onto one of the pulleys attached to a wooden horse that hung from the ceiling of the laundry room. Dry clothes were taken down and ironed, just like my Aunt had done, when I visited her in Great Yarmouth. It helped lift my spirits to relive those childhood memories, as I pressed each garment.

The relentless grind of work was broken up each afternoon from two to four, when we were allowed to rest. We gathered in the lounge, where we could sit, knit, write letters and talk. Promptly at four, we were put to the task of preparing the evening meal. Dinner cleanup followed. From seven until nine-thirty in the evening, we sat around the lounge watching television or talking. Friday evenings, the house was a buzz of excitement, as none of us wanted to miss *Ready Steady Go.* More often than not, the Stones were appearing. *The Last Time* was going up the charts as quickly as news of their escalating scandals was being reported.

※

There weren't many girls at the house when I first arrived. Those who were there had plans on leaving right away, and the others were having their babies very soon. New mothers stayed in the tiny nursery with their infants as much as possible. The room was so small that only three babies and three girls, could fit. We had to walk sideways between the cribs and changing tables. Time with our newborns would be short lived. We only had our children with us until "suitable homes, with two parents who were stable and old enough to raise a child properly" could be found. We weren't supposed to bond with our little ones, "Once you give your baby up, you can go on with your life and live it as if nothing ever happened," was the propaganda drilled into our adolescent heads on a daily basis by the doctor, Mrs. Kent and Matron. That our condition was a shame to ourselves and our families and that we had to return to 'normal' as soon as possible was a constant mantra poured into us, as often as milk was poured over cereal. Our babies would never be ours. We did not deserve them, nor would we able take care of them. I don't remember one girl who, after having held, cared for and kissed the chubby cheeks of her child, ever totally believed the lies we were constantly fed. In our non-believing, we clung to our little ones, until the day they were physically removed from our loving maternal arms.

We each had our own story to share. All were similar: boyfriend's rejecting the girls they had proclaimed to love, over-the- top parental reactions to the news, and a society rigid in its response as to how best to solve our situations. Sadly, not one person believed my story. No one was willing to believe that Brian Jones, of the Rolling Stones, the group we loved to watch on *Ready*

Steady Go, was my child's father. I was labeled a liar and basically shunned. I stopped talking, did my work in silence, and kept to myself. Why talk to anyone if my truth of my situation was to be labeled a fabrication?

Yet, to my dismay, no one doubted the story of a young Iranian woman, who had traveled to England on a yearlong student visa, met and fell in love with another student and became pregnant. She was stunningly beautiful, told us she was part of a royal family and had been promised through an arranged marriage to a man she'd never seen or met. She wasn't labeled a phony, when she described the dowry her parents had received in exchange for her hand. The girls drank in the terror she shared with us at her fear of being found out and stoned to death. They cringed at the knowledge that her parents would be banished from their home. Not one person scoffed when she shared how she was unable to admit that she was no longer a virgin, and, even worse had gotten pregnant and come to Beechwood in secret. Her story somehow seemed heroic and romantic, and completely believable.

Two days before her visa was to run out, she had her child and, because an adoptive family could not be found before her departure, the baby was put into foster care, until a suitable situation could be located.

Jean, one of my roommates, had made a friend named Margaret before I arrived. Like us, Margaret had been forced to let her child go and return home to "live a normal life." A letter arrived from Margaret's mother a few weeks after her departure informing Jean that her friend had died. It was several weeks later that I learned she had committed suicide.

In those days, our mothers, our fathers, and friends expected us to "just carry on" as if nothing out of the ordinary had happened. How many young women returned to society to pick up where they had left off, only to find that it was impossible to ignore and bury an experience that would scar them for the rest of their lives? "How many Margaret's are there that we never hear about. I often asked myself.

Life at Beechwood was far removed from anything I could have imagined or had ever experienced. Lights out at ten was the worst for us all. Never a night went by that the sound of someone sobbing could not be heard. I would touch my growing belly and wonder if my baby could sense my unhappiness and the sadness that surrounded me. As my baby moved, pushing its limbs against my innermost being, I found that there was no comfortable position in which to sleep, and no comfortable thoughts to be contemplated. I hoped my baby would be healthy. I wondered if I would be able to see parts of Brian and parts of me in it, and then my mind would wander to The Tour and how loved I had felt in the arms of my baby's father.

By mid-November, The Rolling Stones had released *Little Red Rooster*. This Willie Dixon song showcased Brian's brilliance on the spine tingling slide guitar. It reached number one on the charts and the Stones were well on their way to fame. Listening to the radio, hearing Brian play, I was heartsick and lost.

Christmas I was afforded the privilege of being allowed to go home for the day. My parents literary smuggled me down to their flat. I wasn't yet showing very much, and my stylish empire dress covered the small bulge that I did have. Still. my mother was terrified that I might be seen, and then our family shame would be out in the open. Being out of Beechwood, even if it was for only a day, was a joy and a luxury that my mother's rantings could not take from me.

Mike my bother called us from overseas. He was on a tour in Aden he seemed happy relaxed, and enjoying talking to each of us and wishing us a Merry Christmas. When I had my chance on the phone, he asked "Do you remember Peter Young from the Anniversary Party?" I said that I did, but to myself I was wondering how he thought I could forget all that drunken groping, "Well, he would like to know if he could write to you. His patrol was scouting one of the roads and a bomb blew up their ferret tank. One of the men was seriously injured. Peter is in the hospital. He was blown clear, but has shrapnel in his head and face."

"I'll think about it. Give me his address." I answered. I did start writing Peter and began to look forward to his letters. I shared my feelings about my imprisonment at Beechwood. He shared what army life was like in Aden. When he returned to duty as a radio operator, we continued our correspondence. It was a relief to have one person who knew my situation and who the father of my baby was without judgment.

That New Year's Eve was a far cry from previous years, when I had celebrated at Trafalgar Square. I remembered the year before and how I had partied and been surrounded by friends, without a care in the world. But at Beechwood, as always it was lights out at ten, with no attention being paid regarding the New Year. That night I became one of the unseen faces, who cried in our room.

Early January, a new girl arrived and was given a private room. She had high blood pressure and was put on bed rest. Her baby was due about the same time as mine. I saw her a few times when we were in the queue waiting to see the doctor. Betty was shy and afraid like we all were. I started our first conversation, the one that never ended so long as we were able to be together. She didn't have to work because of her health and the fact that her father was paying five pounds a week for her room and board. Other girls arrived, other girls left, Betty and I were to be there for months - she for three, me for six. We shared our dreams, discussed our ex-boyfriends, and revealed the details of how our parents acted when they had "found out" but most important of all - at least to me, she believed that Brian Jones was the father of my child.

In the hall was a red post box. Letter writing and letter receiving were big events for us, as we all yearned for news from the outside world.

Thursday's brought some relief from our daily chores, as we queued up for the doctor to examine us. We each took our turn in a quiet room, lying down on a bed as the doctor put a horn shaped instrument to our tummies. He told me he was listening for the baby's heartbeat. As my due date grew nearer, he felt my stomach to see if the baby's head had dropped. Never once did he offer a word of encouragement, nor did he explain what was happening to my body or me, or what was going occur during the birthing process. He was, however, full of advice and admonitions about girls like me, who got themselves into trouble and became a burden to family and friends.

Sunday afternoons, for two hours was visitor's day. Mum and Dad would bring me magazines, personal supplies and news from home. It was awkward - Dad sitting upright ready to bolt when the clock struck four chimes, Mum being cheerful about how well things were going and what I would be doing when I returned home.

Sometime in February, Betty and I bolstered each other up enough to approach Matron and ask if we might be able to go to Putney High Street to the shops and buy some personal items. Granted permission, we rode the bus to town. To say the bus ride was uncomfortable was putting it mildly. Other passengers stared at our protruding bellies, checked out the ring fingers of our left hands, and with eyes and facial expressions let us know that in their mind's we were nothing more than disgusting. Stopping at Woolworth's, the first thing each of us did was to purchase cheap gold brass rings, which we immediately placed on the proper finger. I also ended up buying knitting patterns and wool yarn, to make an outfit, or two, for my baby.

Each of the Beechwood girls had different backgrounds and experiences, we did have one thing in common, and we all shared a collective unhappiness and shame that dominated our psyches. Adoption was the only solution for our "problem." We had no rights or recourse. Once a suitable home was found, our babies would be removed from our immature and inept care. Girls like us had no right, or need, to keep a baby, and each child would be placed into a "good, caring and suitable home." Any girl who voiced the desire to keep her offspring was quickly brought to heel and degraded into believing that a lone parent could not bring home a fatherless child. The system and society was not set up to sustain such an event, and so it was that the fruit of our wombs were torn away from us and handed over to strangers, who were somehow more qualified, more loving, and more stable than we were.

British society was ill prepared for the sixty's sexual revolution that was sweeping the nation. Birth control was just available, but not easily acquired. Good girls didn't know about "those kinds of things, and the boys with whom we good girls dallied, were expected to educate us in the ways of the world. Schoolgirl conversations, naughty books like *Lady Chatterley's Lover*, words looked up in the dictionary, were the sum total of our sexual education. Parent's avoided 'that' conversation by warning us that 'good girls waited until they were married."

But, as my mother pointed out, I was not a good girl, had not used protection, and was experiencing the ramifications of my choice. "Thank God there are so many loving families out there looking for babies to adopt." She told me over and over.

March nineteenth Betty went into labor. Up until that day I had no idea what 'labor' would be about. Watching Betty cringe and wince in pain, as her contractions became harder, scared me. What would come next, when she was closer to giving birth? An ambulance arrived. We said our good byes and Betty was taken away. My personal loneliness was overshadowed by my concern for her and the baby. Two days later, Matron announced that Betty had delivered a baby boy the day before and that she and her son, Christopher, were doing well and would rejoin us after her convalescing period.

The evening of Monday, March twenty-second, I began to feel odd and uncomfortable. I knew I had started labor because that is how Betty had begun hers. I didn't say anything just lay awake in bed all night suffering through the cramping pains. In the morning, I told Matron, who immediately set me to cleaning the silver, and all the cutlery and trays in the house, and, when I had finished she made me do it yet again.

By mid-afternoon, my contractions were nearly doubling me over. Matron sent for the ambulance which took me to St Theresa's cottage hospital, run by a few nuns and nurses.

Upon admittance, I overheard someone say that I was "one of those girls." I was led to a stark cold room, with an iron framed bed and a bedside draw unit. I was given a hospital gown, instructed where to put my clothing, and left alone. Not knowing what else to do, I climbed into the hard bed, where at least I was supported when the intense contractions overtook my body. Eventually, a nurse came in, shaved me and ordered me to turnover, so that a soap and warm water enema could be administered. She was mechanical in her actions and didn't talk to me. As soon as her task was complete, she left, and I was alone once more to attend to my pains as best I could. The room contained a jug of water as my only comfort. I remember looking at the cracked handle, as each contraction swallowed me. Once my pain subsided, I listened to nurses, as they whispered and walked down the halls.

All of Tuesday, I was left to labor alone. No one asked my name, and certainly no one cared to offer me a kind word. By the early hours of Wednesday I was in intense agony. Someone was screaming in the room next to me, and. with every scream, I believed I would die if it got that bad for me. At times a nurse poked her head into the door and take a look at me. Not a word was spoken, just a quick peak.

"Is there anything you can do to help me with this pain?" I asked one of the nurses, who just stared at me, not uttering a word, a hard look on her face, her lips tight.

"Girls like you deserve to have the pain. Maybe you won't be so promiscuous in the future." With that she turned, and left me alone, suffering in that cold uninviting room.

To her retreating back I asked myself how I warranted this. Brian had left me alone to suffer the worst pain of my life. I wished he had cared enough for me to be at my side, as wave after wave of birth pangs engulfed my body, but no, I was on my own, enduring what "girls like me deserved," as the nurse had so briskly informed me.

Five in the morning, a gush of warm liquid flooded down my legs and onto the bed linens. Had I wet my pants, or was I bleeding to death? Panicked I called for help.

"Stay put!" a nurse called, "I'll get the nun to examine you." All business, devoid of compassion or care, a nun came in, had me raise my legs, and probed my cervix." You have a way to go." Another nun came in and without saying a word, changed the bed and left as well. An hour and forty-five minutes passed. My pain was constant and unbearable. I wanted to scream, to shake my fist at a God. I was freezing cold, shaking as if I had been dunked into a river, the relentless contracting continued unabated. Then the urge to push came upon me so strong that I gave into it. I screamed for help and was ignored. Overwhelmed with fear, I pulled myself up in an attempt to get out of bed.

"Stay in bed!" a nun barked, as she marched into the room. "Next time you feel the pain, push as hard as you can." The pain came, and I did not push. It hurt so badly and I was so tired, that all I was able to do was turn my head away, squeeze the pillow until my knuckles turned white and cry. At seven a second sister came in. "It's OK now. I'm here to help you." She said, in a kind and calm voice. "I'm Sister Agnes. I've helped lots of girls have their babies, you have nothing to fear now. Stop pushing. whatever you do, don't push anymore. We are going to get through this in another way. Now pant, pant like a dog. Look at me now." she looked me in the eyes, and her calmness eased my mental distress.

Then she made panting sounds, showing me what to do. "The cord is wrapped around your baby's neck. I have to get it unwrapped. It is going to be all right." I began to pant. With a gentleness and ease of one who knows what she was doing, Sister Agnes unwrapped my baby's cord, and with three pushes, my small bluish child slid into the world. He inhaled, began crying, and soon his color turned from blue to pink. He was amazingly beautiful. Sister Agnes wrapped him in a receiving blanket and held him up so that I could have my first look of his gorgeous face.

"What are you going to name him?" she asked.

"His name is Paul Andrew." I replied, in love already. She took him away to bathe and weigh him.

My baby boy weighed seven pounds and four ounces. I had to have stitches, as I had torn quite badly. After the stitching was completed, another unyielding, silent, nurse remade the bed. Soon after, Sister Agnes brought Paul back to me. The first thing I did was gently unfold his blanket, so I could see his little fingers and toes. I gazed at his sweet little face. He opened his eyes, and I kissed the fluffy down on the top of his head. He smelt so sweet, and he was mine.

"I love you little Paul." I said wrapping him tightly in his blanket.Hearing my voice. he looked around and snuggled close. "How could I have made something so perfect, I wondered?" He was a miracle. I wanted time to freeze forever at that moment, because my future, our future together was on a time line, and the sand in the hourglass had already begun its decent to our ultimate loss of one another.

It was March Twenty-fourth 1965 and while little Paul and I were getting to know one another, Brian was on his way to Denmark, oblivious to the miracle of the birth of his fifth and last child. There would be no pretty blue balloons, no cards, no flowers or gifts, and most certainly no proud daddy handing out cigars. Beechwood had notified my parents. Only Mother came to see me in the hospital. I told her how nice Sister Agnes had been to me, and Mother sent her flowers for her kindness.

No one warned me that the process would be painful, Sister Agnes wrapped my breasts with an ace bandage to keep my milk from coming in. Despite the bindings, my body would know there was a baby to be fed would produce copious amounts of nutrition for Paul. Breastfeeding was forbidden.

Yet, I leaked constantly, my breasts were hard and painful, so a few times I put Paul to my breast, which felt good for the relief it produced, More importantly, the euphoric feeling of nourishing my child, and being so connected to him that breastfeeding provided cemented the love that grew in me by the minute.

Dawn with Paul in the garden at Beechwood March 1995

In the sixties, it was routine that women stay in Hospital for ten days after childbirth. Paul was with me the entire time, and I hardly left my room. What could be outside our little paradise that would be more important than the two of us being together?

Upon my return to Beechwood. I found my belongings had been transferred downstairs to the 'Mother's Dorm.' Before childbirth, I had not understood why the expectant mothers didn't live with the rest of the girls. After Paul's birth, it made sense. If I'd heard from one of the new mothers about what was going to happen to me at the hospital. I think I would have been scared to death.

It was great to see Betty. I hadn't seen her during my hospital stay, because I was too scared of the uncaring nuns and nurses to ask after her. Christopher was not well. He had respiratory problems, and a doctor came in daily to check on his progress. Betty was a good mother and did everything the doctor instructed her to do, with a lot of added love.

*Dawn with Paul Betty with Christopher
in the nursery at Beechwood.*

My daily chores were lighter and revolved around Paul's feedings, changing and bathing. We took care of the nursery, and every free moment we spent with our infants. Lights out was still ten, but nightly feedings allowed us the freedom to be up and about so as to care for infants. Allowing babies in bed with us was forbidden. But every night at three in the morning, after changing and feeding, I stole my baby out of the nursery and tucked him safe and warm next to me in my bed.

The routine of my mother and father visiting on Sundays resumed. My Uncle Andy made a special trip to see Paul, and Helen drove out to see us, as well. Mother stuck to her opinion that her grandson was to be adopted out as soon as possible, so that I could return to a 'normal' life. No one except Helen showed any concern or sadness over my situation or Paul's. What was done was done.

After my delivery, The Adoption Society wrote to prospective families that my son had been born, was healthy, and ready for his new parents to claim him. It was hard to understand why, week after week, my child had not found a home, when others were readily accepted. I had requested that Paul not to be placed in a Catholic home and I hoped he would find a family who was musical.

Wednesdays were dreaded. That was the day when the black car drove up the drive way and Matron came to the nursery and took babies to London, to see if their new parents wanted them. We girls were not allowed to leave Beechwood until 'the call' came in, indicating that the new parents were going to keep our baby. Then it was expected we would phone our parents, who would then drive out to pick us up, and we would resume our normal lives. If a baby were brought back by Matron, the mother would resume her child's care, until a suitable family was found. We all knew our day would come, but all hoped that by some miracle it wouldn't. We all left the nursery on Wednesdays so that the mother, whose baby was to be taken that week, could have time to dress her infant and say goodbye.

Normally, new mothers only had their babies for one or two weeks at Beechwood after the ten day convalescing in at the hospital. Betty and I were two mothers, who kept our babies much longer- Betty, because Christopher hadn't been not been well and had to be healthy before leaving, and me because Paul had been rejected.

I didn't understand at the time why he'd been unwanted, but I do now. The Adoption Society learned from several parents that no one wanted a 'rebel's child.' In order to find adoptive parents, The Adoption Society changed Paul's birth information to read that the father was unknown, white, and healthy.

Every moment spent with Paul was special. I sat with him in the garden, stroked his head, talked to him and sang him the *Golden Slumbers Lullaby*. . . Now, nearly five decades later, remembering the words to that song breaks my heart. I loved singing to my golden haired child.

Every day, I smelled his sweet breath and looked into his clear blue eyes. "Look for me, little Paul, look for me when you grow up. I will never stop loving you." He was such an adorable baby- bright, alert and never cried. He smiled a lot and was smart and lively. I will always treasure the time I had with him. Our bond was deep, and, on the day I knew it was time for him to leave me, I thought I would rather die than live without my little boy.

Finally, a prospective home has been found. Later, I was told that the couple lived near the ocean, that the mother was a piano teacher, and that they had a daughter, who had been adopted two years before. For the first year of his life, if I wanted, I could write to The Adoption Society, who would let me know how he was doing. After one year, all files would be destroyed - forever.

Betty and I were told our babies would leave together in the same car. I packed Paul's clothes, leaving out an adorable blue outfit I had knitted for him expressly for that morning. That night I snuck him into my bed, so as to have every available moment of cuddling and kissing. In the morning, I bathed, fed, and dressed him in the little knitted suit.

NOT FADE AWAY

Dawn the day Paul left in his blue knitted suit April 1965.

"What do you think you are doing?" Matron asked, in a huff, "Take that awful suit off! His parents don't want that!" Sobbing, I changed him into a white fleece night shirt, white matinee coat, tiny bootees, and wrapped him up in a blanket. Paul began to cry, too. He looked dismayed and seemed to sense that something was terribly wrong. Hearing the familiar sound of gravel crunching under car tires, I looked out the nursery window and saw the black car making its way up the drive. My heart plummeted. I held him tightly in my arms and when Matron came in to take him away from me, I would not, could not let him go.

"If you love him, you will let him go - NOW! You don't want to see him in a foster home do you?" Her eyes were hard, her stance stern. Of course I didn't want to see him in a foster home - I wanted him with me. But I was defeated. I kissed my sweet Paul on the forehead, told him 'good bye' one last time, and then planted a last kiss on his soft chubby cheek. She took him crying from my arms, turned and strode away.

Betty and I held each other, crying inconsolably, helplessly watching as our precious babies were taken out to the car, placed in a single carrycot next to Matron in the back seat, and driven away. An hour and a half later, the phone rang and we were told we were allowed to leave.

"You will carry on with your life as if nothing has ever happened." These words, the mantra pounded into my brain during my entire pregnancy, echoed in my mind. Lies! Lies! Lies! I heard my inner being scream. How could I ever carry on again? I didn't call my mother to come pick me up. I just couldn't face going back to my parent's house to be told I did the right thing, when I knew in my heart and soul that it was wrong. How would I ever 'get over' it?

I packed the rest of my clothes and donated unwanted maternity dresses in the cardboard box in the cupboard for other new girls to wear if they chose. I headed for the door. Betty was in the hallway, waiting for her father.

"So, now what?" I asked her, numb, dead inside. She looked at me with unseeing eyes.

"What? What now? My dad is coming. My mum is taking me to the zoo."

"The zoo, whatever for?" It made no sense to me nothing made sense to me. She shrugged her shoulders and pushed her glasses more closely against her nose.

"I don't know, she said it would take my mind off things."

"I'm going to Great Yarmouth. I'm staying with my aunt for a while. Why don't you come with me?" At this point, Betty's father pulled into the drive. She stood there for a few minutes, tears falling as she bit her lip.

"Right. I'll do it." She said, and walked out to the car's side window. I really couldn't hear what she said, but I could tell her father wasn't happy, as he kept looking over toward me. Finally, he rolled the window up, waved to Betty, and drove away.

"You're going then?" I said, stating the obvious. She nodded her head 'yes' and we both picked up our suitcases and headed down the road to the bus stop, where we would take the Grey Green Coach to Great Yarmouth.

CHAPTER SEVENTEEN

It's Not Easy

The ride to Great Yarmouth was a haze. Time ceased to exist I was trapped in a vortex of grief, every cell of my body quaking in anguish. My limbs were numb and my heart was pierced to the core. The tide of my life had been pulled back, leaving a chasm where hours before my chubby cheeked baby boy had filled my essence to overflowing. Tear stained cheeks, sodden hankies, shoulders still quaking from unchecked sobs. I sagged into mental and physical exhaustion. My life was tattered and shredded into a thousand and one irretrievable pieces. The person who had been me was now a hollow shell, tossed into the gutter of life, labeled unfit to raise the little person who had spent nine months growing in my womb listening to my heart. Paul, the possessor of the nucleus of what had been me, had been wrenched from my clinging arms and placed into the embrace of complete strangers, and I was powerless to change the wrong to right.

My only consolation, if it could be called such, was that my fellow grief traveler, Betty, sat next to me, exploring the inner reaches of her own grieving soul. We cried for our lost boys, our vanished childhoods and stolen innocence. That we had been forced to succumb to the brainwashing imposed upon us by parents, church and society - that we unwed mothers were unsavory to the point that the little ones we loved the most would never have a fair chance in the world if left with the likes of us - was sobering. We were the moldy leftovers on the plate of life and, as such, once our purpose as baby makers had been completed, into the rubbish we had been tossed, to be forgotten and discarded.

It had been a small triumph for Betty and me to declare our independence. We'd escaped the oppressive institution that posed as a charming Victorian Home for unwed mothers. We'd rejected the onerous aspect that loomed before us in the form of our parental houses. We'd thrust away the shackles that had told us what to do and when to do it, and were running to a safe place, where the nurture and understanding we both needed would be waiting for us with uncondemning and open arms. Admittedly, our journey would be short lived. I knew that my aunt would not be able to accommodate us for more than a few days, but any distance of days, hours or minutes away from Beechwood and the inevitable return to family was a welcome respite.

I was in no hurry to place myself under my mother's tyrannical thumb. In my mind she was the prime instigator of my banishment and the loss of my baby. Unfair or not, a little voice inside of me whispered that if she had cared enough about either myself - *her* child, or my baby - *her* grandchild, the anguish I was enduring would never have occurred.

Betty and I needed time to grieve for our lost babies, and we were sorely in need of a sympathetic figure that would not only to listen to us but hear, feel and share in our pain. My dear Aunt Eva fit that role. She was the only person I could depend upon to provide understanding, unconditional love, and support.

In an effort to staunch our sobbing and grief, if only for a little while, and as we journeyed towards East Anglia, I regaled Betty with childhood stories of my Great Aunt Eva and about Great Yarmouth and what a fascinating place it was. I wanted her to share a small piece of the joy and love I had experienced in my growing up years.

I doubt Betty heard much of what I said, she was as traumatized me. But imagining Auntie's homey lodging house, her welcoming consoling arms and understanding welcoming ear, was almost enough to buoy us through the storm of a lonely bus ride. It was towards the end of our journey that bits and pieces of the propaganda that had been spoon- fed to us while we were at 'that place' began to seep into my mind.

"You will be able to move on with your life just as if nothing ever happened. It is in the best interest of you both that you give the baby up. No man will ever want a girl who is damaged goods."

A part of me had believed these phrases. I had no background knowledge that would tell me otherwise. However, the thought that the five weeks I had poured myself into the experience of motherhood and had cherished every moment my baby was in my arms would miraculously be erased, once Paul was placed into his 'real' home, seemed impossible. I 'd put to memory the smell of his milk sweet breath, the gurgling sounds he made when asleep, and the feel of his velvet soft cheek. How could it all evaporate as Matron, my Mother and The Church kept telling me? As the coach clocked up each mile, the magnitude of grief that surrounded the loss of my son became the truth I was immersed in, and this reality created the clarity that their words were lies.

Betty and I disembarked from the coach and dived straight into the first available taxi in the long rank. As we made the short trip to Aunt Eva's place on Princes Road, I stared at the little brown suitcase that had been bought especially for my stay in Beechwood. I thought about the little blue baby suit I had knitted. My heart had been pierced when Matron had informed me that my baby's new guardians would not want it. I'm glad now that I was left with the little outfit that has been a treasured possession of mine. What had originally felt like a blow to my soul had turned out to be a gift.

Exiting the taxi, we approached Aunt Eva's home with anticipation. After what seemed an age she answered her doorbell. And the big door slowly widened, Betty and I rushed into her outstretched arms. Her age had not diminished her ability to offer love and welcome runaways into her home and her heart. We held tightly onto Auntie for the longest time, our bodies shaking as our tears flowed again. My great aunt stroked our backs and heads, just as she'd done so many times in the past when I needed consolation. I breathed in the familiar, yet indescribable, smell of warmth. At least with Auntie I knew, if she could do nothing else, she would show sympathy with regard to the ordeal we'd been subjected to and the traumatized state of our young minds.

Trauma can do strange things to a young girl's mind. I remember the trip to Great Yarmouth and my visit with Auntie Eva, but the memory of Betty accompanying me was completely erased until 2011, when Betty's daughter sought me out after reading a newspaper article about me. Forty-five years after the fact, this young woman contacted me via the internet, and, after much correspondence and fact verification on our parts, reunited me with Betty.

It was through Betty that lost memories were dug up from the grave of my unconscious mind. That traveling with a close friend and confidant after the loss of my baby could be wiped away so completely is quite alarming. Betty was, after all, a girl with whom I'd shared a room at Aunt Eva's boarding house. Betty even had photos of us at Beechwood and in Great Yarmouth that she had kept from all those years ago. It was seeing those photographs that broke the fog in my mind and brought the memories flooding back. The tears flowed just as they had done in 1965.

When memories returned, I remembered the two of us walking along the Great Yarmouth beaches, ducking our heads against the brisk winds blowing in from the sea. We watched the shopkeepers spruce up their storefronts, in preparation for the soon to arrive summer visitors. Passing St. Mary's Catholic Church where I'd gone to school, I purposely had us cross the road each time we came upon it, and on every occasion I was glad that my baby Paul had not gone to a Catholic family.

In our ramblings, Betty and I would eventually end up in Leo's coffee bar, where we talked endlessly about our babies, trying to convince one another that we had done the right thing. But, despite the rhetoric, in our hearts we knew that for us, and for our babies, adoption had not been the best answer. Realizing that, we broke down in tears once more.

We spent the cool, chilly evenings with Aunt Eva, huddled in front of her cheerful fireplace. We watched her knit, listening to the rhythm of the needles clicking, clicking, and clicking. We spoke of the previous week, our losses and our families, and wondered if we would ever be 'normal' again. Auntie was caring and compassionate, and kept apologizing for not being in good health so that she might have been of more help.

Finally, we our goodbyes to my aunt and left Yarmouth to go back to London to try and resume our lives. I was so glad Betty had come with me during that desperate week. Betty's dad picked her up from the bus stop and we parted going our separate ways

Home hadn't changed. Mum and Dad were happy and all smiles with my condition out of the way. Now things could return to normal, normal in their minds anyway. I went back to work for Simon, who had kindly kept my job open and was glad to see me. It was good to get to work, but a huge portion of me was lost, gone away with my baby boy, Paul, whom I worried about constantly.

Bronny and Bunty visited and offered to take me out. They were happy and energetic, ready to shop, go to cafes and concerts. It was such a disconnection from the life I had just returned from, and being social and picking up where I had left off was the last thing on my mind, or in my heart. Betty told me years later that she and I spent a lot of time on the phone in mutual commiseration over our shared miseries. To think now that I forgot about our conversations and our time together really blows my mind.

I felt as if I were in a glass bottle, watching what was going on around me but unable to reach out and partake of any of it. I found myself helplessly looking at every baby, wondering if Paul was being loved, was he feeding all right, was he missing me as much as I missed him? I was numb, only wanting to be left alone. I sat writing letters to the Adoption Society, who responded to my mail with encouragement that things would be just fine and to get on with my life.

Home was a foreign place to me now. Mum and Dad wanted to carry on as if nothing had happened. I was still the little girl who went to work every day and brought her paycheck home once a week. I had nothing to say to them, and they had nothing new to say to me.

"You'll get over it."

"Move on with your life, pretty soon it will be as if nothing ever happened." What did they know about how I felt? Mother would never have snuggled against my baby cheeks or kissed my infant head, much less choke and nearly die from grief at the loss of me. Father had fallen into a world of his own, a world I would never again be able to reach.

Chapter Eighteen

You Can Make It If You Try

The only spark of joy in my life was the letters I still received from Peter. He was tired of Aden, living under a tent in the blazing sun, and talked about coming home. My letters were full of the sadness of losing my baby and the difficulty of just getting through another day. Peter was kind and understanding and provided me the consolation I so sorely needed. He answered every letter I wrote. No matter that they were all filled with sorrow and woe, he was faithful in his kindness towards my situation. In June, he wrote that his regiment was due to come home in August, and asked if I might meet him at the airport. I thought that I might as well, since my parents were going anyway to meet my brother Mike. But as the date got closer, I began to panic. I looked back at the photos from the anniversary party to remind myself what he looked like. I had poured my heart and soul out to him, and yet I doubted I could pick him out in a crowd. I began to feel awkward and wondered if he would remember me as I was when he first met me, or as the fallen rose I was upon his return?

Dawn the first day home May 1965

    In the end, did not matter, I decided to tag along with the family. My future sister-in-law, Linda, was joining us, so I had someone to talk to on the way. She and my brother were getting married in three weeks, and the subject of flowers, wedding cakes and dresses were completely occupying her thoughts. My mind was off in the clouds, achingly missing my child wondering about Peter.

"Will you be one of my bridesmaid's?" Linda asked. I was taken aback, a bridesmaid? "You will be wearing an empire dress, floor length, Lime green silk and will carry bright orange chrysanthemums. It will be so lovely."

"Of course, I'll be a bridesmaid." is all I could muster, my mind stuck on the vision of carrying a bouquet of bright orange chrysanthemums, not even close to my favorite flowers.

"Good, Mike has asked Peter to be a groomsman. It will be perfect." I hoped it would be, but I wasn't thinking of the wedding, I was thinking about meeting Peter.

It was nerve wracking waiting for the plane to land, looking for my brother and Peter. We spotted Michael first. He was dressed in civilian clothes. I wondered where Peter was. Then I spotted a good-looking young man, whose face was tan and hair bleached blond from the sun. "Oh, how handsome he is" I thought. He was standing next to my brother and smiling at me. That smile made me giddy, and I had to look away, think of something else. I vigorously hugged my brother. Peter held out his hand, reached for mine and grasped it tightly in his. I could feel my face flush, and started to giggle as if I were a schoolgirl.

We all walked to the car park. He was the perfect gentleman, opening the back seat door for me and helping me slide over next to my brother on the other side. Linda hopped onto Mike's lap, putting her arms around his neck - all giggles and kisses. We talked idly about the war, the flight back home and the wedding, while in the background the radio was playing *I Can't Get No Satisfaction*.

Peter never let go of my hand. He took my breath away every time he smiled, and I could feel my cheeks flush, and was sure that the tremors in my heart would cause me to faint. What a gorgeous man!

Back at the flat, Mother made tea, and the chatter and excitement of the reunion carried on a while longer. When it was time for Mike to take Linda back home to Maidstone in Kent, he took Peter with him, so as to drop him off at his parent's place in Catford. As I walked Peter back to the car, he suddenly took me in his arms and kissed me long and hard. It was the kiss of a man who knew what he wanted. Oh, I swear I heard bells, and instantly my shyness dropped away as I knew what I wanted, too. I wanted to be Peter's.

"I'll call you as soon as I'm settled at my parents' house." And within two hours he was on the phone asking to see me the next day. Despite all of the letters we'd written over the past year sharing our hearts and feelings, I was excited that maybe I had found 'the one,' yet terrified that maybe I was going down the same road I had been on before, and would end up being hurt again.

The next day, he came over in his parents' brand new Austin 1100. He told me that they were not happy with him seeing me. They thought he was taking up with a girl too soon after returning from overseas and being away for so long. We called as often as we could. After that one day, I did not see him again for the three weeks before my brother's wedding, which was August twenty-seventh. Linda kept me busy with wedding plans anyway, and, of course, I still had to go to work. Upon seeing him again, I knew I was in love. He was no child like Brian - he was a man and was committed to me. I knew he would swim through shark-infested waters to bring me a cup of tea.

After the wedding, we could not get enough of each other. He was based in Hoo Aldershot, a few hours away by train. Whenever he had leave, he spent his time with me. He was sweet and romantic, and when he had to return to his barracks, my thoughts and dreams were always about my gorgeous blond haired military Romeo. His kisses aroused a passion in me that I'd never felt before. I could never get enough of them, of him. He was gentle and considerate of my feelings, putting my needs before his own, and I felt like a precious treasure with him. On weekends away from the Royal Engineers, we saw each other every chance. I couldn't get enough of him, or he of me. I yearned for his arms, his lips, and our long conversations getting to really know one another, and what we wanted for the future.

We took long rides into the country, watched the sunset, shared picnic lunches and sweet hours in one another's arms. Our hearts and bodies fit together, our minds and souls fused into one. No one could, or ever would, be able to love me so completely and perfectly as Peter.

※

The end of August, I had a visit from Linda Lawrence. I was surprised that she knew where I lived. It wasn't like we were friends, after all. However, who knew what Brian had told her about me, if he told her anything at all. Did he say I was just his friend? Her baby, Julian, was with her. He was a year old and a gorgeous little blond haired sweetie, who sat laughing on her lap.

"So, where is your baby?" She asked looking around the flat.

"I don't know," I replied. "I had to give him up for adoption."

"Really?" she responded. I had the feeling she didn't believe me. I couldn't keep my eyes off her happy little boy, and wondered if my Paul would look like him. She kept looking around, and chatted about nothing. While playing with our dog, Cindy, she said, "You know, I have a dog, too, the same breed. His name is Pip." Of course I knew that, but why say anything? I was still trying to figure out why she'd come over in the first place. Had Brian sent her, or Andrew, to see if I had really given Paul up?

"Have you seen Brian?" I asked.

"No, he has other girls now, and besides I'm seeing Donavan He's a wonderful man and fantastic with Julian." She left soon after and the whole encounter made me feel sad and uneasy, The worst part of all was that she got to keep her baby, while I had to give mine up. It felt so unfair. The loss of baby Paul never seemed to stop wrenching at my heart.

The end of September, Peter asked me to marry him. Of course, I said yes. Peter was my entire life. Through Peter the smothering loss of my little Paul was nearly bearable. He had helped me begin to breathe again.

"Would you like to have Paul back?" Peter had asked me. He knew my heart still ached. "I will be happy to adopt him." In no time at all, I had called the Adoption Society and arranged to see Mrs. Plummer, the Society's secretary, who was in charge of placing babies. Arriving at the Agency in Knightsbridge, in the heart of London on our appointed day, Peter and I had been especially particular on how we dressed, desperately wanting to make a good impression. He wore a sports jacket and nice trousers, I wore my Mary Quant dress. We were shown into the clinical white wall office, where Mrs. Plummer sat behind a large formal desk. She was tall and very neat. Nothing in her appearance was out of place. Her brown herringbone suit was very formal, and the skirt covered her knees. Her thick tan stockings disappeared into her highly polished brown leather, four inch laced heels. Her long salt and pepper hair was pulled into a tight bun. She gestured for us to sit in the two chairs in front of her desk.

"What is it that you want from me?" Her voice was sharp and to the point. She tilted her head in our direction, looking up a bit, as if she were smelled something distasteful under her nose.

"I've come to get my son back," I said in a voice that was less than authoritative. At that, she laughed at me- laughed as if I had told the most extraordinarily funny joke.

"You've come to get your son back? What are you thinking? He's safe and happy. You gave him up. He's been placed in a good home, a home with two parents who are established, and stable, and can give him everything a child wants and needs. They have maturity, a home of their own, and are certainly more qualified to raise a child than you. Why the two of you aren't even married. No court in the land is going to award a child to the likes of you. "At this, she looked at both Peter and I as if we were a pair of criminals having lurked in off the street. "You gave up your rights to the baby. You were well aware of what you were doing at the time you turned him over to us. There is no going on back on it now. Your child is in the hands of his true parents. You need to move on with your life and be done with this nonsense. You will forget all about the baby as soon as you let it go." With that she stood and thrust her hand in the direction of the door, giving us the clear cue that we were dismissed and should leave. I felt as if I'd been attacked and flattened by a battalion of harpies.

Years later, I found out she had lied to us. The truth was I had not given up my rights at that time, as I had not signed off on the final adoption papers. In hindsight, if I had been able to afford one, I could have hired a solicitor to represent me and perhaps gotten him back.

Why was it that everyone kept telling me to let Paul go and get on with life, and that I would forget all about it? How could I ever forget my baby? What rubbish! Putting his arm around my shoulders, Peter walked me to the car.

"How can they do this?" I wept. "There must be something we can do!" But clearly there was not. Hadn't Mrs. Plummer said that no court in the land would award us the custody of my son? I could feel his little body being wrenched from my arms all over again My mind swore it heard his wails as he was being kidnapped away from me in that black ugly car. My grief burst forth in body wracking sobs. All Peter could do was hold me close, and tell me how much he loved me. I knew he loved me, more than life itself. I needed him at this dark moment.

Peter and I were engaged to be married the following March. We had been prepared to tell his parents about Paul and my past, if we had been able to get Paul back. With that door closed solidly in our faces, we decided not to tell his Mum and Dad. Peter's Mother was a very old fashioned straight-laced Victorian woman, who didn't care very much for me. My taking their baby boy away from them didn't help and my Catholic upbringing pounded the final nail in that casket. If we had baby Paul, it would have been worth the drama of telling them. But without Paul, why cause anymore problems? We decided it was best to keep the past the past.

October rolled around, autumn - drab and gray.

"Dawn," my Dad said, "I received a call from the Rolling Stone's office. We need to go down and sign a few documents in front of Andrew Loog Oldham."

"Why?" I asked.

"I will tell you when we get there," was his answer, and we did not talk on the drive over. I had no idea what in the world this could be about.

When we arrived and parked, I could feel the panic in my heart begin. What if I ran into Brian? What would I say, what should I do? I still had some feelings for him, but I also had a great deal of anger and grief mixed in as well. How could he just dump me like a sack of flour, and move on with life as if I had never existed? My love and hatred of him were mixed together into a stew of confusion. Did he ever think of me, or what had happened to his child? Did any of it affect his life at all, or was I just something to be used and tossed aside like a paper cup?

Arriving at the office, we entered the common area. Bill was sitting in a chair, leaning back against the far wall playing with a pencil. When he saw me, he smiled and waved. I could only muster a faint smile in return. The place seemed unusually quiet. It was as if the walls knew what was about to happen - everyone seemed to know, except me. Charlie walked by, but seeming pretty intent on going somewhere other than where I was, he nodded and moved on.

We were shown into an office and directed to a pair of chairs in front of a large desk. By this time, to me, large desks only meant something bad was going to happen. My hands began to sweat as my nervousness increased. It seemed like we sat there for hours. I examined the grain of the oak in the desk and the large leather chair behind it, which seemed like a king's throne to me. The walls were covered with disks and photos of famous artists: Bob Dylan, Small Faces, and The Who.

Andrew strode in, anger seething from his pores. Mick Jagger followed directly behind. Mick looked like a man who was tired of being put into the position of apologizing for Brian Jones.

"Ello Dawnee," Mick said, in that familiar way he had. Andrew stared through me, giving dirty looks. He was right snot. He spoke a bit with my dad with his 'I am God' air, while sitting on his leather throne. Mick grabbed a chair from the back of the room and sat next to Andrew. Andrew forcefully turned a paper that had been lying on his desk over, and thrust it toward me to read.

"I have received a cheque for 700 hundred pounds from Andrew Loog Oldham LTD, paid to me by the said company on behalf of Brian Jones in full settlement of any claims arising, damages and inconveniences caused, by me, by the birth of my son and I will make no statement about Brian Jones or the child to any member of the press or pubic."

I began to shake. My father put his hand on my knee. Surprised, I looked at my dad, searching his face for any sign of what to do. He was looking back and forth between Andrew and the paper, and I could sense that he wanted to jump up, reach over and deck the man. But he pressed his feelings down. It was not the time to create a scene. It was time to move on with life.

"Sign the bloody thing, Dawn," he growled, breaking the silence. "Take the money. It's what we paid for you at Beechwood anyway. Just get on with your life - what's done is done." I looked at my father, then down at the form. "What?" Is all my mind could register. My father handed me a pen. I looked at Andrew who stared at me, his face showing nothing other than irritation that we hadn't signed the paper and left his office quickly enough. He acted as if this cleanup he was doing for Brian Jones was beneath him - that we were beneath him. Mick looked away, embarrassed. My thoughts and feelings were of no interest to anyone. They just wanted the bloody thing over and done with so everyone could move on as if nothing had ever happened. It was the same old story, just a different day and different location. Shaking, I signed my name. Mick signed his name to the document as a witness, and then stood up and quickly left the office. Andrew handed my father the check and stood, which gave us our clue to stand. We turned our backs on that office, walked out, saying nothing and looking at no one.

"What was that about?" I asked my father. I was in shock and not sure what had just happened. "Why did they give me money?

"I told Brian Epstein what happened to you. He was wondering where you were and could tell I was unhappy about something. He knew that Brian had been hanging around our place, as he'd seen his car parked in Mr. Hopkins parking space in the courtyard last summer. He felt bad for what your Mum and I have been going through and contacted Loog Oldham, told him he needed to 'take care of it as soon as possible.' Also, your Mum wrote to Loog Oldham, and Brian, while you were gone asking for help. So it was agreed that, to keep this unfortunate incident from getting into the press, that you should be paid in exchange for your silence." I was flabbergasted at all the intrigue that had gone on behind my back. "You will put the money into the bank. You will give me 500 pounds in repayment for the expenses your Mother and I paid to Beechwood, and the rest you can do with as you choose."

Peter in the Austin Seven.

    I chose to buy a bright red used Austin Severn. It didn't matter that I couldn't drive - I would learn. I gave it to Peter so he could drive back and forth from the barracks rather than wait for the train.

    Late one night not long after, there was a commotion in the lobby. Someone was crazily ringing the entrance bell. Opening the door, my father came face to face with a wildly drunken Brian.

    "I want to see Dawn and my baby," he slurred stumbling through the door.

"You'll not see her. Get out!" my father ordered. "You'll clear off now, if you know what's good for you!" Angry, out of control, Brian pushed his way past and was making for the stairs. Peter and Mike were on their way up them to see what was going on.

"What do *you* want?" Mike shouted in Brian's drunken stupefied face.

"I want to see Dawn and my baby! Get out my way. I'll see them by God!" The men grabbed Brian and forcedly pulled him away from the stairs, ejected him through the entry door. "I want to see Dawn and my baby!" he yelled. But the three of them bore down again, and Brian stumbled then ran away, they chased him down the entry drive and around the square, until he was out of sight. They returned laughing and joking about the entire scene.

"What's going on? What's so funny?" I asked hearing and seeing them return in such high spirits, unaware of what just happened.

"Oh, we just chased off a vagrant. Don't need any of those hanging around here." My father answered, as they laughed some more. I didn't know the truth until years later. At the time I couldn't have cared less about Brian He was seeing Anita Pallenberg, and Peter was the center of my universe.

CHAPTER NINETEEN

I'm Free

November nineteenth was not only Peter's twenty-first birthday, it was also the day we got engaged and we had a big party at Chelsea Barracks to celebrate. My dad invited some of his army buddies to play background music, while a few of my friends and family members enjoyed a buffet style meal, cake and booze. The wedding was set for the following March, but two weeks after the party I knew there was a problem, I was pregnant again.

Peter was shocked when I told him, and we both worried at what our parents were going to say.

"What were you thinking?" my father railed at me, full of disgust, "How could you have gotten yourself caught again? You silly girl! well at least he's marrying you this time." I hung my head in shame. Would I always be the outcast? Mother wasted no time in calling Peter's parents, who in turn wasted no time in coming over to our flat to let me have it.

His Mother barked, "Are you trying to trap my son into marriage? If he wasn't already twenty-one I'd keep him from making this mistake, but it's out of my hands. My son wants to marry you and there is nothing I can do. But getting married just because you're pregnant will never work. That's no way to start a marriage.

His Dad said nothing, but gave me a wink as he left."

When they had gone, Mother, not surprisingly, went ballistic and wasted no time in taking matters into her own hands. "How stupid can you be?" she yelled. "Didn't you learn your lesson the first time? Now I have to bail you out again! You are getting married! You're lucky he wants to marry someone like you."

Determined that no one should know the truth, she told people that Peter had to go back to Aden in January for a year's tour, and that we didn't want to wait to get married. As I heard my mother passing this new lie around the family, I asked what she would do when people found out that Peter was not going overseas again, and her response was "I'll cross that bridge when I come to it."

She called the St Mary's Catholic Church in Cadogan Square, told the Father her 'little' lie, and asked that he marry us as soon as possible. The Father was very sorry, but the church was booked full. However, out of courtesy to Mother, he would fit our wedding in at nine in the morning of Saturday December eighteenth - two weeks away. The year was 1965

That task completed, she called Peter, "I have the church booked and expect you to be there on time and ready to marry Dawn." Peter didn't have much to say other than "Yes, mam" and "No, mam." It was obvious my mother was on full throttle storm mode and no one was going to contain her. Peter felt bad that I was left to deal with the families on my own. He kept reassuring me to hang in tight. as he would be home soon and ready to marry me. I had no other choice.

For Peter to be married in the Catholic Church, we had to make arrangements with a Father who would teach him about the faith. We were lucky to be paired with a younger, new Father, who proclaimed that he could tell we were deeply in love and that if Peter promised to raise our children in the Catholic Faith he was more than happy to perform our wedding ceremony. Of course, Peter agreed.

In her continuing quest to take care of everything expeditiously, Mother soon found that buying a suitable ivory wedding dress was next to impossible. The ones she did find were too expensive. Eventually, she was forced to purchase a white dress from C&A on Regents Street. It was a long empire satin sheath, with a lace coat attached to it - not quite what I had envisioned when I was a child, and it was certainly not a fancy handmade work of art like my Auntie made when she was designing gowns. But, under the circumstances, it would have to do. Still upset that she couldn't get an ivory dress, Mother went to a fabric shop and bought five inch lace trim with blue flowers embroidered on it and ordered me to sew it around the bottom of the dress, as it would not be fitting for me to wear pure white as a bride, with my history. Unbelievably, I was allowed the choice to buy a pretty tiara that would hold my veil on.

It was arranged that a cousin from each side of the family would act as a bridesmaid. Once again, Mother, in full form, picked the pattern and had a seamstress make their dresses, an awful peacock blue empire style with white fur muffs.

The night before our nuptials, Mum told me to go to confession, so that I would be able to enter my marriage with a clean slate. Fearing the worst if I didn't comply, I did as I was told and confessed my sins, the latest being that I was pregnant again.

The morning of our wedding, it was pouring rain - considered a lucky sign, but I didn't care. I just wanted to get it all over with and start my new life with Peter, and get away from my parents and the past. When my flowers arrived at the flat, I was very upset because, once again, Mother's choice didn't remotely match anything I would have picked. I was presented with a bouquet that contained teeny tiny white chrysanthemums tied together with a white paper ribbon to carry down the aisle. "Mother," I wailed, "I hate chrysanthemums and you know it."

Turning on me, she hissed "You are the most ungrateful person I know. I can't believe you don't appreciate one thing I do for you, especially considering the circumstances. You get yourself into trouble and expect me to help you out again!"

It was about that time that my two bridesmaids, my brother, and mother had to leave for the church. I watched them go with a feeling of sadness, because the day was not going like I had dreamed it was supposed to many years ago. It was with relief that I would be left alone for a few minutes without anyone, except my father.

Dad was pacing, looking out the window, waiting for the Bentley that Mr. Hopton had loaned to us as a wedding gift. We were to ride to church in style and, as tradition dictated, Father and Daughter would arrive last at the church. When he started to cry, I was taken completely by surprise. I'd never seen my father cry before and really did not know what to do. "What is it Dad?" I asked.

"You look so beautiful, Dawn. I am pleased that you and Peter are getting married, and I do hope that the two of you are very happy." As he choked up and stopped speaking, my heart went out to him. It must be hard on fathers on the day their little girls marry. Maybe it was more difficult on my dad considering the circumstances. Hugging and looking out the window we saw our car had arrived, with Mr. Hopton's chauffer at the wheel. We hurried outside, and my dad opened the car door for me to get in.

The car was black and decorated with white silk ribbons, tied from the mascot to both the driver's seat door and the passenger side door. It was splendid, and made our drive more special.

Arriving at the church, I was finally at peace, and soon found myself completely captivated by the beautiful white flowers that were everywhere. They'd been set up for all the weddings that would be following ours, but we had the good luck of being able to use them for our ceremony as well.

Peter's parents had not yet arrived. They were supposed to have been there before Dad and me. We waited as long as we could, but, as there were other weddings after mine, the Father indicated that we had to begin without them. We found out, after the fact, that they (or should I say Peter's mother) had delayed their arrival, so as to make a final statement that they did not approve of our marriage and especially did not appreciate the wedding being held in the Catholic Church. His father apologized, but reminded us that Peter's mother would do as she would do, especially considering our situation.

Dawn & Peter December 1965

    Our wedding breakfast buffet was held at London's King Cross above a restaurant, with a nice three tier wedding cake. Happily, both Bunty and Helen came to the wedding. After our celebration meal, Peter and I returned to the flat, changed clothes, and around lunch time we left for the train station. We were to honeymoon in Great Yarmouth at Auntie's for a few days, Auntie had paid for our travel as a wedding present.

While we enjoyed our time together as happily married newlyweds, mother was busy with her own plans. She quickly sold my wedding dress, knowing I wouldn't be handing it down to any of my daughters. At first I was angry, then after a bit of thought realized the dress didn't represent any joyful thoughts, other than that Peter and I were happily married. I would not have made any daughter of mine wear it, and considered it a back handed blessing that she had sold it and it was gone.

Sadly, it was during this time that my father was given two months notice to find other employment by Mr. Hopton. Dad was told that a scandal like mine, getting pregnant by one of the Rolling Stones, would not sit well with the tenants in Chesham Place if it ever got out. He told my father that he was sorry, because he liked and respected Dad, but that he had to leave. A few weeks after the wedding they packed up and moved.

My parents decided to leave the busy life in London and buy a new house in a peaceful village in Derbyshire. They used the money from Andrew Loog Oldham for a down payment.

Peter was still in the army so we had housing, although we never lived on base. We rented homes that were subsidized by the military. Peter had always said he never wanted us to live on base, because there were too many pitfalls when men went away on tours, leaving lonely wives. He rented us a house on a lovely quiet street in Ditton, near Maidstone Kent

Chapter Twenty

Mother's Little Helper

Betty came to visit, and bought me a beautiful white shawl she had knitted, which has always been very special to me. All of my children and grandchildren have been christened in it. Betty was still living at home and working. Seeing her brought back painful memories that were still fresh. But I was so excited to think that I was carrying a child that no one was ever going to take away, my mind quickly switched into anticipation of the baby I was to have, and not the one I had lost.

At that time in England, if a mother had had a normal delivery with the first baby they were expected to have the second and up to the fourth at home under the care of a doctor/midwife. I was assured that if something were to go wrong, a "flying ambulance," equipped with an operating room, would be standing by. So as to be in ready, the midwife would alert the ambulance when I went in to labor. I found this bit of information soothing, as I was somewhat nervous about not going to the hospital.

It seemed that every month the Stones were releasing a new song now I was hearing *Paint It Black* on all of the radio stations.

I enjoyed getting to know Mrs. Wardlor, my midwife, on her monthly, then bi-monthly, and finally weekly visits. As my due date drew nearer, she reminded and reassured me that she was always on call and ready to come to our home and deliver the baby.

Sadly, a home birth was not meant to be. By the ten-day overdue mark, everything had been done to induce my labor. I drank cod liver oil and went for long walks, all to no avail. I was sent to Pembury Hospital, in Kent, for induction. Husbands were not allowed in the labor rooms, so I was alone again. At least during this labor period I knew that Peter was just outside my door, and that was calming. June fourteenth 1966, I had a beautiful baby girl, whom we named Sherry Anne, Just like Paul, I unwrapped her blanket and inspecting this little miracle, touching her tiny fingers and toes and sweet little face.

The hospital room soon filled up with pink balloons, beautiful flowers and hosts of cards from well wishers. The visitors were all happy faces, and wanted to coo and " ahh," over our little girl - . quite a contrast from what happened over a year before. My mother was happy to welcome her new baby granddaughter into the family with kisses and hugs and whispered love. I thought of Paul, and wished that his room had been filled with blue balloons, flowers and joy.

Two days later, baby Young and I were released and allowed to return to home. Peter's mother was waiting to see our family's new addition, and Mrs. Wardlor arrived every morning to help me bathe and feed her. I could not put her down, and as the first child of a generation, she was showered with gorgeous gifts and love from both sides of the family.

As always, it seemed that the Stones followed me, this time with their release of their hit *Mother's Little Helper.*

When Sherry turned six weeks, I remember holding her tight as sad memories of Paul being wrenched away coursed over me. It was hard not to think of him. I wondered if he had started to walk yet. Had he said his first words? How was his little life proceeding? Was it possible he missed me like I missed him?

Out of the military, on his own with a little family to support, Peter was finding it difficult to obtain employment. To take care of us while he found a suitable desk job, he took on night shift work at the paper mill, unloading barges. This was hard work, and after a year he injured his back. To help out, I took Sherry, safely wrapped in her pram and spend my days picking strawberries. We couldn't make ends meet, so we packed up and moved to Derbyshire near my parents, where Peter was able to obtain a job working for Rolls Royce. Finally the kind of job he had been looking for! They hired him as a draughtsman, which is the trade he had earned his HNC degree in.

By August of 1967, I was pregnant again. I was thrilled because I wanted a big family, and we were well on our way. The news at that time was full of stories describing how Brian had been arrested on drug charges and sentenced to Wormwood Scrubs Prison. He managed to escape this punishment by paying a huge fine. Newspaper photos showed pictures of a man with dead eyes peering out of a sunken face. It was a caricature of the man I had once known and loved. I was sad for him, because, despite his fame and fortune, he had turned into a hollow shell of the man he once was, and could have been.

Barely four months later, November fifth, Guy Fawkes Night, I miscarried. I have never enjoyed the Guy Fawkes celebrations with all the noisy fireworks. Walking I was walking home after a trip to town, a group of boys threw lighted pinwheels in my direction. I thought I was under some kind of attack and panicked. Within hours the pains of birth, and ultimately another loss, began. I was hospitalized and *my* Mother's Little Helper, Sherry Anne, who'd looked forward to a new baby sister or brother, was as heartbroken as I was.

I don't know what I would have done, if I didn't have my little Sherry. She was such a little pickle, and I told everyone that she was going to grow up and be a scientist. She had such an imagination for mixing things together to see what she might create. That summer piles of dirt, blended with sand, became whatever her little mind imagined it to be at the moment. In the winter, snow was combined with things she found laying around the house or back garden area. Inside, at the table, her food would be jumbled and stirred with sugar and tea, and then managed to be splashed everywhere. She was a handful and kept my mind occupied

At work, Peter made friends with colleague, Allen, and his wife Dianne. Dianne quickly became my best friend, it is a friendship I still hold dear to this day.

September 1968, I was pregnant again. I refused to tell anyone about what I knew was good news. What if I lost another baby? I didn't think I could handle people looking at me from across the street with pity in their eyes. By my fourth month, I was assigned a midwife, whose name was Ann Daly, who was also about the same age as I was. We soon became fast friends.

On the tenth of March, 1969, Derbyshire was getting more than its fair share of snow. Ann had been out to visit a few days before, and everything was going well and nothing out of the usual was expected. I had experienced a backache all day, but, with a lively toddler to carry around and housework to attend to, I thought nothing of it. Sherry's night routine was the usual bedtime stories, cuddles, kisses and 'I love you's. Going downstairs after tucking her in, the pains suddenly became harder, more insistent and familiar. I was in labor.

"Peter, it's time. Call Ann, you better hurry." Peter jumped up from his chair, called and looked out the front window. There was three feet of snow outside. Peter went out and shoveled a path up to the front door, while I tried to slowly make my way up the stairs to ready the bed. The length and strength of the cramping let me know that I didn't have long before our new arrival would be making an appearance. Out of my mind in pain, I tried to take my dress off halfway up the stairs. Things were going fast, and I knew Ann's arrival and my ability to ready the bed or get up the stairs for that matter might not be in time.

Seeing me shaking and struggling on the stairs, Peter ran to me and helped me to our room. Once in the room, it appeared he was trying to back away from me, from the situation. Was he thinking he shouldn't be in there when I had our child? Was he as overwhelmed as I was and trying to escape the inevitable? I couldn't have that. I needed him at that moment, more than I had ever needed him in my life.

"Open the box in my bottom dresser drawer. You'll find the plastic sheeting we need to cover the bed." I told him, grimacing. With the sheet quickly on the bed, I collapsed and let nature take over. At that point, Peter had no more choices. He was about to get his credential in being a midwife.

While we wrapped our slippery newborn in a towel, not knowing what to do about the cord that still attached us together, a gust of fresh air entered the room, "Oh, I'm too late." Ann stated. We were so relieved to see her. "So what did you have?" which was a perfectly logical question under normal circumstances. We looked at one another perplexed. What did we have?

"Well, we haven't looked." Peter answered and opened the towel, "We have a girl."

"Tara Jane." I announced, "Perfect in every way." Ann and Peter could not agree more. Sherry blissfully slept through the night.

I was still in bed when Sherry entered the room, bright and early, the next morning. Looking at the sleeping baby in the crib that she had helped me set up, she spun around in joy, clapping and ooohhhhing the presence of her new baby sister. I gave her a new baby doll to take care of, so we would be mummies together. She was such a good little mother, too.

Sharing the news with neigbours of our good fortune at having another healthy child, and while out walking Tara in her pram, people, stopped to have a look inside invariably they would say, "What a shame you did not get a boy." At the mention of a male child, my heart always clutched. Little did they know that I did have a boy, almost four years old - always in my mind but never spoken of.

CHAPTER TWENTY-ONE

Paint It Black

The papers were constantly filled with stories of the 'The Rolling Stones' and their antics. 1969, Mick Jagger and Keith Richards, went to Brian's house to let him know that the band was firing him. Reporters stated that band members said "that his decadence was more than they could bear." Brian stated that "I no longer see eye-to-eye with the others over the discs we are cutting." Whatever the truth was, it was headline news and no one in England could escape it.

Brian had removed himself to recoup at Cotchford Farm, his beloved country home located in Hartfield. Once owned by author A. A. Milne, and his son, Christopher Robin. Brian must have relished the idea of running away to the Hundred Acre Wood that Milne wrote about in his popular book *Winnie the Pooh*. The garden around the home displayed statues of the adored characters, and I wasn't surprised when I'd learned that Brian had bought the estate. Milne's home must have taken him back to the childhood years when he cherished the animal creatures, whom he had told me were so "innocent" and loved reading about. I had imagined that Cotchford Farm was a new beginning and a place where the new band he was starting up might find roots and become successful.

The pool at Cotchford Farm Hartford 1969

AA Milne once owned the house where Pooh & Friends were written

The news that Brian and the Stones had parted company was only a few months old when on the night of July second I had a vivid dream. I was in an underwater abyss, looking up towards the surface of a swimming pool, where I saw a struggling Brian. He looked down and saw me under water and reached his hand out to mine. His hair was floating out around him and he had a terrified look in his eyes, I tried to take hold of his hand, but could not reach it before he floated away. I awoke with a start, trying to catch my breath as if I was taking in water, "Peter, I whispered hoarsely, I just dreamed that Brian drowned in a swimming pool."

"Oh Dawn," he said more dead to the world than awake, "don't be silly. Go back to sleep." The next morning, the front page headlines were nearly screaming off of the newsprint. Brian Jones had drowned in his pool. "Death by misadventure," the coroner had reported, and the press was in a feeding frenzy, trolling about, trying to beat one another out of a scoop. Peter and I were petrified that news about my affair and subsequent birth of a son would leak out. We had not told Peter's parents or any of our friends. It was one of those secrets we had planned to take to our graves.

Selfishly, but happily for me, Pat Andrews, who had had Julian Mark, and Linda Lawrence, who had had Julian Brian, were singled out, interviewed and reported upon. It saddened me greatly when I learned how much Brian had kept from me. He'd fathered four other children and had not been a part of their lives either. How much more had he kept from me, With his death. I knew I would never be able to sort out all of the pieces of this complicated man.

I watched the funeral on the television alone in my living room. Local school children had been released from class to watch the procession. Flowers overflowed the gravesite, where the solid bronze casket would be lowered into the Cheltenham ground of Brian's hometown. Photographers literally crawled over people to get pictures of mourners, who would have preferred that their grief remain private. I cried as if I were back in Torquay, being turned out of his life all over again. This was something else I had to deal with on my own - just as so many other things that revolved around my time with Brian were experienced alone. Of course, my thoughts were drawn to little Paul, just over four years old not knowing that his father was no longer alive.

I immediately sat down and wrote to the Adoption Society.

July 3rd 1969

Dear Mrs. Plummber

My Name is Dawn Young "nee Molloy, my Son Paul Andrew was born March 24th 1965, sent to adoptive parents in April and had his birth certificate changed November 23rd 1965 at Ilford court.

Would you please inform his parents that his real Father has died, He died as you may have read in the News Papers on July 3rd 1969, his name Brian Jones.

I hope Paul is happy, as you may know for hundreds of mothers like me he is never far from my thoughts; I should like to know if Paul's parents will eventually tell him of his Fathers death.

Yours Faithfully

Dawn Young

They replied:

July 9th 1969

Dear Mrs. Young

Thank you for your letter. We are very sorry to read about the death of Paul's Father in the Press, it was very tragic. I am sure that Paul's parents will inform him about his death at the appropriate time. Paul continues to make excellent progress and is looking forward to going to school.

Mrs. Halpin.

General Secretary

1969 was the year that Peter and a partner decided to start their own air conditioning company. He was still working at Rolls Royce, but the new business required that he travel back and forth between Portsmouth and home. As the company grew, Peter decided to leave Rolls Royce and manage the new company full time.

Still the good little mother, Sherry was a wonderful big sister to Tara Jane. Tara managed to shadow her big sister everywhere, and they played together all the time.

March 1970, I was pregnant again, despite having faithfully taken the birth control pill. To say we were shocked is an understatement. I had Ann, our midwife, out to visit and help me get ready for my confinement. No problems, except, when I went onto labor, Peter had to call the pub where Ann was to tell her to come. She arrived at our house cheerful and ready, she and Peter had a few drinks while they waited for me to present them with another bundle of joy. On October fourth 1970 Ann delivered our third beautiful daughter Samantha Claire. Again I have never got over the joy of inspecting my new baby. She was perfect in every way. As soon as my ten days recovery ended, Peter was off to Portsmouth. During that time Sherry and Tara walked with me as I pushed Samantha in her pram. Neighbours once again, peered at the gorgeous little face inside, and commented on how sad it was that once again I didn't have a boy. Paul would be five and experiencing his first year of school.

The evening that Peter had left, I put Sherry and Tara, to bed at seven. I had Samantha in her carrycot beside me, so I could feed her while watching a bit of television. It was eleven, and everything should have been blissfully perfect, but sensed something was wrong. Out of nowhere I experienced the odd feeling that someone had poured ice-cold water over me.

Chilled to the bone, a flash jolted through my mind to go and check on Sherry – now! Something was very wrong. I wasted no time running up the stairs to her room. When I opened her door, the light from the hall shone on her face. She was as white as marble. My God! Terror convulsed my body and I ran to her, touching her face. "Sherry, wake up!" I shrieked in terror. "No! No! No!" I wailed, shaking her cold little body, trying to wake her up. What could be wrong? What could have happened? "Oh my, God! Sherry! Sherry!" My thoughts raced what could I do?

Leaving my lifeless child, I tore down the stairs, out the door over to the neighbour's house. "Help me! Help me!" I screamed pounding on the door. Tears poured down my face, and it seemed an eternity before they answered. As coherently as I was capable of, I told them what was going on with Sherry, and they followed me running back to the house.

Shaking and listening to her chest, there was nothing they could do. There was nothing any of us could do. I fell into the nursery rocker holding her, rocking her, sobbing. An ambulance was called. Peter was called and made it back in less than two hours. My parents were called as well. "This can't be happening. This can't be happening." I moaned over and over again. Once more, I was living a nightmare that must be endured. "My God, what had I done to deserve this? Why is there so much loss in my life?"

"There is nothing more we can do," a disembodied voice announced and the neighbour had to pry the limp and lifeless tiny body away from me.

"Why God? Why give me this adorable little person and then take her away from me? Why? Was it because I had allowed Paul to be taken away?" Was I so bad that I was to be punished in this manner? "Sherry, Sherry," I kept saying, hoping that by hanging on to her name, in some miraculous manner, she would be able to stay with me forever. She was such a unique little person, not a day went by that she didn't make us laugh or glory in having her as one of our daughters. I completely lost all of the faith that had been left in me.

The doctor and police arrived. It was a blur, and I was helplessly in shock. My Mother pitched a wailing fit, telling anyone who would listen how her first-born grandchild had tragically died and now how could she go on?

Somewhere in the distant background of that ominous night, Tara woke up and added her tears to the ocean of grief we were all feeling. The Officials were courteous and professional. "Had she been sick at all? No accidents? We will have to do an autopsy to determine cause of death. We will find the answers and get back to you." It was all a blank in my mind. They could have been speaking a foreign language. I might have been a blind person, for all that I saw and understood that night. It was a blank, a blur. My friend, Dianne, fed Samantha, as I was unable to do anything more than stare. Over and over, I relived the moment when I opened the hall door and the light shone on the cherubic face of my baby girl. My mind mulled what I might have done better, what I could have done right. What had I fed her the day before? Should I have read her an extra bedtime story before I tucked and kissed her into bed? Did she know how much I loved her? Had I told her that I loved her before I said good night? How would I ever learn to live without her? It was as if my heart had fallen to the other end of the universe and then drifted away. This loss was worse than any I had ever experienced. I was inconsolable and there was nothing that Peter could to ease my grief, nor could I ease his, And so we just sat and held one another.

At five, an unknowing Paul would never have the opportunity to meet his little sister, and Tara and Samantha would never enjoy being mothered by our little sunshine girl.

The onerous task of picking a casket, making burial arrangements, discussing the service and how things should go, fell onto Peter's shoulders. I was in limbo. little Sherry wasn't supposed to be in a white casket with satin lining. A short service at the side of a grave was not the place a young daughter should be. Funeral directors, graveside ministers, and mourners in black - I looked at what was going on around me and saw nothing but soundless moving mouths. I wanted to leave. It was too much to take in.

Tara was confused. She wanted her big sister, her playmate. She could not understand what happened to Sherry. How does one explain death to a two year old? She became clingy, and wouldn't be alone.

The autopsy seeking an answer to my baby's death came back as a case of SIDS. It was noted as unexplainable, and the death of my little Sherry was documented as one of the oldest children to be recorded.

The day of the funeral, our entire cul-de-sac was festooned with flowers. Neighbour's, friends, family, even total strangers came and lay bouquets in front of, and along the entrance to our home. The sight was unbelievable, and extremely touching.

Returning from the cemetery, our small family group retreated inward. For a while, our curtains and our hearts were shut away from the world. The first day we went out, me pushing Samantha in her pram and Tara clutching my hand, I looked down the sidewalk and saw friends who had only a few days before offered their condolences with cards and flowers, crossing the street so as not to encounter our little threesome. I was deeply hurt. I longed for a soft gaze, a kind word, or a gentle touch from friends and neighbour's. I desperately needed to hear and feel that I could go on with life, and that there were people "out there" who would always support me. I suppose they feared that, by acknowledging Sherry's death, I wouldn't be able to stand up and move forward. The truth was that I desperately needed to talk about her and to relive happy moments from her life with other people around me, who had known my little angel as well.

Peter was more often the two hundred miles away in Portsmouth, than he was at home. I could not live in the house where my daughter had died and stay sane. It was decided that we move to Lee on Solent, and begin again. Dianne, dear friend that she was, helped me pack and within three days of tipping all of my drawers into plastic bags, we were off.

I suppose I had expected it to be a new beginning. In looking back, a part of me wonders if I believed that moving out of the house where Sherry had died would somehow push the tragedy back into the most closely locked vaults of my mind. The truth is that, with Sherry's death, parts of both Peter and I died as well. We seldom spoke of her. The pain was too consuming. In looking at each other, we both saw bits and pieces of our little lost child. She was in Peter's eyes and peeking out from my nose - bits and pieces of each of us, formed at conception to create a perfect little girl. We hurt unbearable, and yet we could not ever completely fall into total despair because Tara and Samantha were still in our lives, were still our little sweethearts, still needing their Mum and Dad. We lived on a roller coaster of emotions, there was such a huge hole where Sherry's laughter used to be. It was hard not to feel anger at God, devastation, and somehow that I had failed in some way. We reached out to one another but for some reason pulled back, to each deal with the loss on our own

Sherry's death ravaged my soul and I never slept through another night after that. I constantly woke up went to my babies' rooms to awaken them, to make sure they were well and alive.

Sherry Anne 1966-1970

Peter put all his energy into making his business grow, leaving me to raise the girls. I decided that having another child would fill the gap. I wanted to spit in the face of fate, and have the three children I once had. After a few months Peter agreed to try for another baby. It took a couple of years, but by February of 1972, I was pregnant again.

We needed a larger home, and purchased an eighty- year- old stone cottage in Frampton Cottrel. South Gloucestershire This move took more time and effort than the three days it took after Sherry's death. This time, Peter and I were taking the time to sort through things - discarding what we didn't need, keeping what we did. Then Peter found the brown suitcase with all of the memorabilia that I had kept from my time with Brian.

"What's all this?" he asked, holding up the shirt that Brian wore for the photo that appeared on the sleeve of the Stones' first LP. Looking at pictures of Brian and I in my courtyard at Chesham Place, he asked "Do you still love him?" The look of hurt and regret on his face nearly broke my heart.

"Of course not." I answered, because it was true. I loved Peter. I suppose I had kept Brian's things as a touchstone between myself and the child I bore with him and me. Brian would always be gone from my life, and even if Peter did not realize it at that moment holding an old shirt from days long gone, he was my present, and my future, and forever love.

That weekend, I gave the shirt to Peter's brother, and the harmonica he'd left on my nightstand was given to the girls. I tore up the pictures that had been taken of Brian and me, and tossed them into the rubbish bin. But Paul's pictures, his birth certificate and his tiny blue knitted suit were lovingly put together and stashed inside the brown suitcase. Paul would never be completely out of my life, even if we were never to meet again.

August the third, Nadine Anne was born, our fourth beautiful daughter, in Southmead hospital. I was not allowed a home birth, and she came into to world screaming her objections about her new circumstances. She soon developed a rash that covered her entire body. That earned me a private room in the isolation ward. I will admit I was somewhat disappointed that after so many girls, I had not given Peter a son.

"What's the matter?" the night nurse asked me. She seemed to sense my disappointment and wanted my thoughts out in the open.

"I was hoping that after three girls I might have a boy for my husband. I have to admit I'm a bit sad about, that is all."

"A bit sad?" She answered "Put your housecoat on and follow me." I did as she asked, and followed her down the hospital corridor. She stopped in front of a glass window where babies with all kinds of deformities were in their cots. Some had wide gaps in their spines called spina bifida, others had cleft palates, and one had a huge head on one side with a shunt coming out to remove water from the brain. Two of the babies had Down's syndrome, and one had been born with no limbs because its' mother had been given thalidomide when she was pregnant. She turned to me and very seriously said "You have a beautiful, normal healthy baby girl, be very thankful." I felt sad and ashamed that I had ever felt those sorry feelings.

"Thank you." Was all I could say for a gift that was bigger than she would ever know. When I went home, I held my head high and ignored the remarks from neighbour's and acquaintances, sighing and frowning that I hadn't been able to give Peter a son. "Oh, what a shame," I always smiled and answered that both Peter and I were very lucky to have such beautiful and happy girls.

More often than not, in the closet of my heart I thought about my now seven-year-old son. He would already have been in school for two years. Always, I wondered how he was doing.

Chapter Twenty-Two

You Can't Always Get What You Want

Ever since the day I married Peter and settled into 'domestic bliss', I felt this certain something in Peter - a sense of uneasiness and a nervous restlessness. He was always striving for something better for us, and nothing ever seemed to quite settle him down. He was a caring and affectionate father, a loving kind husband, and as a family man he took to the role and excelled. But there was always more than family and friends inside Peter. There was always a constant soul-searching going on within him. This manifested itself in a merry-go-round of upping sticks and moving to new pastures. We'd been living in the cottage for a little over a year and it was already time to move on.

This was August of 1973 and we had found a house in Charfield still in Glostershire It was a hard move for me, as I was not feeling well, being run down and tired all the time. The thought crossed my mind that if I didn't know better I'd think I was pregnant again. But I'd been taking the pill faithfully because Peter and I didn't plan on having any more children. Imagine my shock when November rolled around and I missed my period. I went to the doctor, who told me I was at least five month's gone, and he was concerned because he didn't think that the baby was normal.

Peter wasn't pleased He was tired of seeing me in maternity dresses, and everyone thought that three children were enough. My father was in the last stages of breast cancer, and he and my mother had bigger problems to think about than my being pregnant again and maybe not having a healthy child.

In my seventh month in January, the doctor ordered an x-ray be taken to see where the baby was situated, He also he couldn't hear the baby's heartbeat. At my February appointment, another x-ray was ordered. This one wasn't of much use, as the placenta was blocking the view. The official medical opinion was that our child had hydrocephalic, or some other birth defect, and not to expect a live birth.

Stricken with grief, we rode home in silence. In an effort to ease or maybe ignore the pain, we made no plans and did not speak about our child. Of course, ignoring the situation did not make it go away, but we did the best we could to go on with life.

By February twenty-third, the baby had stopped moving altogether. I was losing weight, and it was decided that an induction would be the safest way for me to deliver, rather than taking on the risk of surgery. Peter dropped me off at the hospital and took the girls the three hours' drive to his parent's house in London. They were the only people we had told about my pregnancy.

Admitted and laying alone on the gurney, I gave in to my fears and grief and wondered why these kinds of things happened to me? Those thoughts were soon put out of my head, as the contractions brought on by the induction took over. They were harder and stronger than any I had experienced before. In a short while, the nurses were running for the doctor with the news that the baby's head was emerging. He was delivered before anyone could stop me from seeing him. What I saw was a perfect baby boy, but not breathing and blue. The doctor and staff rushed to put electronic nodes on his tiny chest to send a current through him.

I was overwhelmed and confused. What was going on? Was the baby alive? Then I heard a cry, and I saw him begin to turn a healthy pink. They rushed him to NICU. When I delivered the placenta, it

You Can't Always Get What You Want

was purple, almost gray in color. And the doctor remarked that all the nutrients had gone, and that had we waited even a few more hours it would have been too late. His concerns at that point were if the baby had gotten enough air to his brain soon enough and that he'd taken in a lot of mucus while trying to breathe, which could cause pneumonia. But his biggest fear was of brain damage from lack of oxygen. He would let me know within four hours how things were, once the Guthrie Test was completed.

Our baby boy might be lost, and I had no idea what to do or who to tell. The doctor took care of the situation. He called Peter and told him he had a son. He had to tell him more than once because Peter just could not believe it. By the time Peter had returned to the hospital, all of the tests had come back indicating that our baby was normal. However, he would be staying in NICU on a new medical innovation, which looked like a mattress, but monitored Arron's vital signs. An alarm would sound if his breathing stopped, which it did one night. I was wheeled down to see him. He couldn't be missed! He was the biggest baby in the nursery area, weighing in at eight ponds two ounces. Over his incubator, the nurses had placed a sign that read "B-U-S-T-E-R".

I was settled into a ward of four. The only telephone available was a coin-operated phone out in the hall. I took my turn in the queue and called my mother. I knew it must have sounded odd to the other women waiting their turn when I opened my conversation, " Mother I have something to tell you," and continued our conversation with the news about the birth of a grandson.

Mother had trouble taking it all in. After all, we had been out only two months before to celebrate what was to be my father's last Christmas. Rut, as always, I didn't show. How could she have guessed? Of course, the game of twenty questions followed. Why hadn't I told her sooner? The baby wasn't to be viable so you kept it a secret? Oh yes, Dad's condition, I understand. Who else knows? What were you thinking? When I had the chance to talk to my father, whose condition had continued to spiral downward, I could hear true joy and happiness in his voice. A boy at last!

A new baby - joyously welcomed but not expected. We tossed around names and decided to call him Arron. Arron and I wouldn't be allowed to leave the hospital without suitable baby clothing and supplies. Peter and the girls made a trip to Boots Chemist on the day we were to be released from the hospital. Peter purchased blue baby gowns, nappies and a carry cot to take him home in. The girls were thrilled with the arrival of their new baby brother. It had been nine years since I had held a son in my arms. Looking down at Arron's tiny sweet face, I wondered if Paul would have been as happy to have a little brother as his sisters were. I wondered if was he doing well in school, was he healthy, what were his interests? As always, when I thought of my lost son, I experienced the feeling that he was walking across my heart and I had to gasp and catch my breath.

Sadly, my father died shortly after Arron was born. It was an overwhelming to lose him at the very young age of fifty-seven. He had been a heavy smoker and had hung out in smoky environments, but still the thought of breast cancer is in a male is never something anyone believes will happen to them or someone in their family.

My pain was tempered with the knowledge that he'd made his peace with me. He had tearfully told me that he'd let me down as a father, especially in my greatest time of need when he should have been stronger. It meant everything to me to hear him utter those words of comfort. I also felt great elation for the lifting of the burden of guilt he had so deeply felt. My father's death a few weeks later held a great poignancy in my mind's eye. I still treasure those words he shared with me from his troubled soul, along with the trumpet he used to play on so many royal occasions and the buttons off his red coat he had worn so often at Buckingham Palace. These treasured mementos remind me of a man I would love to have known as the good father he had wished he could have been.

With me being busy raising three girls and a baby boy Peter's company continued to do well and the need to move urged us to pack up once again. Seizing a good investment opportunity in Southsea Hampshire, Peter purchased a Hallmark Card store and a Model Village. We purchased a huge Victorian house that had been used as separate flats, and decided to convert the home back to a single family home. Peter called it "the money pit." Peter's parents came and lived in the basement flat of our house and ran the two businesses.

It was a good and satisfying life for the children and me, but, as always, Peter had his sights set elsewhere. A very old tobacconist shop was offered for sale in Petersfield. Peter couldn't resist, and we were off to a new home in a village called Horndean. It seemed that every business Peter set his hand to flourished. But none was able to capture his imagination as a lifetime profession. Once again, true to form, Peter's wandering spirit beckoned once more, only this time he was looking at prospects overseas.

Mother had moved to Australia after my Father's death, so it was agreed that we would take a trip there to see if there were any opportunities for our family. We were off to Sidney for a month to take in the sights and look for the next pot of gold. We soon discovered that it was not for us. A petrol strike was in force and only certain license numbers were allowed to fill up on specified days. This made it difficult to get around and see things with the children. We also learned that the Australians don't like the English, who were subject to endless remarks about being 'Pommy Bastards' and requests for us to 'go home.' Mother, thinking they were joking, laughed and ignored their remarks, and wondered why we had a problem with it. Needless to say, we did what the Australians suggested and left.

Peter left his parents to run the shops, while he took a job in London that sent him to Hong Kong, Singapore, China, and most Asians countries. Having him gone so much was difficult on all of us. We are a family that thrives on being together, and so Peter's coming and going all of the time left the children in a state of uproar. They missed him terribly.

Eventually, Peter sold the model village and the rest of the stores. It was time to move to the United States. It was 1982, and Peter had been sent to Los Angeles on business. He found he could make a good living there, and decided it was time to move us all to the States. We sold our home in three days, and Peter's parents found a flat in the neighborhood where their friends were. We were immigrating.

June 1982 we arrived at Heathrow. Looking out the window as the plane flew over London was a haunting experience. Somewhere down there in on of those houses is my son was all I could think. It felt like I was leaving him all over again. As London became smaller and smaller on the distance, I realized that the chances of Paul ever finding me were diminishing as well. He was seventeen, I wondered if he would have come with us, if given the choice. Now we would be 5,000 miles apart. How would he know to look for me in a land overseas?

Peter had already bought us a house, and the children were excited at the prospect of living near Disneyland, seeing the sun year round, and having drive-thru hamburgers. Arron was ecstatic at the prospect of playing baseball and soon the 'The Los Angeles Angels' baseball team had the biggest fan.

Settling i to American life, Peter and I decided that public school was not what we wanted for our children, since we'd been warned against it. I started my quest to find a good private school, and immediately became overwhelmed. I didn't realize that there were so many religions, and all of them had private schools. I had only known of Church of England, Catholic and Jewish schools.   In America, I was confronted with Mormon, Seventh Day Adventist, Baptist, Lutheran and many others. The only religion I knew was Catholic, and I was not too happy about the prospect of sending my children to a Catholic private school. But I guessed it was 'better the devil I knew' than the one I didn't, so it was nuns and fathers all the way through high school for my children. Of course, my mother was as thrilled over this as I was upset, but I overlooked the religion for the better education.

During summer holidays we traveled the country, learning more about our new home. When we weren't traveling, we hung out in the swimming pool, which was a real novelty for us British.

CHAPTER TWENTY-THREE

Something Happened To Me Yesterday

What more could I wish for in my life? I was in Los Angeles, California, living the dream. We'd been in the wonderful and wondrous United States for a number of years, and it was definitely living up to our expectations. Each day brought something new and exciting. Peter had bought a business in Maui Hawaii, where the family would enjoy holidays Life was good. By now the children were more or less grown and managing their own lives. Still, in our family of four there was always something coming up to rock the status quo. So there I was, on that warm and sunny Sunday September eleventh morning, with the luxury of some time to myself, and the dubious pleasure of my own company and my ever- constant nagging memories. I looked at the pool, it was wonderfully inviting. Maybe I could fix myself a Margarita, find a good book, get out there for a quick dip and then spend a relaxing hour or so stretched out on the lounger, reading about someone else's romantic dreams.

The reality, though, was at that very moment the damn phone was ringing itself off the wall, seemingly more insistent than usual. To say this would be the single most important phone call in my life would be doing it some considerable injustice.

"Hello," I said, perhaps with a little bit of ire in my voice at being inconvenienced. I was guessing one of the girls had run into some kind of trouble or other, and I'd be getting into my car going off somewhere to meet them and sort out a problem.

However, this wasn't a family member calling. The voice on the other end of the line wasn't one I knew, but still I could pinpoint the accent precisely. This caller had the unmistakable slightly abrasive East End of London twang.

"Is there someone called Dawn Young, formerly Molloy, who lives there?"

"This is she." I answered, but I didn't give a moment's thought as to whom this voice belonged, let alone ask the caller who he was. His next few words, or question as it turned out to be, completely and utterly grabbed my attention like a clap of thunder overhead.

"Does the twenty-forth of March 1965 mean anything to you?"

"Of course it does." How could I forget the birthday of my first born son? Before I could come to my senses and ask just whom I was talking to, the caller came back with words that would ring in my ears every day for the rest of my life.

"Well, unless I've made a very big mistake or you are not the person you say you are, then I am your son Paul Andrew Molloy." Paul Andrew, those words knocked me for six.

"Are you OK? Are you still there?" I was dumbstruck. My vocal chords must have constricted with the shock of my son's revelation. I had no doubt in my mind that this was my boy. Who else could it be but Paul? Many times while we still lived in England I'd dreamed that one day I'd hear his voice. But the day we flew away from home, off to the United States, I clearly remembered looking out the window of the Boeing 747 and thinking that there would never be a chance that my child would be able to find me. From that day onward, I never again allowed myself to believe that my dream of seeing him again would become a reality. And yet, there I was on the phone and on the other end of the line was my precious little baby boy.

I pictured myself holding him in my arms, his golden hair and tiny face - an image that had never left me. Wincing from the pain of my memories, I began to tremble, the trauma and heartbreak of handing my child over for adoption flooding through my veins. My heart was pounding hard and fast in my chest, and my hand, I realized, was clamped tightly around the telephone. I relaxed my grip and took a few deep breaths in attempt to recover some composure.

"Sorry, I'm still here," I managed to choke out. My shock had taken total control of my mind, body and vocal cords. All of my senses seemed to be numbing as I fought to understand what was going on. My brain just couldn't seem to cope or know where to start. Luckily the Margarita I'd made was close at hand. The alcohol and the coolness of the crushed ice seemed to help, and I managed, "I can't believe it's really you."

"I assure you, it is. My adoptive parents named me John Peter, but my birth name is Paul Andrew Molloy. A flash of disappointment charged through my mind. His new parents hadn't kept even one of the names I'd given him.

"Do you want to call me Paul?" He asked me very sweetly.

"I'll call you John," I answered, maybe too quickly. "If that is your name, then John it shall be." (Each birthday since John and I have been reunited, a phone text is always sent to Paul Andrew, although I still use his adopted name in general conversation.) "How on earth did you find me?" I was feeling a lot more at ease with this man. I couldn't believe he had been able to track me all the way to the other side of the world.

"I've been looking for you for the past ten years. As soon as I moved out of my parent's home at eighteen I started looking for you." I sucked in a deep breath and sighed silently. My baby boy had spent some of the most important parts of his formative years with unresolved issues troubling him. "Your trail went cold when you moved to the United States. I was ready to give up, but decided on one last try and hired a private investigator. He located your mother in Derbyshire." I felt both honored and ashamed that he'd gone to so much trouble.

His finding my mother must have been fate, as Mum, after sixteen years being out of the UK had only just returned two months before. Since the situation was a delicate one, the investigator invented a story about an old school friend trying to contact me. My aging mother was only too willing to be helpful to reveal my whereabouts to my old 'friend' and provided him with my telephone number. I wondered what she might have done if the true identity of the 'friend' had been provided. Would she have rejected his need to find me as she had rejected my need to keep him so long ago?

"You're a hard woman to find. You must have gypsy blood, as many times as you have moved around." He laughed out loud at that. It was the first time I'd heard my son laugh, it was the first time I'd heard his voice. This was to be a day of many firsts for us. In spite of my emotions being totally at sea, my concentration was completely focused, and I was picking up some good vibes across the phone line.

"Yes, we have. My husband's work keeps us on the move."

"I found out that you got married later in the year after I was born. You've been married a long time. Is Peter Young my father?" he asked nervously. I was taken aback at that.

"Didn't your parents tell you who your natural father was?" I asked, shocked.

"No" came John's reply.

"Well, I'm afraid Peter isn't your father." I answered, completely confused by the conversation. How could he not know who his father was?

"Then who is my father? What is his name?" I felt myself tighten up.

"John, your father died in July of 1969. He drowned in a swimming pool." My mind went back to the airless, dry, hot small hours of July third 1969, when I dreamed of seeing Brian at the bottom of a swimming pool and watched his hair float around his face. I had shot bolt upright in bed and screamed out, "Brian has died!" I remembered how Peter, who, of course, had no good feelings for the man who fathered my baby, patiently listened, and gently and quietly calmed me down, and how the following morning I was double shocked to read reports of Brian's death in the newspapers. Now, twenty-six years later, all alone in my house with no Peter to turn to, I was going to have to hit my baby boy with the news that his father had tragically died.

"You were four years old. I wrote to the adoption society and told them I was assured they would let your parents know." I was shaken. How could I tell my son who his father was?

"Tell me John, are you around five foot six inches tall and do you have thick blond hair?"

"Yes," John answered. I envisioned that he might look just like his father. In my heart, I wished that he could guess who his father was without me having to tell him. I didn't want to go through the heartache of telling him my story. It was a sorry tale, and the sad end of his father's life did not make it any better.

"So what is my father's name?" he asked again, seeming a bit frustrated at my dancing around the subject.

"Well, John, you are not going to believe me when I tell you."

"Okay." His response was confused and guarded at the same time.

"Have you heard of the Rolling Stones?" A little perplexed and probably thinking I was a bit of a nut job, John responded," Well of course I've heard of them, who hasn't? Have they got something to do with my father?" With all of his research in trying to find his mother Dawn Molloy, he'd never run across my name and that of his father Brian Jones connected to it.

"John, the man who founded the Rolling Stones was Brian Jones. I don't know if you know of him, but that's who your father was." The line went quiet, had we lost our connection? It seemed an eternity before he responded. "No way. Get out of here. You're joking, right?"

"John, I'm not joking," I replied earnestly. "Brian Jones is your father."

"You're telling me, I'm the son of the guy who started the Stones?"

"Brian and I went out for about nine months, and then I became pregnant with you. There is absolutely no doubt that Brian is your father. I know it's a lot to take in all at once. Your parents should know all of this." I wondered if his parents had told him anything about me over the years, or if had they'd received any of the letters I'd written.

"Listen John, I don't know how much you know about the Stones and the sixties, but I'm sure you know their image has always been portrayed as that of being wild boys." I felt John should know the Brian I knew and loved and not the Brian that the newspapers reported about.

"I was sixteen the first time I met the Stones. They were just a group of boys trying to get something going. I attended the first few shows they put on, where only a handful of people watched. They were my friends, nothing more - a group of boys I hung out with. Really, they were a sweet bunch of boys in those days, courteous and friendly. The rebellious image you hear about them is really not who they were, not a reflection of what their real characters were. For a couple of years after we first started to hang out, I went my own way, got a job. Over those two years they had begun to achieve some fame and I had a chance meeting with Brian at a party I had gone to with a friend. That was when we started to date.

"He was the easiest guy in the world to talk to, and it felt as if we'd known each other all of our lives. We had some great times together, and I met loads of other pop stars of the sixties. I always knew that Brian was a shining star amongst them, and I can honestly say that, at that time, your Father was the kindest, most gentle man I had ever met. However, I cannot comment about what he was like after 1964.

"I'm telling you this, so that, when you go research him and his life, you think of him the way I remember him and take what you learn with a pinch of salt, when you read about the Rolling Stones persona with all the hype that goes with it." It felt strange extolling Brian's virtues. After all he had left me to deal with the trauma of being an unwed mother, whose child had to be forcibly taken away.

But I needed John to hear the truth about the father he had, before drugs and alcohol took over his life. It felt good to unburden my memories of Brian to our son. I felt the same kind of ease with John that I had felt with his father. I guess John's "No way. Get out of here. You're joking" had been a real icebreaker. I felt a connection to John at that point, and felt his acceptance. In that one phrase, he was using language you would normally only find with close friends and family. I knew I liked this young man as a person, but where would I fit in his life? I had no idea where to begin. It would be a challenge. John closed our conversation about Brian stating that he wasn't looking for his father, he had pinned his hopes on being able to find me, his mother.

We talked a while longer. I was amazed at how much he knew about me. He had copies of all of the birth certificates of his half siblings and, of course, knew about my marriage to Peter. I wondered if he ever wondered what it would have been like to be part of this large family, and what his place in it would have been like.

John had a family of his own, and I learned that I had two more grandchildren, a six-year-old granddaughter, Emily, and a four-year old grandson, Luke. It was unnerving to learn that my baby had grown up and started a family of his own. My memories had no room for him to be grown up, become a man, and a parent on his own. I had missed so many of his birthdays and family occasions. I was so grateful he was back in my life.

John and I talked like two people who had known each other all of our lives. It was comfortable and easy. We pushed the traumatic circumstances of our parting into the backs of our minds. I let the lies that the Church, my mother and the attendants at Beechwood had told me fall to the back of my mind. The moment of our reunion was for drinking in the ecstasy of what we wanted and needed to learn in that moment. It was perfect. We had no cares, and there were no recriminating thoughts or accusations. We had talked for just an hour. That sixty minutes of hearing my son's voice, after the many thousands of hours I'd been denied that pleasure put me into a state of total elation. My baby boy had found me and I'd heard him talk, heard him laugh, and he'd joked with me. So much pain just floated away. knowing that he had grown into a well adjusted young man with a great personality.

"Can I call you tomorrow?" John asked

"I'd love for you to call tomorrow, but I need to give it a couple of days. I have to tell Peter about this I know he'll need to adjust to this news."

"Okay, I understand," he answered, "I don't want to cause any stress or interfere in your life beyond your wishes."

"John, I don't want to lose you again. I couldn't bear it. As soon as I talk to Peter and let him digest this, I'll get back in touch with you. Give me your telephone number and address."

"I'm happy at how you are taking all of this. You better make sure that Peter is sitting in a very deep chair, is comfortable and has a couple of strong drinks in him when you deliver this bombshell," he laughed

"Oh, telling Peter will be easy," I said flippantly, knowing in my gut that it would be just the opposite. To say that Peter would need a soft chair and a couple of drinks would be an understatement. Telling Peter the monumental news that mine, and Brian's son had found me definitely required all of John's flippant recommendations, and maybe a bit more besides.

After we finished our goodbyes. I held the phone to my ear, listening to nothing but silence. It took a lot of willpower to put the phone back in its cradle on the wall.

"Now, where are you Peter?" I voiced to the empty kitchen walls. Within thirty seconds I'd lost my bravado. Would Peter be the supportive rock he'd always been over our twenty-nine years of marriage? In the cold light of day, I realized this news might have some life changing ramifications.

My firstborn had found me! I wanted everything to be right! My euphoria was tempered with fear. It was weird having such elation and such trepidation at the same time. I remembered Nadine's comical impersonation of Mick Jagger earlier in the year. How were our children going to react to the incredible secret Peter and I had buried away for all of our married life?

How were my daughters going to react when they learned that their mother, who had never been short on opinions regarding relationships and sex, had gotten herself pregnant by one of those outrageous Rolling Stones? I could feel the pedestal on which I imagined I sat, crumbling from under me. My thoughts were running wild. I needed Peter to get home and soon, if I didn't unload all of this soon, my head would burst.

I looked at the Margarita mix and considered making myself another drink. But I've always been a useless drinker. Such is my need for order and control I tend to avoid anything that alters the fine balance of the emotional baggage I carry around. How could I let alcohol invade the lifeline my most recent telephone caller had presented to me? I knew what I had to do. I had to face the facts with the past, but this time the past would not hold all the trump cards. At long, last I had something to bring to the table.

Chapter Twenty-Four

That's How Strong My Love Is

As soon as I hung up the phone, I raced up the stairs to my bedroom. I took in the lovely smell of the fresh sheets, which I'd put on the bed that morning, mixed with the floral scent wafting in through the open window. Outside in the trees the sparrows tweeted sweet chirps of contentment. My senses had kicked into overdrive. How glorious! Everything was wonderful! I was so alive. I quickly moved across the bedroom, opened the closet door and reached up to the topmost shelves. It was quite a stretch, but my groping hand soon found the handle I sought. I pulled it over the spare blankets, out through the closet door, and placed my prize on the bed.

Thinking back now, it seems unnatural that I didn't immediately flick the catches open, but I didn't. For its part in this drama of mine, the small brown suitcase sat defiantly on the bed, challenging me to do something. I stood for a moment eyeing the worn leather. I remembered the first time I'd opened the little monster and loaded it with baby clothing, personal items and the heavy weight of sadness. This was the very case that my mother had purchased for me to use during my Beechwood confinement. Memories of Mother sitting on my bed and overseeing its packing, while castigating me as a trollop and the lowest and worst kind of daughter filled my mind.

It hurt remembering how I had then closed it up and carted it off with me and the child growing in my womb to Beechwood - the maternity home for the bad, worthless, promiscuous slut my mother would have me believe I was.

The thought of my heartless mother soon had me sitting right next to the little brown case. My anger filled me with courage. My fingers flipped the catches, which pinged a dull thud against the stays. I flung the top open. Of course, this wasn't the first time I'd secretively unlatched the brown leather case. Always before, I had closed the lid with a thud and felt sorry I'd opened it to begin with. This time felt completely different. Thanks to my firstborn's persistence and the hope he had held in his heart, the memories in the suitcase now brought new meaning.

The case's contents held a treasure trove of my family history that was so precious and private that I'd made it completely off limits and had shared its contents with no one. The emotion this open box tossed out was overpowering with bitter sweetness.

I pushed my hand past the other mementos and tenderly lifted out the tiny little blue suit I'd so carefully knitted nearly thirty years before. Instinctively, I pressed it to my face and breathed its' scent.

I wanted to will myself to cry over the loss of my boy, but the anger that had stalked me, since the day the gray green bus had carried me away from the Beechwood gates, held me in its grip. My true and unadulterated hatred for the system that had put me into that slavish 'legal' baby adoption farm flooded through my pores. I reviled once more, as I had a hundred times over the years, the systems - both church and societal, that had allowed the growth and implementation of such an inhumane establishment of confinement. Talk about preying on the vulnerable! Young fertile girls just like me, who'd gotten themselves pregnant, were the vital cog in their factories. We were used in the production of a continuous supply chain for healthy white babies needed by thousands of barren women. I'm sure they were unaware of our plight probably thought they were doing us, the girls in trouble, a favor by taking our 'unwanted' children into their homes, so that they could have happy families. Maybe in a few instances this was true, but the girls with me at Beechwood held a different point of view.

We were brainwashed on a daily basis to accept that, if we loved our babies, we would give them up in our child's best interest. To those of us who dared strike back with the thought of keeping what was about to be stolen, those authoritarian despots took every opportunity to undermine and belittle us and fill our heads with the lie that our babies' prospects would be ruined if kept by such as we were. Naïve, overwhelmed, emotionally bludgeoned, we stood by helpless as our infants were confiscated and given to parents deemed more worthy and deserving, while we were left to cope with a lifetime of regret, humiliation and grief. I'll never forget their deceit, along with the utter conceit that we should be thankful for their help and guidance in dealing with our 'mistakes'.

I picked up the tiny blue knitted baby outfit, put it to my cheek, smelled it again and again while saying, "You found me baby boy. We will never be separated again, I promise you." His baby scent, albeit faint, still clung to the garment that I had been forced to strip from his tender little body on the last day I'd ever see him. Now, I was grateful that Matron had informed me that his new 'parents' wouldn't be dressing him in the clothes I'd made for him. I looked at the tiny little baby's helmet, mittens and booties, and thanked the lord I'd been left with this. Breathing in his faint scent once more, I looked inside the case again, reassessing the small bundle of riches I had assembled over the years.

On top lay the white knitted shawl given to me by Betty. Tucked underneath was Sherry's beautiful lace christening gown - a joyous and at the same time tragic garment. A storied gown of my family history, a precious possession for the joyful memories of each girl baby in the family wearing it for their blessing. It felt good to be able to pause and face, with a new perspective, the cruelty life had doled out to me. Nothing could bring Sherry back. However, my forever dream that one day Paul would return had always been a sweetness that had helped me deal with the pain.

It was time to end my sentimental journey. As much as I wanted to keep trawling through the contents of the suitcase, it would have to wait. Peter's car had just pulled into the driveway, and my news for him quickly pulled me away from my trip down memory lane. Caressing Sherry's christening dress and quickly replacing Paul's suit, I fastened the case's clips and returned it to its place in the back of the closet. I straightened the bed and felt strangely confident, as I ran down the stairs, preparing to drop my bombshell on my husband of thirty years.

Pausing at the kitchen door, I listened to the clatter of his coming in. I could hardly contain my joy and excitement. My biggest dream was coming true, and the prospect of being reunited with my baby boy made any lingering doubts, about immediately revealing my news, inconceivable. I wrung my hands trying to contain myself, while listening to Peter chatter about his day's events.

Finally, I was able to coax him to the patio, offer him a drink and sit him down. The news of my amazing telephone call poured out of me. I wanted to dance with joy from the excitement, but I also wanted to watch Peter, waiting for his reaction. "I'm not surprised" he said, "I knew he would be looking for you one day." Searching his face I saw nothing but kindness and support, "Really?" I said.

"So, tell me, how do you know it was him?" he asked, a note of concern in his voice.

"Well, he has all of the information on his adoption. He's even has been to all of our previous houses."

After a long pause, Peter said, "You should be very cautious, until you have complete proof. So what are you going to do now?"

"I'm calling him tomorrow. I wanted to wait until I told you, before I did anything else." That night I was unable to sleep, as over and over I relived our first phone call.

Luckily, no one was home the next day when John phoned. "I thought you were going to wait till I called you?" was the first thing I said.

"I just couldn't. I was up all night thinking about it!" I laughed, knowing exactly how he was feeling.

"I bet I know what you were doing." I teased.

"What?"

"You were reading about your father, weren't you?"

"Well, yeah, how did you know? I don't like what I read about him either. Did you know that we are mentioned in quite a few books?" Now that surprised me and I told him I didn't know about that at all. Living here in States, I wouldn't hear about the Stones too much, unless they are on tour.

"You know, John, most of the books written about Brian are probably written by people your age. They didn't know Brian personally and a lot of what has been written is hearsay." As strange as it may seem, I didn't want John to have a completely bad opinion of his father, the man written about in all of those books was not the same man I'd known. The man I remembered was kind and sweet and vulnerable. I told him that the only book I would give any credence to would be *'Stone Alone"* by Bill Wyman. Who better to tell about Brian than a man who lived with him twenty-four hours a day?

We bounced away from the subject of John's father, instead talking about his childhood and his family, and then my life and family. It seemed like we could never say enough or share enough. At the end of our call, we promised to put pictures in the mail.

After hanging up, I rummaged around in a recent photo album in search of current pictures of myself. It wasn't an easy task finding any of me, as I am usually the one taking all the photos. Eventually, I found one taken of me at a recent bridal shower, and then I scrounged for some of the children. I didn't think any of the photos were all that good, but they would have to do.

John called again the following day and I swear my heart was nearly trying to beat out of my chest the entire time we were on the phone. I just couldn't wrap my mind around what was happening and how euphoric I felt.

That evening after dinner, Peter said, "Well, I guess you're going to have tell the kids. No doubt he's going to want to see you at some point. I think you'd better arrange a dinner party, so we can tell them about John together."

He was right of course. So, the next day I called them all and told them I expected them for dinner with their spouses on Friday evening, as I had something important to tell them. The girls panicked, thinking I had a serious illness, but I reassured them that this was not the reason and that they would have to wait and see. In the calling and inviting, I could feel my fear and excitement, and wondered if it came across to them as strongly as it was overtaking me.

John continued to call, and we were both floating on air. I spent some time making a small photo album with all of my baby Paul information in it: the birth certificate, the letters I'd written to the adoption society, his adoption papers and the photos I'd taken while we were still together. I had very few pictures of Brian. Years before, I'd given or thrown away most of the things that had been his. The album was finished off with a beautiful eight by ten black and white photo of Paul that the Adoption Society had sent me when he was four months old.

I called John and excitedly told him that I was having dinner for all the family on Friday and was going to tell them about him. "That's great." he kept saying, and then changed the subject. "Is it alright for me to come and visit on October twenty-ninth for a few days?"

"Of course, you can come!" I was so excited. We went silent for a few minutes. When he spoke next, he caught me completely off guard.

"Did you ever think of me?" His question took my breath away, and I held the receiver in silence, staring out the window.

"Yes, John," I said, looking down at the middle finger of my right hand. "I've been wearing you all the time. When Arron was born, Peter had seven separate gold rings made for me to represent the most important people in my life. These are my six children and Peter. I've worn them for twenty years. So, yes, John, I do think about you.

My excitement never abated from the moment I hung up the phone until the Friday I was to announce my big news to the children. I wanted to shout it from the mountaintops, tell cashiers at the grocery store, and write letters to all of my close friends. But I reined in my excitement enough to keep my undisclosed news to myself – at least until I told the children. There was so much to do, and think about. I imagined how I would tell them, dreamed of what they would say and do, wondered what they would think of their mother who had kept such a secret for so long. I predicted every scenario and all of them turned out perfect in my mind. However, the afternoon of the announcement party, as I set the table with my best china and crystal glasses, situated the fresh flower arrangement and lit candles, my excitement began to turn into dismay. All of my great planning seeped out of my mind, and I began to worry about how to tell them.

The roast beef and homemade Yorkshire pudding, both family favorites, created a heavenly smell in our home. I wished that my cooking preparations might calm the nervousness that was quickly beginning to overtake me, as the time for their arrival approached.

As each of my family arrived, the knots in my stomach twisted tighter. A part of me wanted to shout "how can you act so normal, when everything in our lives is going be dramatically changed?" Our family life would never be the same again. Dinner was so routine, with everyone sharing in the idle chitchat about their day.

Such a typical get together, yet I couldn't keep my hands, arms and face from flushing hot and then turning goose bump cold. I could barely eat and hardly looked up from my plate, as news and pleasantries were exchanged.

As I cleared the table and served dessert, my heart plummeted when Peter said, "Well your Mother has some news she wants to share with you." My mind went blank all over again, and I just looked at him, my face blushed in embarrassment I felt as if I was sixteen and caught doing something I ought not to have been up to. How was I supposed to start? I had gone over it a million times in my head and, now, faced with the reality of it, I was lost. Looking down, I gripped the photo album I'd made, It was on my lap, in readiness of sharing it when the big moment came.

As tears welled in my eyes, Peter reached over and took my hand, cleared his throat and spoke the words I was unable to. "Before we were married, your Mother had a baby. She was sent away to a mother and baby home and was forced to relinquish the infant up for adoption. I knew about it and it has not mattered to me. Now, that child has found your mother and it seems he wants to see her. However, the story does not end there. You see, your Mother was once the girlfriend of one of the Rolling Stones and that is who the father of her son is." There was a brief stunned silence, and then questions all at once.

"Mum," Tara burst out "how come you never told us? No wonder you don't ever want to watch all those reunion shows."

"Mum," Nadine interjected, "I can't imagine what you were feeling when I came home with those Stones tickets. If I'd only known."

Samantha, holding her own counsel, sat in shocked silence.

Pushing his chair back, Arron got up, walked around behind me and put his arms around me. "Wow," he said, "I have a big brother. The Rolling Stones! Way to go Mum!"

I pulled the scrapbook from my lap and passed it around for everyone to see. Of course, the book raised more questions and comments. When all of the excitement wore down, I shared the news that John was going to arrive October twenty-ninth. Everyone was in a state of shock.

In addition to telephoning, I wrote long loving letters, and sent photos to my newly found son. The postal service seemed to take forever. Daily I checked the mailbox for something, anything, from this son of mine whom I'd waited so long to see. Finally, the day arrived when I reached into the box and pulled out a brown airmail envelope. This was it! I would get to see what he looked like at last! I felt the photographs through the paper. I looked at his handwriting and ran my finger over the turns from his pen - my son's handwriting!

Dancing into the house and headed to the kitchen bar stools. Tara was visiting and I sat down next to her. I showed her the envelope, then jumped up and spun around holding the treasure to my chest, joy and smiles radiated from me. Then I pulled it away, looked at the writing, and clutched the package close once more. I just couldn't bring myself to open it. Suddenly, Tara snatched the envelope from my hand, ripped it open and handed it back.

"Now read it." Handing the photos to Tara I began to silently read what my son had written to me.

> Dear Dawn,
>
> Sunday September 11th now ranks as one of the best days of my life, thanks for the phone call and thanks for saying everything I always dreamed you would say, thanks for making me feel that I belong to you even after 29 years

The letter then went on to tell me about his family and his life. While I read, Tara examined the photos, "Oh Mum, look here he is! Look!" I gasped as I saw my son, a grown man - not a little blond haired baby. My face started to hurt from all of my smiling. To see him all grown up for the first time! To be able to search for some recognition on his features that he had inherited from his father or me. He had Brian's jaw, mouth and thick blond hair. He was built just like his father, too. In looking at his face closely, I recognized my eyes. He was a handsome young man and I couldn't get enough of looking at him. Here was my lost son at last.

He had also included pictures of his children. I had two more grandchildren! I was happy and sad about that news. - sad for the years I'd missed watching those little tikes grow. My heart somersaulted with anticipation I would see my lost son, and then at some point meeting his wife and adorable children.

First picture of John 1994

Of course, the days leading up to October twenty-ninth inched by. I was as anxious as a five-year-old on Christmas Eve! I counted the days. John called almost daily and wrote letters full of questions. We learned that we both love music, that he worked almost constantly, and dearly loved his children. The phone bills grew along with our marathon conversations. We couldn't learn enough about one another. I hated leaving the house for fear I would miss a call. He was constantly on my mind.

Finally, the end of October arrived, and my time was spent getting the house ready, the guest room set up, the big family gathering meal organized and deciding what I would wear when I met him at the airport. The girls gave their advice. I wanted to look nice for him and have everything be perfect. Would we recognize one another from the photos we'd exchanged? Should we wear a flower, or something, so we would not pass each other in the crowd?

The day before, to my surprise, John had arranged to have flowers sent to the house that read

> Dear Mum
>
> Only a few more hours & we will be together again forever!
>
> You're Son John

I was a wreck the night before his arrival. My nerves kept me awake the whole night. In the morning, nothing suited me, and I changed outfits three times. I probably drove Peter crazy, while we drove down the 91 Freeway to the Los Angeles Airport, as I kept saying, "I can't believe I'm doing this! It's so surreal. I thought I'd never see him again. The adoption society said they were going to destroy the files and, if he came looking for me no one would know where I was." I was so happy and kept asking Peter to pinch me to make sure this was not all a dream.

CHAPTER TWENTY-FIVE

We Love You

The arrival board for his plane indicated his flight was on time. I paced in front of the exit gate, my heart racing, my palms sweating, and I feeling like I would bounce out of my skin. Peter had the video camera ready to film everything. Passengers began to exit, rushing into the arms of loved ones, laughing and crying. We waited and watched, and waited and watched some more. All of the travelers seemed to have disembarked, and still John had not made his appearance. I began to wonder if he had lost his nerve and never boarded the plane at all, or had stopped and gotten a return ticket home.

I began to panic. Tears choked my throat and were threatening to flow down my cheek, when I saw a smiling, blond haired young man. I knew it was John! My boy! I ran towards him, and, putting his bag down he encased me in his arms. They were strong like his father's were. We hugged tightly. I couldn't let him go, and he did not try loose his hold on me either. "I can't believe it's really you!" I kept saying into his ear. "I know, I know." He repeated. " Hmm I recognize your smell." That precious moment will always stay with me.

First touch October 1994

Eventually we broke free and it was time for the mundane 'get to know you' chat. How was his flight? Was he nervous? Yes, he was and could hardly muster his courage to walk through the gate. Yes, I was nervous too and knew just how he felt and was concerned that he might have changed his mind. I signaled for Peter to come over. John shook Peter's hand, and we made our way to the car.

John became quiet and shy on the drive home, "Peter, we need to turn the car around and find a phone booth so John can call. He talks non-stop on the phone." We all laughed at that and he seemed to feel more comfortable. I kept turning around in my seat to look at him and make sure he was really with us.

I could tell he was tired from his journey. We were both running on adrenaline. He wanted to see the house, so I gave him the grand tour and let him settle into the guest room. As I fixed a light meal, I watched him pace about, move his hands and cock his head in the same manner as Brian had done. Seeing him act like his father, even though they never had the opportunity to meet, was really quite unnerving.

We talked well into the night, too wound up to go to bed. Eventually, he gave in. His body could take no more, he went off to the guest room and I stayed up a while longer, cleaning the kitchen and pondering all what was going on at that moment in my life and the miracle of it all. Finally, it was time for me to try and put the joy and wonder that surrounded me to sleep. Before I went to bed, I crept into the guest room to take one last look, to make sure he was really there and that I wasn't in some kind of giddy dream state. He was sound asleep I bent down and kissed his forehead and whispered, "Goodnight my sweet boy." I went to bed a very happy woman. At last after an eternity of years, my firstborn son was sleeping in the same house and under the same roof as me.

John bounced into the kitchen early the next morning. I was already having a cup of tea. His smile literally made his face glow "Good morning!" we kissed and embraced, we really didn't know how to act.

"Would you like a cup of tea?" I asked, and of course he did. How he did like his tea - with milk and sugar just like me. What else did we have in common? We laughed as we compared our hands, our feet (size 8 just like me), and looked at our faces for similarities. Did he have any illnesses or surgeries, I asked? How strange it was to ask my own son if he had any illnesses or surgeries in his life. His facial expressions his hand gestures were both familiar and unfamiliar at the same time. I still had a nervous feeling inside that I might wake up.

After breakfast, Peter went to work and it was just John and I. We took some cold drinks outside and sat by the pool, sitting as close to one another as possible. He touched my arm, then apologized. "I'm sorry, I don't want to make you feel uncomfortable, but I just need to make sure you are real." He said shyly. Oddly I was thinking the same thing.

We talked some more and then he went to his room and brought out his adoption information to show me. He'd gone to the Society and picked up his file, which contained his birth information and all of the letters that I had written to them so many years before. He told me that he'd spent a large part of his flight reading over the content of that file.

Those hours by the pool enjoying the sun, just John and I, were warm and special. I shared my story, reliving the good and the bad moments. John listened and watched my facial movements so closely that I was reminded of the early days when Brian and I had talked for hours on end.

"That's bloody awful," he reiterated over and over, as I told him of Beechwood.

He took my hand, looked at me intensely and said "I'm so sorry." He reminded me so much of his father, and I was filled with complicated feelings. I remembered myself as that lost girl of 1965, and now being reunited with my son again, after all the time not knowing him, I had trouble comprehending that he was a grown man and that I'd missed his childhood.

It seemed like only moments had passed, when Peter had returned from the office. Neither John nor I was ready to give up our private musings, but, with another person present, our conversation somehow felt too personal and vulnerable to continue.

We decided that a trip to Hollywood and a visit to all of the tourist places were in order. We visited Mann's Chinese Theater placed our hands into the imprints of stars, walked Rodeo Drive, and lunched at Cantor's, a wonderful Jewish restaurant by the Farmer's Market. Knowing John liked muscle cars, we stopped at the Peterson Car Museum. I think he was a little overwhelmed trying to take it all in, and we weren't able to stay too long because I had to prepare dinner.

It was the evening when all of the kids were coming over to meet their newfound brother. Conversations had been furiously flying back and forth amongst them all. This evening had been eagerly looked forward to.

John swam in the pool and relaxed while I prepared the meal. We were becoming more and more comfortable with one another as the day wore on. However, as the hours ticked by, and the family reunion dinner drew near, I became anxious. How would they take to one another? Would they have things in common? I wondered if I would have been as brave as John was to fly to the other side of the world and meet a family full of strangers.

WE LOVE YOU

I set the dining room table for a party. My best China, perfectly matched tablecloth and napkins, flowers and candles. This was going to be a celebration. I couldn't hide my happiness. John seemed surprised at how much trouble I was going to, but that is how I am. I love to entertain for Easter, birthdays, Christmas. Holidays have always been special at my house and welcoming John into our midst was the best observance I was to ever have. It was no trouble, only pure joy. I lovingly prepared the family favorites: roast beef, Yorkshire pudding, roast potatoes, parsnips and veggies.

Six-thirty came and right on time Nadine, Dave and baby Ashley arrived, followed by Samantha and Tony, and behind them Tara and Gary, and then lastly Arron. I am an affectionate person and hug and kiss my children anytime I get the opportunity. I made introductions all around and left them to get to know one another, as I dished up the feast.

Dinner conversation that evening was more of a question and answer session, with bits of humor tossed about amongst the siblings. I suppose John was as relaxed as anyone could be, considering the situation. I'm sure he must have been pretty overwhelmed. I know I was inundated with joy and a heart filled to capacity with love. While clearing the dinner dishes, I was completely content listening to happy conversations.

I had made a cheesecake especially for John. While making it, I'd poured every ounce of love I had into it. This was to be his first birthday cake with all of us.

Birthday cheesecake with 29 candles 1994

My heart ached at all of the birthdays we had missed and I wanted this to be perfect and memorable for him. I put twenty-nine candles on top, lit them and carried it into the room full of revelers. Everyone began to sing Happy Birthday and my eyes filled with tears. John appeared to be touched, and my heart nearly broke when he shared that he'd never had a birthday cake before. How very sad.

Periodically, John disappeared into his room. I assumed it was because he was not used to being with a lot of people and was uncomfortable. When the evening ended and everyone had left for their own homes, John told me that he couldn't believe what a great family I had and how loved everyone was. I'm sure he was missing his family and thinking about them, too.

That night I tossed and turned in bed. I just could not sleep. I'd been so happy knowing that I had him back, and had been so excited that he would soon be coming out to visit, that I hadn't really allowed any negative feelings to sneak in the back door. Now that he was in my life and the years of wondering and worry were over,

I had not cried a tear. But now sad thoughts overtook me and my heart was heavy.

It was two in the morning. Still not sleepy, I put on my robe and slippers and padded down to the kitchen for a drink. I turned on the light and saw John leaning against the sink. He looked away and asked me to turn it off please.

The moon illuminated the room, and I saw tears streaming down his cheeks. I walked over and touched his shoulders. He turned and embraced me and we both broke down into sobs. "I always knew you loved me," he cried. "I've missed you always. I've always felt your presence, like you were treading on my heart."

The knife of realization that I had missed his childhood jabbed me to the core. That was exactly what I had felt all of my life when I thought of him as well. The pain is something I will never forget. I had no idea that the revelation of this truth would break me down and cause me to become an emotional wreck. It was a defining point in our reunion. I became so incredibly sad, and the tears that wracked me were as emotionally laden as the ones I cried the day he was removed from my arms. I later learned from other adoptees and First Mothers that this emotional trauma is normal (I had to admit that it seemed natural and familiar that we should both feel that way), but, at the time, a part of me wondered what was going on and how we would ever cope with it. We sat for a long time on the sofa, comforting each other, holding one another's hands, he swearing to me that nothing would keep us apart ever again, me being in total agreement that we would work the distance out by phone, and visit often. Things were going to be fine.

When we finally went to bed, I found myself still not able to sleep. I lay awake until morning thinking about my son and all of the things we'd shared so far and what we would share in the future.

I got up with Peter, We always start our days together. Since Peter was going off to work, it was decided to take John out to Hemet to see Tara and then over to Riverside to see Nadine. Unfortunately,

Samantha and Arron were unavailable. It was a busy visit full of lively conversation and sharing.

John seemed captivated by America, taking in every bit. I learned his wife was a stay-at-home Mum, and that he had worked at the same motor company since he was sixteen. His life with his adoptive parents had been a good one, and they had never hidden the fact that he and his sister were adopted. He was sad that his mother was not too happy that he had searched for and found me. He'd had a falling out with his sister over it, as she was afraid her mother would be hurt. I could understand his sister's worries. After all, his adoptive parents had brought them up, protected and loved them. I know she had no idea about the grief and turmoil my life had been in, not having the opportunity to raise my own son. These kinds of situations are hard for everyone involved.

In telling me these things, he paced back and forth, stopping to think, looking at me for a second or two, then turning and starting off again – just like Brian used to do. He was his father's son.

When I learned that his family knew he was visiting me, I imagined what an upsetting time it must be for them. I contemplated how they must feel, and asked John if he would mind if I wrote them a letter. I suggested that he give it to them. That way I wouldn't know where they lived and their privacy would be protected. He agreed to give them a letter and hoped it would help them to understand why he had felt so compelled to search for me.

In my letter, I expressed my heartfelt thanks to them for raising John into such a fine man, and how grateful I was to meet him at last, after worrying and wondering what had become of him for so many years. I also let them know that he would always be their son and that nothing would change that.

On his last night with us, we went out to dinner to one our favorite restaurants. When we returned home afterwards, I stood in the bedroom doorway and watched him pack his bag, getting ready for his imminent departure. I wasn't anywhere near ready for him to leave. We still had so much to talk about.

We Love You

Dawn and John the day he left 1994

    We hardly spoke on the drive to airport. We waited with him until his flight was called, hugged and said our last goodbyes. As I watched him disappear through the gate, all of my being wanted to run after him and figure out some way to make him stay. I sobbed all the way home. I thought my heart would break. I could feel his familiar footsteps crushing my heart. It felt so heavy, and thought I would never be able to breathe again. We had just found one another and I feared I would lose him once more. Peter was so kind trying to comfort me, but it was all to no avail.

    I was a complete wreck and simply obsessed. Once again, I would not leave the house for fear I might miss his phone calls. We resumed our phone conversations and talked everyday for hours. When we weren't on the phone we wrote letters full of emotion and honesty. I am so thankful now that the internet was not around, because I still have all of those handwritten letters and cards. It was like some strange love affair - we talked, we wrote, and I thought about nothing except him.

Chapter Twenty-Six

Pain In My Heart

Peter was so supportive. He could see how unsettled and sad I was, and arranged for us to go to England to meet John's wife and children in late November, only a few weeks away. November is such a beautiful time, because the trees have changed into their showy fall colors. That was something I'd missed living in Southern California.

A smiling John picked us up from Heathrow and drove us to his bungalow. His lovely wife, Amanda, welcomed us into their home, introduced us to their gorgeous St. Bernard, Roxy, and most importantly to me the grandchildren: pretty six year old Emily and handsome four year old Luke. The children were amazing and we bonded instantly. I imagined them visiting us in the States over holidays and how happy we would be investigating new places and enjoying first time experiences. I loved everything about their little bungalow, especially the fact that it was warm, cozy, and full of love.

The next night we went to dinner at a pub and met Amanda's mum, dad and two sisters. We talked freely, sharing our lives and were surprised at how very much alike our lifestyles were.

The following evening we went to John's adopted sister's house. She let her feelings be known that she did not like it that John had gone out and found me. She was adamant that she had no intentions of searching for her biological mother as she had a Mother already (eight years later she did meet her First Mother, and all is well). I respected her opinion, even though it made me feel uncomfortable and unwelcome. Of course, I knew this might happen before going to visit. She had a baby girl Alice, seven months old, who didn't like strangers. But for some reason she took to me, which seemed to soften John's sister's opinion a bit.

Our trip was for only four days. I was sad that John and I had so little time alone to talk. We stayed up late every night, going on and on about our lives and staring at one another.

The time evaporated and, too soon as always, it was time for Peter and I to leave. I kept telling myself that we would be seeing them all in March for Samantha's wedding, which was only three months away. John's daughter, Emily, was to be in the wedding as a flower girl, along with Nadine's three-year-old daughter, Ashley. Three months seemed like an eternity and, once again, I fell apart as soon as we were on our way back to the States.

Thank God that I love weddings, and love arranging them. My thoughts were kept busy helping Samantha with the preparations. I had decided that I would make the dresses for the flower girls. After gathering their measurements, I spent many carefree hours cutting patterns, pinning and sewing. I couldn't wait to see how pretty they will look in them.

Peter brother and niece, as well as John and his family, were to arrive a few days before the wedding. John seemed excited at the thought of meeting his maternal grandmother. I wasn't sure how Mother would take the news.

Mother had moved to the States fourteen years after leaving England for Australia. I'd been hurt when she made the move after Dad's death. I suppose there was still a little girl inside, wishing she would look my way and say, "I have always loved you, Dawn. You were the best daughter a mother could ever have." Sadly, I was never going to hear those words. When she left the England, the move was made with a man, a friend she said. She never looked back, until over a decade later when her 'friend' had died after spending all of her money.

She had nowhere to live, desperate, broke and lonely, so Peter offered to have her live with us. We finally settled on putting her up in her own apartment in Riverside, where she lived for the next six years. Even though she tried, she never fit into the American culture and had been unable to make friends. When she made the decision to move back to England, to the old neighborhood, we all agreed it was a good plan for her.

I had tried, and always would try, to be a good daughter. It is true that I had always held resentment over the part she played when I was pregnant with John. To the best of my ability, I never let her see it. I always called, never missed her birthdays, and made sure she was never alone at Christmas. She adored my children and was a doting grandmother, a far cry from the woman who had raised me.

After their first meeting, John took my mother aside and asked if she could tell him a little bit about his father. Without a thought, Mother immediately and venomously snapped back, "Thank God that bastard is dead! He deserved what he got!" John stepped back in total surprise and said, "Oh, right, thanks very much." After that he had nothing more to do with her, and she couldn't understand what she had done wrong!

During rehearsal at the church, John's son, Luke, suddenly decided he wanted to be a ring bearer. It sounded like a wonderful idea to me and I spent that night quickly making a pillow for him to hold. Fortunately, I had fabric left over from the flower girl dresses. John was worried that Luke wouldn't behave himself during the ceremony, and of course he did, but what a comedy act!

The day of the wedding, John walked me down the aisle to be seated. I turned around to watch Samantha, this beautiful bride, walk towards her future husband. This was a day that became one of my many 'I wish I could freeze moments.' At last, all of my children were together and I was blissful. And Peter's brother, niece and all my friends were meeting my newly found son and his family. I was so proud and enjoyed showing off my delightful grandchildren.

Getting to know my newest grandchildren was a highlight. I loved reading them bedtime stories, laughed at the fun they had when we took them to Disneyland and watching them swim in the pool. The best part was being near John. I couldn't stop looking at him and reflecting on all of the years we'd missed together. I was in seventh heaven.

.As always, John and I were inseparable. This proved to be aggravating for Peter and Amanda. John was attentive to my needs, opened my car door, and helped me with whatever I was doing. He was outwardly affectionate, probably because that is the kind of person I am. But I later learned being affectionate was not part of his normal makeup, John told me that his normal behavior was standoffish and distant when it came to expressions of outward affection. "I didn't have you to imitate, so I made up my own personality. I'm different from all of you. I don't let anyone get close, I don't trust."

It was hard for everyone around us to understand. We were the best we could be together, which I suppose made everyone else feel like we might prefer that they be excluded.

After the fact, I learned that it is important that everyone in the family be consulted and prepared, when a First Mother and her child are reunited. If we had had the knowledge and books to read then that are available now, it would have been a less difficult time for everyone. I now know it is important to make sure that all family members are one hundred percent on board with meeting a lost child, and that they also understand that the reunion might bring up intense emotions for everyone involved. The two books that I read two years later, which would have been a great help at the time of our reunion, were *'**Primal Wound**' by Nancy Verrier* and *'**Synchronicity & Reunion**' by LaVonne Harper Stiffler*.

For twenty-nine years, my feelings had been repressed. I'd never been allowed to grieve the loss of my baby, and never been allowed to speak of him or my feelings about him. I didn't bury him like I had Sherry. All of my life I knew he was alive and living somewhere. The most agonizing part was that nearly every day I heard Stones music, which acted like salt on my open wounds.

John returned to London on March sixteenth with a promise that he and his family would be back in August for their summer holidays. It was terribly sad, especially since his birthday was on the twenty-fourth and I had wanted to share this special day with him. He apologized a explained that he would not be able to call, as he would be in Germany on business.

The twenty-fourth arrived and I was down, I felt like my soul was being destroyed, I could not even wish him Happy Birthday because he was unavailable! In an effort to cheer me up, Peter suggested we go to our favorite Italian restaurant and have dinner. I really didn't want to go. I was too depressed and wanted to stay home, but he insisted. Why couldn't I just lie around and feel sorry for myself?

Arriving at the restaurant, I was surprised to see that the entire family was there. "How strange," I thought. We exchanged ordinary chit chat for a short while, when, from behind me, in walked John with a bouquet of flowers. Stunned, I stood up, put my arms around him and cried. He looked into my eyes and smiled mischievously, "You didn't think I'd let you spend my first birthday without you did you?" Oh my God! I was in total shock. It had been set up as a surprise. John had arrived the day before and Tara had picked him up and kept him at her place until dinner. What a wonderful thing to do, and best of all he'd arranged to stay another three days with us.

We spent two wonderful days sightseeing and continuing to catch up with our lives. It surprised me when he revealed that he had gone to all eleven of the houses we'd lived in while looking for me. He had also obtained all of his sibling's birth certificates, my marriage certificate, and even Sherry's death certificate! He had even visited the hospital where he'd been born, but it had been torn down and something else was being built in its place. I was amazed at the lengths he'd gone to find me.

He happily shared his excitement over his purchase of a muscle car, a Dodge California, police vehicle, in June of 1982 – the very month and year we immigrated to the United States. He shared that something inside told him he must have that car. He was proud of the hours he'd put into restoring the car to pristine condition and even bragged a bit that a magazine had written an article about him and his lovingly rebuilt vehicle. His animation when he described the overhauling process and the work he put into his pride and joy showed me how much he loved it. I couldn't help but smiling, as I listened to him describe it as a proud father would a newborn child.

Our time together once more passed too quickly. Leaving him at the airport, I felt my heart would collapse with grief. Once again I cried all the way home.

Over the next six months, John and I called and wrote to one another often, pouring out our souls. He related funny family stories, told me about his dogs, his passion for boating, and his business travels. We talked for hours, and both agreed that we were looking forward to August when he and his family would be visiting again.

Sadly, during that time, Peter's business had trouble, and we were forced to sell our home and the business in Hawaii for what was owed on it. President Clinton had cut our McDonald Douglas contract, and within one week the company went from one hundred employees to eight.

By the time John and family arrived, we had moved into a nice rental home, which wasn't far from our original property. Peter was struggling to keep afloat and worked day and night. But even with all of his worries, he found time to take us on a road trip, so that John and his family could see the sights of San Francisco and places in between going down the coast. John loved being in America, and especially enjoyed driving on Pacific Coast Highway

The trip was everything a trip should be. The weather was fantastic and we managed to get nicely tanned. One evening at dinner, Amanda surprised us with the fantastic news that she was pregnant. Another grandchild! Could life get any better? I was ecstatic. I was going to be 'Nanma' to my son's new baby and be part of its growing up life.

All my children together at last 1995
Left to right, Peter Arron, Dawn, Tara.
Samantha, John and Nadine
(Photography by Scott Nelson)

Inevitably, they had to return to the England.

John still wanted to move to the United States, and asked me to get his green card. But the reality was that he had a very good job, and it would have been a difficult upheaval for his family.

John and I were still in what is now known as the *honeymoon stage* of our reunion. The truth is that, given time, the honeymoon aspects would have calmed down, and real life would have been reinstated, and all would have found happy compromises. But, unfortunately, we were so wrapped up in the euphoria and happiness of getting to know one another that our spouses felt abandoned and left out.

Peter had been supportive and explained to me that it was strange that I had a son who was not related to him, while his children and I were all related to this young man. He felt out of the loop and didn't understand. Of course, neither did John or I, we just knew that the distance of an ocean between us was nearly unbearable and that our spouses didn't get it.

John did call me first to share the good news that he and Amanda had had a healthy baby boy, Connor. We laughed that, since I was on California time and it was eight hours behind, which meant his son wasn't technically, born yet.

During my second trip back to the England to see John, I had the privilege to meet his parents. It was a day I will never forget. His mother had received the letter I'd written to them in which I had explained that I understood she might feel upset that John had found me, but that I was not looking to take him away from them, because he would always be their son. To my surprise she wrote back and told me she always knew John had a missing part, and was glad he'd found me. She added thatm "In my opinion, there is always enough love to share." And since she knew I was coming out, asked if I would visit them and have lunch.

John and I drove three hours to the small village in Devon, where they lived. We were having a great time talking and listening to the radio, when John said "Well, we are nearly there." As we drove up the drive to their house, I became cold and started to shiver I felt the blood drain from my face. John noticed, "We can turn around and go back. You don't have to do this you know."

"No, I want to go in, just give me a minute." I answered, taking deep breaths, trying to shake the overwhelming feelings I was experiencing. Soon I was able to get out of the car, face my fears and head up to the house. They opened the door and greeted us with joy and love. It surprised me that they were in their sixties, having imagined them be my age. But then I remembered that in order to adopt a child in those days, a couple had to prove that they were stable, professional, and owned their own home. The laws had been quite strict and I know that they must have had these credentials in order for John to become their son. It surprised me that they were very well spoken, unlike John who speaks more cockney (must be the shop floor motor industry). We went to the lounge to unwind and get to know one another.

I could smell the salmon she was cooking for lunch. The house was nicely decorated, no pictures of family on the walls, just oil paintings. Sensing my awkwardness, his mother asked how our trip was and general questions about my life. My stomach was in such a knot, and I was so uncomfortable. Thank goodness for her kindness and understanding.

Lunch was held at a beautifully set table. Cut glass goblets, china settings, cloth napkins, and a flower arrangement in the center made me feel welcomed in style. It was all so lovely, and I thought how I would have done the same for her. But would she have felt as sick as I was feeling? I didn't want to appear rude, but I had to excuse myself and went to the bathroom. Standing in front of the mirror, I looked at myself, "What am I doing here?" I wondered. "They have had all the years I've missed." At that point I threw up. Washing my face, sitting alone, eventually I felt better and rejoined John and his family. "I'm sorry; I guess my nerves are getting the better of me."

"I understand." His mother responded. She was so kind, the perfect hostess.

I managed to get through lunch, learning that she had been a piano teacher at the local school and that his Dad was a professor of science. Both were so intelligent and it must have seemed strange to have a child who showed no signs of being musical and having no interest in math. I thought to myself that math has never been my best subject, either. At that time she did not offer to share any photos of John's childhood. Perhaps she thought it would be too painful for me. In thinking back to that day, I think she was right. Their taste in music was classical, along with theater and shows tunes. Since my father had enjoyed the same music, we were able to share that in common. She brought up the subject of flowers and gardening. I told her about my love of Bluebells, and how much I missed seeing them in America.

After lunch, a walk along the cliffs was suggested, it was hoped that the fresh air would do me some good. She was right again. The wind seemed like a gale, pushing against us with each step, but it felt good on my face and cleared my mind. As I walked with John's mother, John and his Dad wondered ahead of us.

"You know, every birthday I thought of you, and sent a voice out to the void to tell you he was alright." She said. I broke down in tears and she hugged me, "I know it must have been painful for you, but he gave us happiness we would never have known. We have enjoyed watching him grow, and I thank you for that."

The next day I sent her flowers, and apologized for not eating her lunch after all the trouble she'd gone to. She is such a thoughtful person, and that Christmas sent me a card with Bluebells on it.

I have enjoyed staying in touch over the years and have attended family functions when I'm in England. I will always be grateful to them for loving and protecting John, until he became an independent young man.

CHAPTER TWENTY-SEVEN

Blue Turns to Gray

John began his own journey of self discovery at eighteen years of age. When he finally found me and learned that his father was Brian Jones of the Rolling Stones, he'd had ten years to imagine who his parents might be. Maybe finding that a man like Peter was his father would have made John's journey easier. I know that there would be a lot less press and baggage surrounding a man who was a "regular" person, instead of the son of a famous musician

Brian was no regular man. His fame followed him even after death. Maybe his death helped create the constant speculation and glorifying of the story that had become the specter of the person who was John's father. Brain Jones had become a phantom, and truth had become enmeshed with untruth. Brian was an icon of the sixties, a famous man who did more than his share of drugs, and had gotten five young women pregnant, and abandoned them when he was needed the most. I remember him as being loving and caring, charming and witty, childish and also intense. John had inherited many of Brian's characteristics along with a strong resemblance.

During one of my trips to England, I arranged for John to meet some of the people who knew his father and me in those bygone days. I contacted the Stones' office to ask if any of the boys were around and might be able to meet John. Both Mick and Keith were abroad, but Bill Wyman was glad to hear that John had found me, and was more than happy to meet with us and disclose what he remembered.

We met Bill at his second floor office in London. It was a joyous reunion, and Bill and I shared a heartfelt hug.

He shook John's hand and remarked that he was the same height as his dad, and how much they resembled one another. We made our way down the stairs to a coffee shop across the street, where stories about old times flowed. Bill retold the story of my involvement with Brian, and John asked questions about his father. Many of the answers provided were not what John would have liked to hear.

Bill declared that John was better off not knowing his father. Being brought up in the shadow of the Stones only brings trouble and greed." I think John was surprised to hear that. The subject turned to Bill's book, *Stone Alone*.

"So why did you put my mother's picture in your book?" John asked

"Because Dawn got a raw deal - Brian was a cold bastard." Consider yourself lucky your out of all this –that you had a normal life. Your best out of it.

The conversation moved to catching up on our lives, John told how he had been searching for me, Bill spoke of his wife Suzie and I talked about Peter and living in the States.

"I went to the Steel Wheels concert in LA in 1989 with a friend." I confessed, "I wondered if I should have tried to go backstage to see you boys. I thought you probably would have forgotten about me. Also, I didn't want to tell my friend how I knew you." Bill laughed at that.

"No, you should have tried. It would have been nice to see you."

"Yes, I was sad to learn of Stu's passing." I told him. We reminisced a bit more, and realized that the day had gotten away from us. It was time to say good bye. Bill suggested we have lunch at his restaurant, Sticky Fingers, up the street, He asked us to give him time, and he would let his staff know we were coming. John and I spent some time looking at the memorabilia that was on the walls at Sticky Fingers, a few pieces which belonged to Brian. I felt John was wishing he had known his father, it was a good day.

John Dawn and Bill Wyman in the Café 1995

I contacted Pat Andrews, another of Brian's conquests who'd fallen pregnant by him. She agreed to meet us at a nightclub on Regent Street along with her and Brian's son, Mark. - one of John's four half siblings. Rather tellingly, Mark never turned up to the meet us. Either Pat had not told him, or he was not interested.

Unfortunately, we couldn't meet all of the people that I remembered from those days. There wasn't the time. I provided John with as much information as I could, along with names of those I could recall as being close to Brian. I couldn't do anymore, and left it up to John to follow his own instincts. I knew John had to do what John had to do.

Brian and I were history. I never gave any credence to the sensationalism some commentators had dredged up. Generally, news stories were nothing more than melodramatic fiction printed to sell papers. I had my own special memories of a very unique and extraordinary person in my life. I have always been happy to remember Brian in my own way. Whatever conclusion John came to about his father would be personal to him.

My reality with regards to Brian Jones is that he was my first love I gave him everything I had to offer. I'd become pregnant. I had wanted to pin the blame of Brian's abandonment of me on the pressures of or the attitude of the Rolling Stones management; I wanted his rejection to be anything accept that he, of his own volition, had chosen to move on to someone not encumbered with his child.

The truth is that Brian's history is smattered with exactly the same scenario I had found myself in. Brian had had four other children by different women and, each time the mother would find herself in the same state I had been left in. Brian was uninterested in being part of it. He seemed to have had the heartless capacity to disassociate from his responsibility and emotional involvement in the procreation of his children.

My confinement, where I saw Brian's success story splashed across newspaper and magazine headlines, or witnessed frenzied fans adoring the boys through the television, was a depressing time. My heart grew heavier and heavier, as I realized that Brian and I would never be together and I was going to face the unknown alone, with no one who cared about me.

In the end, the adoption turned out to be a deceitful business, wherein against my will and without full knowledge of the truth of my rights, John was wrenched from my arms and given away. It was a tragic point in my history that left me sad, lonely, and broken.

Chapter Twenty-Eight

Not Fade Away

I felt John begun to pull away. Of course, he had his own family to take care of and maybe the distance played a huge factor. I know that the 5000 miles of separation never used to precluded opportunities to talk our problems through, share triumphs, or have special occasion dinners and get-togethers. Whatever the reason was, he'd thrown himself into his work, and this was the beginning of the end of having any kind of family memories or my grandchildren being world travelers. My girls and Arron couldn't understand John's decision to back off after wanting to know all about us at first. They saw how much I was hurting and became protective of me. I always had excuses for John's erratic on again, off again, behavior. I now realize he had inherited his Father's personality.

John's calls dropped drastically. He told me that his family and business kept him busy. I heard from him barely once a month. I had a feeling of abandonment and fear of losing him again, and fell into a spiral of depression, I had no one to talk to about my out of control feelings. Peter, still supportive grew tired of my moods and told me "to get over it." How many times had I heard that in my life?

No matter how many days passed without a phone call, no matter how many promises were broken, I loved my son (as I love all of my children) no matter what. My immediate family didn't understand.

What they did know was that I was at the lowest point they'd ever seen me in my life.

At that time the internet became popular, and Peter purchased our first computer. I researched, looking for sites in England for chat groups searching for women with similar experiences as me. The only site I found was based in the United States, it was a Yahoo chat group called Sunflowers. Then a spin off from them was FMR, First Mothers Reunited. I joined, and what I found was a haven of kindred sisters, who like me had reunited with their lost children.

I learned that adoptee's feel they can't trust another person, and that some are angry with their mothers, and lash out at them, even many years after reunion, while others simply refuse to meet their First Mothers. Many mothers never saw their babies before they were taken. Others kept them for a day or for months before they were placed. One thing they all had in common is that they remember quite clearly being belittled and brainwashed into thinking they were not good enough to keep their babies, and their infants would be better off with "real parents."

I discovered that some reunions were going well, while others had suffered rejection and heartache. I learned that I wasn't going mad and what I was feeling was normal in 'our world.' Very soon, I understood that the 'adoption triad' was complex for everyone involved.

We call ourselves First Mothers, not Biological Mothers, or Birthmothers. The truth of the matter is that I was John's first mother. Only I nurtured and loved him the first moments and months of his life.

I have made many good friends through this group. Many have written books about their journeys. One such author is Anne Fessler who wrote **The Girls Who Went Away.** Another is Susan Mello Souza who wrote **The Same Smile,** and Lorraine Dusky wrote **Birthmark.** An NBC movie was made from Carol Schaefer's book, **The Other Mother.** Carol has also written a follow up book called **Searching**. As a group we celebrate when a mother hears from her firstborn, and generally give love and support in their life long journey.

We try and meet for one long weekend annually in different states. FMR has provided me with support and has helped me heal from an experience that only someone who has walked in my shoes can understand.

After our move to the States, and even though family ties with my brother, and his family and my mother weren't strong, there were times that I was so homesick for the England that I flew out with the hope that things would change.

My relationship with Mother had improved over the years. I made the trip to Derbyshire on a regular basis to visit her. With age, she became frail and her heart softened. However, she never lost her sharp tongue, and was always quick to judge. I never spoke back, or challenged her opinions. She had cleverly instilled in me a strong sense of duty, ably abetted by the religious folk who schooled but never taught. They generously poured their cup of gospel hokum, and the oft-nrepeated stanza about respect for my elders into my head. I learned my lessons well and did unreservedly respect my mother right up to the end. In spite of living on different continents, I did my duty by her.

A few times we spoke of my unwed pregnancy. I told her how it had affected my life. She never acknowledged that she might have been wrong, nor did she ever offer an apology for her actions. I forgave her, as hanging on to the wrong would have done me no good. I'm so glad that I did, because within six months of my letting go, she suffered a stroke.

I flew out to see her, crawled into her bed to at night curled up with her, while she said her Lord's Prayer. She was a very lonely lady, and it made me sad to see her left with only the Catholic beliefs she had clung to all of her life. Within the year she would pass.

Always a highlight when returning to England, and Derbyshire in particular, were my visits to Sherry's grave and visiting my friend Dianne, who had helped me move on after Sherry's death, and has always been ready with a hug or listening ear. She's always been the rock that I, the ever flitting-butterfly, could depend upon. For forty-six years, we've shared in one another's highs and lows, laughing like lunatics and crying most wretchedly.

Over the years, whenever I flew out, John would come and get me wherever I was, so I could stay for a few days or overnight so I would be able to see his family. Amanda always made me feel welcome, but the dream that our two families would blend was obviously gone. John continued to withdraw into his own thoughts, opening up when he chose to and on his terms only. From one visit to the next, I never knew which John I would encounter.

I grieve the lost opportunities that John and I had to build memories. I felt blindsided by the whole reunion. I had honestly thought that, since John and I seemed so alike, that we could all blend as an extension of our whole family. Sadly, I was wrong.

In 2004 we moved from California to Northern Idaho. John made the trip out to see our new home in 2007 and enjoy our beautiful town. As always, he was more than welcome and I was thrilled to see him.

Our relationship continues. We have had lots of ups and downs. John and I text message and call one another sporadically. But he prefers to keep his distance.

Looking back on all the years, remembering what the Adoption Society social workers, the nurses at the hospital, the church father, and my mother who all said to me: "You will continue on with your life like nothing ever happened" and "It won't affect anyone else," I have one thing to say and that is that they were wrong!

It took my husband, Peter, the one who has been with me and has loved me unconditionally, to point out the obvious error in these statements. The day he shared his viewpoint as an 'outsider,' I was left completely speechless.

"The point is that you not being allowed to raise your first child *has* affected all of us. I've watched you swing from one emotion to another when it comes to John. I've watched you close yourself off and cry for what I think is no good reason. This affects me, because I can't fix this for you. There is no fixing it, and I've come to the realization that this will never go away. It hurts me to see you get excited over some contact, then watch all of your hopes get crushed.

They say 'adoption is the best choice', but it is not - look at what it has done to our family. It affects our children as well as us. Here they have a brother, a half brother, who was never allowed into their lives. They never had the opportunity to get to know him and vice versa. John had no idea that he had four sisters and a little brother, who would look up to him and love him because he is their brother. There's a void in this family, a void that will never go away and will continue with them, through their children and their grandchildren. Adoption doesn't just affect their mother, it affects everyone connected to their mother."

Then he said something that caught me completely off guard. He let me know that he'd told Ashley, our granddaughter, "When one of your friend's ends up pregnant, bring them to your Nanma. She'll let you know that the crap about adoption being a loving, selfless act is bullshit. Let your Nanma explain to them what it really does to the mother and to the unborn child."

Peter's words opened my eyes. My experience had touched so many areas of my life. My mother never had the opportunity to be in her grandson's life. My brother never had the chance to get to know his nephew and spoil him. Other family members never had the chance to pass along our crazy family stories before they passed away. My 'kept' children and their future children will never have their uncle in their lives, and will never have the opportunity to spend time with their first cousins.

When *they* said, "it will only affect you," they were lying. Losing a child to adoption scars the family and leaves a void, an empty space that can never be filled. It doesn't affect just the mother; it affects everyone connected to the mother, and continues on to the next generations.

I've always said that adoption is a permanent solution to a temporary problem. Everything good about who we are, stems from our families and our history. Life is short and we have to love ourselves, our families, and continue to love those lost to us.

Adoption is not like a death of a loved one. It's not final. The pain retreats, maybe fades, but it comes right back. There's no such thing as "over" with this grief.

Afterword

Let me add a final note to my readers. I am not against adoption. What happened in the past - when no choice was given to young women like me, and the right to keep our babies was denied us - was an injustice that can never be made right. Hundreds of thousands of young women suffered unimaginable heartbreak. Dare I say that millions of family members have endured sorrow. all because society was unwilling to stand by young mothers and help them raise their children?

We were sent into confinement, forced to work at sanctioned institutions like Beechwood, treated worse than animals during our birthing time and then kicked away once our babies were placed in "appropriate" homes.

Thank God, that today these kinds of things do not happen. Counseling is available to help young mothers-to-be make informed decisions as to whether or not they will place a child in an adoptive home. Open Adoption, where the adopted child has the right to know about their parentage, is becoming more common although those sometimes fail. In England many adoptees are given the name and location of their birth parents, because it is recognized that they have the right to know their origins.

Sadly, in America there are still adult children searching in different States for biological families because not all adoptions are open. It is my hope that children and birth parents are not kept in the dark in the future as to the whereabouts of their blood relatives.

I am in no way trying to undermine, or discount, the love, nurturing, and real family ties that adoptive parents provide to their adopted children. Everyone needs emotional stability and the knowledge of belonging. Adoptive homes provide for those needs. But, it is my hope that someday Adopters will only think of themselves as guardians to the little ones they bring into their homes and love. The truth is that inevitably the child will want to know, and whether what they learn is good or bad, they have the right to know, so that their heritage does *Not Fade Away,*

Acknowledgements

Situations seem to happen that changed the course of my life. I had no intentions of writing about my experience, but acquaintances and friends I've met along the way, who heard bits of my story have said, "You should write a book." So I have.

My decision to take their advice and put pen to paper was made when I first reunited with my son John, in 1994. In a conversation, a person in her late twenties said, "Nobody would take my child away from me!" I was stunned to realize she had no idea what it was like back in the early sixties for an unmarried pregnant girl. How many more are as uninformed?

I hope that reading this book will give the younger generation a better understanding of those times. and for those who have lived that nightmare realize they are not alone.

I would like to thank :

To Bill Wyman: For his advice and friendship.

To Alan Miles: For his memories.

To Malcolm McDonald: For his input and encouragement.

To Carol Schaefer Author of *The Other Mother* and *Searching* For her invaluable time and advice.

To all my First Mothers on the internet for keeping me sane.

To Dianne: For always being there.

To Jackie: 'Thank heaven for shoes!'

Helpful Resources in England and U.S.A.

In England:

Tracing your Roots (for adoptees)
Sara Jones.
Tel: 0151 608 0503 (answerphone)
Email: sara@tracingyourroots.co.uk
www.tracingyourroots.co.uk

Adoption Services for Adults
Jean Milsted. PO Box 4621,
Marlow, SL7 9DG
Tel: 01628 481954
Email: jean@milsteds.plus.com

BAAF Adoption Search and Reunion website
Birthlink After Adoption
Saffron House, 6–10 Kirby Street,
London EC1N 8TS.
Tel: 0207 421 2600

Post Adoption Centre:
4-5 Torriano Mews,
Torriano Ave, Kentish Town,
London NW5 2RZ.
Tel: Advice Line: 0207 284 5879

After Adoption:
Unit 5 Citygate,
5 Blantyre Street,
Manchester M15 4JJ.
Tel: 0161 839 4932
NPN internet group support
Natural Parents Network UK
http://n-p-n.co.uk/

UMAA.: UK Movement for a Adoption Apology

In the U.S.A.:

American Adoption Congress
http://www.americanadoptioncongress.org/
1000 Connecticut Ave NW
Suite 9
Washington DC 20036
800-247-OPEN

Concerned United Birthparents (CUB)
http://www.cubirthparents.org/
With support groups in some States

First Mothers Reunited for birthmothers only
membership@firstmothers.net groups.yahoo.com/group/firstmothersreunited/

Adoption Healing
www.adoptionhealing.com/

Bio

Dawn grew up in England was one of only a handful of people who first watch The Rolling Stones perform in the earliest days as a band. Now, fifty years later, the music of the Stones can be heard playing somewhere in the world every minute of every day.

Dawn appears from time to time in books and papers. as one of the women who, courtesy of Mr. Brian Jones, the founded the greatest rock and roll band in the world, has had a child by him - in her case a son Paul Andrew.

Dawn was made to suffer, like so many other teenagers of the sixties, from a system that didn't allow them a say in the fate of their children. She decided to share her story in the hope that it would strike a chord with others who have been through tough times and were victims of harsh and unjust systems, and for those who feel isolated as a result.

Dawn now lives in Northern Idaho with her husband.

Disclaimer

Note regarding copyrights. In instances where the author of a work was known, we did our best to secure the rights to use the work and copyright attribution was made. In a few cases, we either did not know the author of the work or we were not able to locate the author. We apologize to these authors. This work is educational in purpose and meant to impart knowledge; hence, we reasonably believe the copyright doctrine of fair use applies. Nevertheless, if the author of an unattributed work is known to you and you have their contact information, please let us know

Printed in Great Britain
by Amazon.co.uk, Ltd.,
Marston Gate.